THE GRAPHICS COACH

by Kathy Murray

New Riders Publishing
Carmel, Indiana

The Graphics Coach

By Kathy Murray

Published by:
New Riders Publishing
11711 N. College Ave., Suite 140
Carmel, IN 46032 USA

Printed in the United States of America 1 2 3 4 5 6 7 8 9 0

Library of Congress Cataloging-in-Publication Data

Murray, Katherine, 1961-
The graphics coach / Katherine Murray.
p. cm.
Includes index.
ISBN 1-56205-129-6 : $24.95
1. Computer graphics I. Title.
T385.M88 1992
006.6-dc20 92-43500
CIP

Publisher
David P. Ewing

Associate Publisher
Tim Huddleston

Acquisitions Editor
John Pont

Managing Editor
Cheri Robinson

Product Director
Rob Tidrow

Production Editor
Lisa Wilson

Editor
Peter Kuhns

Technical Editor
Jonathon Ort

Book Design
Amy Peppler-Adams

Proofreaders
Cheri Robinson
Tammy Tidrow

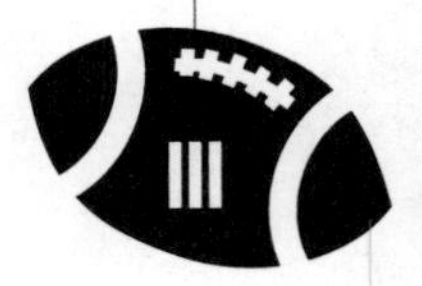

DEDICATION

To anyone who's ever stared at a graphics program and thought "Maybe later."

ABOUT THE AUTHOR

Kathy Murray is the president of reVisions Plus, Inc., a writing and desktop publishing company that specializes in the production of microcomputer-related materials. At the present time, Katherine has authored over twenty books on a wide variety of computer topics.

TRADEMARK ACKNOWLEDGMENTS

New Riders Publishing has made every attempt to supply trademark information about company names, products, and services mentioned in this book. Trademarks indicated below were derived from various sources. New Riders Publishing cannot attest to the accuracy of this information.

Adobe and PostScript logo are registered trademarks of Adobe Systems, Inc.

Appletalk is a registered trademark of Apple Computer, Inc.

CompuServe Information Services is a registered trademark of CompuServe.

CorelDRAW! is a registered trademark of Corel Systems Corporation.

Intel is a registered trademark of Intel Corporation.

Logitech is a registered trademark of Logitech.

Lotus 1-2-3 is a registered trademark of Lotus Corporation.

Microsoft is a registered trademark of Microsoft Corporation.

PC Paintbrush is a registered trademark of Z-Soft Corporation.

Targa is a registered trademark of Truevision.

Ventura Publisher is a registered trademark of Xerox Corporation.

Trademarks of other products mentioned in this book are held by the companies producing them.

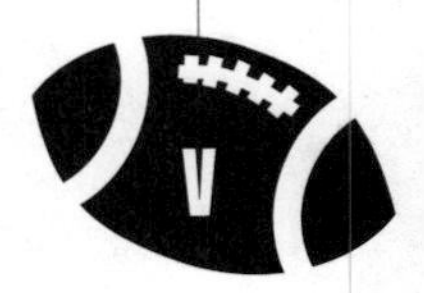

WARNING AND DISCLAIMER

ACKNOWLEDGMENTS

Computer books are more fun than they used to be. This one in particular has been a great project, thanks to the following people:

Rob Tidrow, Development Editor, for his helpful advice, quick feet, insightful comments, and pleasant phone voice;

John Pont, Acquisitions Editor, for finding me in the first place (sort of);

David Ewing, for having the vision to break the mold with a line of books we can all believe in; and

Claudette Moore, for taking such good care of all the left-brained stuff so I can keep on writing.

CONTENTS AT A GLANCE

TABLE OF CONTENTS

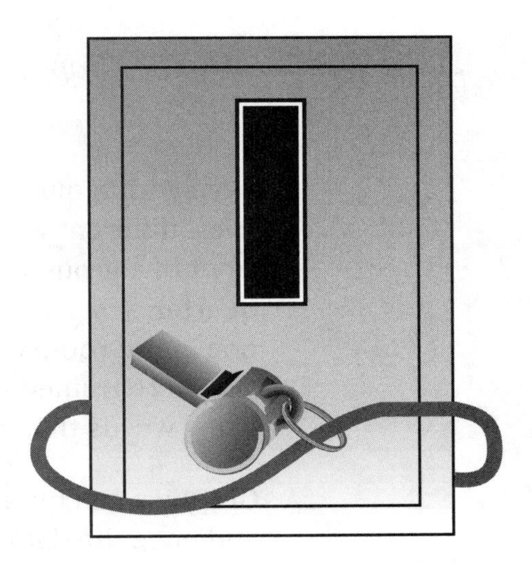

INTRODUCTION

You've probably noticed—everything is graphics these days. Road signs let us know where to walk (or where not to walk) by showing us, not telling us. We understand from roadside pictures where people cross, where deer cross, and where parking is not allowed. Almost without knowing it, we've learned another language—this one universal—that relies on common symbols to communicate thoughts and ideas beyond the limited vocabularies of our respective native tongues.

Why pictures? Surely with the information overload in our country and our world, the average person is beyond the level of picture-book communication. But here's the catch: You may be a first-class world genius in Brazil, but if you don't understand the language when you're visiting Italy, finding your way around is going to be difficult. That picture on the door of the public restroom is a great thing to see.

Graphics. The universal language.

Even within our own language boundaries, within our own industries, different words mean different things. When you're up in front of a group of people discussing sales projections for the next quarter, you run a chance of being misunderstood. Perhaps everyone in the room is not as financially savvy as you are. Or, perhaps you were trained in a different environment and are accustomed to using words that make everyone else go "huh?"

Graphics can break that language barrier for you. Show your audience the data trends, illustrate your argument, graph the sales results in different regions. Pictures can state your message clearly, when words just get in the way.

Computers have, in large part, been responsible for the wildfire-like spread of graphics. Mega-popular programs, like Microsoft Windows, provide us with a graphical way of interacting with our computers. Gone are the unfriendly command lines. We no longer have to spend days memorizing DOS commands. With a simple click of the mouse on a small on-screen picture, we can carry out complex and powerful operations.

Artists have been able to trade their airbrushes and sketchboards for graphics tablets and palettes with millions of colors—no mixing required. And no longer is the artwork vulnerable to studio elements, like dust, coffee, or stray toddlers; it's saved on disk, ready to be reopened, revised, and reused at a moment's notice.

Computers have also made it possible for those of us who are not artists to create artwork of our own. We can illustrate magazines and newsletters, create company logos, display graphs for board meetings, and even design elaborate on-screen animation.

But the advantage of having and using graphics in your work brings with it a downside: Where do you start? How do you learn to create the graphics? Of the different kinds of programs out there, how do you decide which one you need?

In *The Graphics Coach*, you'll learn all the basics about creating and working with graphics. What types of graphics is your system equipped to create? What kinds of graphics programs are out there? How can you make sure that the graphics you create in one program will be supported in another? *The Graphics Coach* provides you with basic hardware information about your monitor, video card, and input devices—such as the mouse, graphics tablet, scanner, or light pen—and explores the kinds of equipment on which you may be printing or plotting your work. In addition, *The Graphics Coach* is accompanied by a disk containing three sleek graphics programs—for DOS PCs, Windows PCs, and Macintoshes—that you can use throughout the book to view, edit, print, and convert graphics files.

WELCOME TO THE PERSONAL TRAINER SERIES

This book represents one subject in the new Personal Trainer Series, a common-sense, no-frills approach to shortening the learning curve involved in using today's technology. In *The Graphics Coach*, for example, you'll find a wide range of usable information relating specifically to graphics—how to create graphics, understanding graphics hardware, finding a graphics program, managing graphics files—the list goes on and on. We won't tell you who created the first graphic ever or make you wade through pages of unnecessary descriptions about examples you'll never use; we give you just what you need to know in order to begin using graphics productively in your work.

Think of *The Graphics Coach* as your personal trainer, ready to help you understand hardware and software considerations, answer your questions (see Chapter 1), and lead you through concise, to-the-point examples. You'll find simple, understandable phrasing and clear illustrations to accompany you along the way.

Additionally, each book in the Personal Trainer Series comes equipped with a special disk, provided to help you get a head start on learning the subject area you've chosen. For example, the disk in *The Graphics Coach* provides you with three different graphics programs, which enable you to work with the examples in this book and build your own graphics repertoire.

WHY DO YOU NEED A BOOK ON GRAPHICS?

Graphics is another computing area in which the technology changes faster than we can learn it. The minute we begin to feel comfortable with what we've learned, new features—and improved hardware—bring us additional avenues to explore and conquer.

For users new to the graphics area, mastering the learning curve may seem impossible. Buzzwords fly around the graphics field like lightning bugs in May: Paint, draw, rastor, vector, RIP, object-oriented, bit-mapped...the terms all seem vague and provide us with no real clue as to their use or meaning. Why call them draw and paint programs when you can paint in a draw program and draw in a paint program? And what's all the fuss about video cards and file conversions?

Most computer users today have an extremely limited amount of time in which to learn new programs. Why bother learning something new if using it will take more time than the something you're using now? *The Graphics Coach* makes deciphering and understanding graphics possible in a short amount of time by giving you simple explanations and examples that reinforce the concepts you're learning. You won't find a million and one tips for using your particular software program in *The Graphics Coach*—just simple, concise text that helps you learn and use graphics in as short an amount of time as possible.

Most books you'll find on graphics speak to one of two groups of users: people who've purchased a particular program and want to learn how to use it (like PC Paintbrush or SuperPaint), and people who write programs that make use of graphics files. Both of these audiences are important and need books to help them in the mastery of their computing goals.

But *The Graphics Coach* is different.

This book explains the hows and whys of graphics from a more general perspective—not related to a specific program or programming language. From a broadbrush perspective, how can you get started with graphics? What can you do with a stylus? Is it possible that you—the same person who used to cut art class—are now the electronic artist who illustrates articles for the company newsletter?

The Graphics Coach won't teach you everything there is to know about graphics. When you close the back cover of this book, however, you'll have a much better understanding of how you can use graphics in your own applications than you had when you opened the front cover.

WHO SHOULD USE THIS BOOK?

Put simply, *The Graphics Coach* is for anyone who has flirted with the idea of creating home-grown graphics but who has not known where to start. Perhaps, even, you've started creating a few art pieces of your own and want further direction on fine-tuning your computer system and display. Specifically, *The Graphics Coach* includes something for you if you are:

★ New to computer graphics but not necessarily new to computers (you may, like many of us, have mastered the basic tasks of several software programs but not previously learned graphics software)

★ Responsible for learning a new program in a limited amount of time

★ Interested in the possibility of creating your own graphics but overwhelmed by the number of programs and options available

★ Confused about hardware issues such as monitors and video cards

★ Hesitant to invest in a graphics program until you are certain that the new program's files will be compatible with files you already have

★ Uncertain about the best kind of graphics software to use on your particular computer system

In addition to providing the answers to these issues, *The Graphics Coach* provides an accompanying disk that gives you even more value. Now, with the valuable graphics programs on the disk and the accompanying file conversion utilities, you truly have nothing to lose as you begin your graphics exploration. You can be assured that the artwork you create will be usable in other programs.

HIGHLIGHTS OF *The Graphics Coach*

The Graphics Coach is divided into three parts. Part One, Elementary Graphics, explains the basics of working with graphics from a general perspective: What are graphics? Why might you want to use graphics in your publications or in your work? What types of graphics programs are available? What are the differences among the different types of graphics files?

Chapter 1, "Introducing Graphics," takes you through a brief question-and-answer session to find out more about your graphics undertaking. Although the answers to common graphics questions

here are brief, references are provided so that you can turn to the appropriate chapter for more information. Also in this chapter, you'll find a graphics glossary containing terms used often in the graphics arena.

Chapter 2, "Why Use Graphics?," highlights the different benefits graphics can offer you. Change the personality of your work by adding an eye-catching piece of art. Follow the evolution of art from traditional paste-board to on-screen design.

Chapter 3, "Graphics Programs," explores the major differences among paint and draw programs. Additionally, you'll find out about CAD programs, presentation graphics, and multimedia and animation graphics programs. A checklist near the end of the chapter helps you decide what type of program you need. You also explore the programs included on *The Graphics Coach* bonus disk and find out how you will use the disk in subsequent chapters.

Chapter 4, "Graphics File Formats," wipes away some of the mystery about creating files of different file types. What does compatibility mean? What types of differences exist among file types? What types of graphics formats are available, and for what program types? This chapter should clear away some of the confusion about the wide range of graphics formats used today.

In Part Two, "Graphics Nuts-and-Bolts," you find out how the hardware you use to create and work with graphics files affects the type of work you do. Organized into six different chapters, with each chapter concentrating on a specialized area of hardware, Part Two will help you build a basic understanding of display and output options as well as the overall systems themselves.

Chapter 5, "Understanding Basic Hardware," introduces you to the important elements in the system unit. How does the microprocessor affect the way you work? Is RAM important? How much room do you need to store graphics files? This chapter answers these

basic questions and provides you with a checklist so that you can determine which considerations are most important for you.

Chapter 6, “Understanding Monitors and Video Cards,” tackles perhaps one of the most overwhelming areas of graphics. How do you decide which monitor will work best for you? What do video cards have to do with graphics? This chapter will help you understand how monitors and video cards work and provide you with information about the most popular monitors and cards currently available.

Chapter 7, “Understanding Art Tools,” introduces you to the various devices you may use to create electronic art. You might, for example, use a mouse, trackball, graphics tablet, stylus, or light pen. Or, perhaps, you might use a scanner to bring the file into your system initially. A checklist helps you decide which tool suits your artistic style.

Chapter 8, “Understanding Printers and Other Output Options,” discusses the various output options you have for your graphics. Learn how the type of printer you have, available fonts, and printer memory all contribute to the way your graphics appear in print. Will you be printing to a color printer? Black and white? Using a plotter? Outputting to film? This chapter ends with a checklist helping you target your output goals.

In Part Three, “Working with Graphics,” you go through hands-on examples of creating and using graphics in your own work. From a basic discussion of graphics do’s and don’ts to more specialized examples of creating, editing, printing, and converting files, this part makes heavy use of *The Graphics Coach* bonus disk.

Chapter 9, “Graphics Do’s and Don’ts,” gives you a full-scale design reference that will come in handy as you set out to create your

own graphics. Learn how the white space on the page is as important as the graphic itself. Find out how creating a graphic aimed at a specific audience can improve the effectiveness of the piece.

Chapter 10, "A Graphics Primer," explores the basics of working with graphics. You'll learn about the different features that paint and draw programs have in common. Investigate the tools you'll use to create objects and control the style, color, and brush shape of individual items.

Chapter 11, "Creating and Editing Graphics," starts with a basic discussion of creating your own graphics. From a beginning discussion of opening a file, through selecting tools, drawing the art, filling areas with color or patterns, and saving the file, this chapter shows you how a typical work session with both paint and draw programs might unfold. Learn to use a variety of editing features to enhance and modify the files you create, and use the shareware programs on the bonus disk to view and edit graphics.

Chapter 12, "Printing Graphics Files," explores the options you'll consider as you prepare to print the files you've created. First make sure everything is connected properly; then enter your choices by working with your program's print options. Finally, this chapter concludes with steps for printing from each of the three shareware programs on the bonus disk.

Chapter 13, "Converting and Managing Graphics Files," explains what happens during file conversion and shows you how to use the file-conversion utilities included on *The Graphics Coach* bonus disk. Additionally, you'll find out about file compression and decide whether it's in your future.

The Graphics Coach winds up with two appendixes and a glossary. Appendix A explains how you can professionally finish the graphics you create; and Appendix B provides installation steps for installing the programs on the bonus disk. The glossary contains the definitions to words used throughout the book.

Now that you know the overall game plan for the book, let's get started...

PART I

ELEMENTARY GRAPHICS

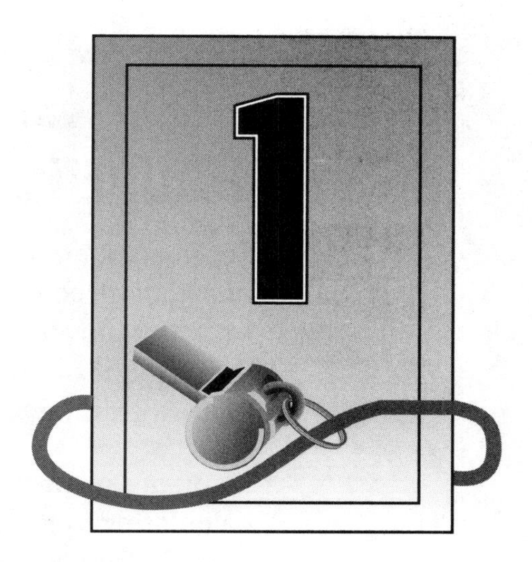

INTRODUCING GRAPHICS

Graphics can do for documents and presentations what the traditional words-on-paper approach cannot: teach visually. In a fraction of the time it takes to read the same information in text form and decipher its meaning, you can look at a picture, graph, or drawing and know almost immediately what the speaker or author is trying to say.

In this chapter you are introduced to the following points about graphics:

GAME PLAN

- What graphics are and why you should use them
- What types of hardware issues you need to worry about when creating graphics
- The types of graphics programs that are available
- The ins and outs of file conversion
- Understanding clip art
- Exploring *The Graphics Coach* bonus disk

A PICTURE IS WORTH A THOUSAND WORDS

Suppose, for example, that you are giving a presentation to the board of directors, explaining how your department can benefit from the purchase of new computers and software. You compare the amount of time and effort employees spend in their manual tasks with time an automated system could save.

If you are using words alone, chances are that the directors are calculating in their heads as you speak, trying to figure out your point before you explain it. If you pull out a graph and show them a visual representation of the same information, you are going to get their attention—and possibly their support.

Graphics these days have gone far beyond the spreadsheet-graphing kind of role. Today, fun paint programs are available that bring out the artiste in even the most technical-minded. Sophisticated graphics program help architects, professional graphic artists, and designers trade their artboards and airbrushes for graphics tablets and pens. Multimedia capabilities turn the desktop computer into a small video studio, enabling users to transform their favorite pieces of art into an interactive video complete with video, music, and animation possibilities.

Most people have graphics needs that fall somewhere between creating simple graphs and producing on-screen animation. You may, for example, need to add an illustration to the cover page of a newsletter, create a business logo, make a presentation to the board of directors, or create artwork for an employee handbook to illustrate company growth trends. You can do all this in an interesting and informative manner by using graphics.

This chapter begins with a graphics question-and-answer session and provides a glossary. You also find an introduction to the Graphics disk, the software that accompanied this book.

GRAPHICS Q&A

All you want to do is create a simple picture to illustrate a key point in the report you are about to turn in. It seems simple enough. You sketched the picture on the back of an envelope, but now you are stumped. How do you get the drawing into your computer?

This section presents some basic questions and answers that are bound to infiltrate your thoughts as you wonder how to get started using graphics. Chapter references are provided along with each answer so that you know where to turn in the book for more information.

What are graphics? In the most basic sense, graphics are pieces of art you create on your computer. When you are drawing a simple on-screen picture, designing a logo, scanning a photograph, or creating a chart in 1-2-3, for example, you are working with graphics. See Chapter 3 for more information about different graphic types.

Why should I use graphics in my documents? Professional-looking documents today do not cut it without some kind of illustration. You can use graphics to create a series of charts for a report or design an elaborate flowchart. You also can use graphics to create more artistic documents. You will find that using an art program saves a considerable amount of time and provides art that can be saved and used again later. See Chapter 2 to learn the benefits that using graphics can offer.

What kinds of graphics can I create? If you are armed with the right graphics program, you are limited only by your imagination and the storage space in your computer. Whether you want to use predrawn art, known as *clip art*, or create your own custom artwork, programs are available today that help you achieve your graphics goals. Chapter 3 provides an overview of the different types of graphics you can create.

What kinds of graphics programs are available? Basically, two different types of graphics programs exist: bit-mapped and object-oriented. Programs that create bit-mapped graphics often are referred to as *paint* programs. A bit-mapped graphic is formed by a pattern of small dots called *pixels*. Programs that create object-oriented graphics often are referred to as *draw*, or *illustration*, programs. These programs create images by using shapes rather than dots. These shapes can be resized without loss of clarity or jagged edges. For more information about bit-mapped and object-oriented graphics, see Chapter 3.

> **The Coach Says...**
> You also see the term *raster* used to describe bit-mapped images and *vector* used for object-oriented graphics.

How do I decide which type of graphics program I need? Your answer to this question depends on the reason you are creating graphics. Are you designing a company logo to place on all your office stationery? Do you need to illustrate a quarterly report complete with charts, free-hand art, and cartoons? Do you need high-quality art with smooth edges and a wide range of colors? For high-quality professional graphics, illustration programs are more widely used. Paint programs programs, however, enable you to fine-tune color and create pictures that are remarkably similar to photographs. Although paint programs are often less expensive than their object-oriented counterparts, they sometimes consume much more of your computer's memory (or at least the bit-mapped files they create do). For more information on these two graphics types, see Chapter 3.

Will other programs accept my graphics files? The answer to this question depends on two things: the graphics program you use and the computer system you have. Just a few years ago, file compatibility was such a problem that you needed a Ph.D. in Computer Science just to use a file in a program other than the one in which it was created. Today, many programs support a variety of file formats, and programs called *graphics file conversion utilities* make it easier for us to use files in a wide range of applications. Now some compatibility between PC and Mac applications exists with a few graphics programs capable of saving files in formats supported by both systems. Chapter 4 explains more about graphics file types.

The Coach Says...

The Graphics Coach bonus disk includes three disk conversion utilities: one for DOS, one for Windows, and one for the Macintosh. For more information on using these programs, see Chapter 13.

Is it difficult to incorporate graphics into text documents? If you are using Windows, placing graphics may be as simple as opening the Edit menu and selecting Paste (assuming, of course, that you already copied the art to the Windows Clipboard). If you are using a program other than Windows, placing the picture may require that you use your program's Import command. If the art you are importing was saved in a file type supported by your program, importing should be a painless procedure. (Other considerations, such as available memory, can botch things up, however.) For more information on importing graphics, see Chapter 4.

The Coach Says...

You can turn a bit-mapped (paint) graphic into an object-oriented (draw) graphic if you have the right tools. Many object-oriented graphics programs, such as CorelDRAW!, include an autotrace feature. An autotrace feature enables you to bring the bitmap into the program and trace the picture, turning it into an object-oriented graphic. If your program does not have this type of utility, you can buy a stand-alone program, such as Adobe's Streamline, to accomplish the same thing.

How do I know which type of graphics software I have? In most cases, you can tell whether you are working with a paint or a draw program by the kinds of tools you see on-screen. Do you have a wide variety of shapes, curves, and lines? Is there a pointer tool (resembling a small arrow) in the tools row? These tools are part of the draw toolkit. A paint program, such as Windows Paintbrush, however, includes only simple rectangle and oval tools, but will show a paint bucket, paintbrush, or spray paint tool. Additionally, most paint programs display a color palette on-screen, while draw programs store color selections in a menu. Chapter 3 explains more about the differences between paint and draw programs.

Here is a foolsafe way to determine whether you are using a paint or draw program: when you magnify the screen display, do you see dots before your eyes? Only paint programs produce bit-mapped images, which are actually collections of pixels. When you zoom in, the pixels are easy to see (see fig. 1.1).

All paint programs have a Zoom In or Magnify option (usually in a View menu) that enables you to enlarge the display of the picture

on which you are working. When you enlarge the view, you easily can see the square pixels that comprise the picture. Figure 1.1 shows an example of an on/off switch created in Windows Paintbrush, a paint (or bit-mapped) graphics program. Notice the small picture of the zoomed area in the upper left corner of the display window.

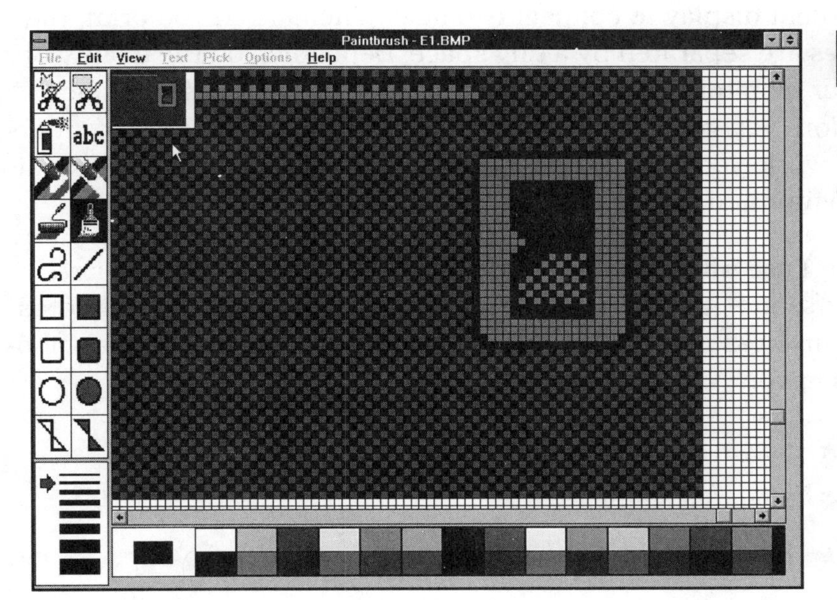

Figure 1.1:

Displaying pixels in a paint program.

Can my printer print high-quality graphics? A thousand-dollar sophisticated graphics program is not going to help you if you are outputting to a dot-matrix printer that is incapable of printing graphics. Before investing in a printer, think carefully about the output you want. If you want color, you need an ink-jet, thermal, or color laser printer. If you want black-and-white PostScript output, you need a PostScript laser printer. If you want only simple, quick printouts of on-screen graphics, one of the many good quality dot-matrix printers could meet your needs. Chapter 8 explores more about your output options.

Will my graphics files print exactly the way they look on-screen? The image that you see on-screen may be only a rough representation of what you actually see on the printed hard copy. If you use a monitor with low screen resolution—meaning fewer dots are used to create the screen grid—you might not be able to place graphic elements accurately. You might, for example, zoom the view to 200 percent display to connect two lines. Then, when you print, the lines are separated by a tiny space. Depending on the quality of your monitor, you may have to place something several times before you get it right. (If you plan to do a large amount of graphics work, you should invest in a good monitor.) Chapter 6 explains monitor and video card considerations.

Can I use photographs as graphics? Newsletters, business reports, and catalogs all look better when real-life scanned photos are used as part of the artwork. The problem with including photos in your work is that you must have the following:

★ Scanner

★ Scanning software

★ Plenty of disk storage space

Scanned photos, however, rarely look as good on-screen as they do originally and the quality may suffer even more when you print the image. The type of scanner you use and the editing program you work with will greatly impact the quality you can expect from scanned photos. See Chapter 7 for more information on scanners and scanning considerations.

> **The Coach Says...**
> Scanners are devices that turn your hardcopy photo or art into electronic format—a file usable by your computer.

What tools are available for creating graphics (do I have to use the mouse)? Most users are accustomed to using a mouse with their favorite programs. Macintosh users have been mouse enthusiasts longer than the PC crowd because of the graphical nature of the Macintosh interface. With the introduction of more graphical interfaces in DOS, such as Microsoft Windows, PC users now are comfortable using the mouse in their daily work. Although most people are comfortable with the mouse, drawing or painting with the it might seem cumbersome. Users who work with graphics for a living often use a different kind of input device—something similar to a pen or paintbrush—with which they are more comfortable. These additional devices, such as graphics tablets and pens, pucks, and light pens, are the subject of Chapter 7.

Will programs other than graphics programs work with my graphics files? The capability to use graphics files in other programs is an important consideration for users who plan to use desktop publishing or incorporate graphics into a word processing report or manual. If you are using a graphics program that saves files in commonly accepted formats, chances are you can import the file into the leading word processing and desktop publishing programs. You might, for example, want to add a piece of art you created in Windows Paintbrush to a WordPerfect document. See Chapter 4 for details.

What does file conversion do? Earlier in this chapter you learned that programs exist that can change a graphics file from one format to another. What exactly does this process accomplish? Aside from what many beginning users think, file conversion is more than a process of renaming file extensions. Usually, in the file conversion process, a file with a PCX extension, for example, is renamed with a TIF extension. A file named ART.PCX becomes ART.TIF after the file conversion process. When you convert a file, you actually change the way the data is written to the file. This is why programs that read PCX files give you an error when you try to open a file type they do not recognize. The program is not difficult; it simply cannot read the file you told it to read. You learn to convert files in Chapter 13.

What are the differences in graphics file types? The biggest difference among graphics file types is the programs with which they can be used. The BMP files are great for Windows users, but are supported by few programs beyond the Windows family of applications. Similarly, GIF files are popular on CompuServe and can be translated into both Mac and PC applications, but not without conversion. Another difference among file types is the size of the file created in that version. Some graphics file formats take up more room than others (TIF files, for example, require more disk space than a similar piece of art in a PCX file). More about graphics file types can be found in Chapter 4.

Should I use a color or monochrome monitor for graphics?Just a few years ago, you did not have a choice. If you wanted to display graphics (which at that time were limited to Lotus 1-2-3 charts), you needed a color monitor. Today, you have a full range of choices with terrific quality monitors available in both color and monochrome. Generally speaking, if you are creating graphics that will be printed in color, you better be looking at a color screen to get the full impact of what you are creating. If your graphics will be printed in black-and-white, you may prefer to use a monochrome monitor (although some people prefer color no matter what their output options may be). For more information about choosing monitors, see Chapter 6.

The Coach Says...

Many monitors—both monochrome and color—are capable of displaying images in various shades of gray. If you're working on a color monitor, changing the display so that the image is displayed in various grayscales gives you an idea of how the image will look when printed in black and white.

Can I purchase predrawn art? Those of you who will never paint a *Mona Lisa* will appreciate clip art—pieces of predrawn art that you can incorporate in your own work. Many packages of clip art are available for both PC and Mac systems. These packages have a wide range of applications such as business drawings, world maps, cartoons, and circus animals. Figure 1.2 shows an example of a symbol file, which is a form of clip art that is included with Freelance Graphics for Windows. For more information about clip art, see Chapter 4.

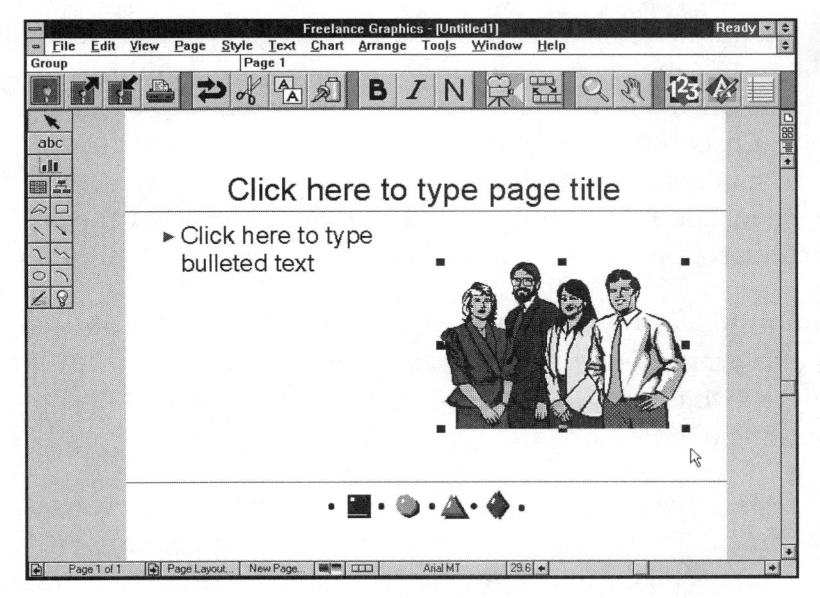

Figure 1.2: An example of clip art in Freelance Graphics for Windows.

Can you edit graphics after you create them? It is impossible to type for long periods of time without making a few typos, and it is even more impossible to create a piece of artwork that is perfect from the moment of creation. As you work with the art you create, you will want to move things, change colors, erase images and lines, and perform a wide range of editing operations. The way in which you edit graphics depends on the type of graphics you

create. You edit bit-mapped graphics by manipulating the individual pixels. You edit object-oriented graphics by changing the shape's size, color, placement, orientation, line width, and so on. See Chapters 3 and 11 for more information about editing graphics files.

What products are available for creating graphics? Depending on the type of graphics you want, any number of popular programs are currently available. One inexpensive (it's free, with Windows) and popular paint program is Windows Paintbrush. The tools are limited, but for simple graphics work it has served many a budding artist well. Popular programs for PCs include PC Paintbrush 5+, Picture Publisher, Aldus Photostyler, Micrografx Designer (or Draw), CorelDRAW!, and the list goes on and on. On the Mac, SuperPaint is a popular choice, as is MacDraw, Painter, Aldus Freehand, and Adobe Illustrator. For more information about specific programs, see Chapter 3

What products are available for converting graphics? Several popular programs are available for converting graphics files, the leader of which is HiJaak, created by Inset Systems. Other programs include HotShot, Conversion Artist, and Collage Plus 3.2.

Many other popular programs are available in the shareware realm, including the three programs included on *The Graphics Coach* bonus disk: Paint Shop Pro for Windows, Graphic Workshop for DOS, and GIFConverter for the Mac.

How can I manage the graphics files I accumulate? Graphics work requires plenty of disk storage space to keep and work with numerous graphics files. Often, no matter what the size of your hard disk, you must compress the graphics files you are not using. Chapter 13 explains how to work with the files you create.

In the next section you learn some of the graphics technology discussed in this book and other books about graphics.

A QUICK GRAPHICS GLOSSARY

This section introduces you to some of the terms used throughout this book. Remember, however, that a more complete glossary is included at the end of the book.

bitmaps: a shortened term for a bit-mapped, or paint, graphic. A piece of bit-mapped art is actually a pattern of small dots, or pixels, that are displayed in varying colors (or gray-scales) on the screen.

CAD: computer-aided design. CAD applications represent the high end of the graphics spectrum, enabling users to design sophisticated architectural plans, schematics, and other materials that must be based on precise measurement and accuracy.

color palette: the area on-screen (or perhaps in a menu) that enables you to choose the colors used in the graphic. Paint programs usually display the color palette on-screen; draw programs often provide a color palette command that displays the current palette. (Some programs also enable you to create your own custom color palettes.)

fill color: a term used to describe the color in the area of the shape you are working with. In most paint programs, you can create filled shapes (such as a filled rectangle). In draw programs, you create the shape and then specify the color or pattern with which it is to be filled.

graphics tablet: a square or rectangular surface on which you can draw, paint, or plot (for CAD applications). A pen or puck is used in place of the mouse to send electronic signals to the computer; the graphic is drawn on-screen as you create it on the tablet.

gray-scale: a term used to describe the tones of gray used in place of color to show graphic shading. Up to

256 different graytones are possible on black-and-white monitors, and up to 64 shades of gray can be displayed on most color monitors.

jaggies: a term used to refer to jagged edges on a graphic image. Bit-mapped graphics often suffer from jaggies, although you can purchase programs (or use a trace feature in your draw program) to smooth jagged edges.

light pen: an electronically light-sensitive pen that sends information to your computer, enabling you to draw on a graphics tablet or on-screen. For graphics work, a light pen used on a graphics tablet may provide the most comfortable input option if you are accustomed to working with more traditional media (such as pens, markers, and paintbrushes).

mouse: the hand-held pointing device used to select tools and options and draw or paint on-screen.

object-oriented: the term for the type of graphics that is vector-based; that is, built from a pattern of shapes, lines, and curves rather than from individual pixels.

pixels: the dots that make up a bit-mapped graphic created in a paint program. Pixels may be individually assigned different colors or shades of gray.

plotter: an output device, similar to a printer, that produces high-quality output by using a variety of colored pens on paper. Plotters often are used for CAD applications.

puck: a small hand-help device that is used with a graphics tablet in CAD applications to plot points of a diagram, schematic, or blueprint.

trackball: a supercharged mouse cousin, in which the ball inside the casing—not the entire mouse—moves to position the pointer on-screen. Some computer

keyboards come equipped with a built-in trackball (some laptops have tiny attachable trackballs), but overall, trackballs are not as popular as their manufacturers expected them to be.

vector image: the type of image created by a draw program (also known as an *object-oriented graphic*). A vector image is actually a combination of shapes, lines, and curves placed together to form a graphic image.

video adapter: also called a graphics card, the video display adapter controls the way your computer interacts with the monitor. The adapter is the piece of hardware that really does the work when it comes to determining screen resolution, the number of colors available, and screen update speed. The most common adapters are the Hercules adapter, CGA (an outdated and substandard graphics display adapter), EGA (a level higher than CGA, providing workable text and graphics), and VGA (provides the highest screen resolution and supports the greatest number of colors). SuperVGA is a cousin of VGA and is currently the highest standard of adapter available for PCs.

USING THE GRAPHICS COACH BONUS DISK

In this section, you are introduced to another important part of *The Graphics Coach*: the graphics disk. The disk contains three graphics programs—one for DOS PCs, one for Windows PCs, and one for Macintoshes—that enable you to create, edit, view, print, and convert graphics files.

The first program, Paint Shop Pro for Windows, is a shareware product popular with Windows users. You can start this program right from Program Manager (installation takes care of placing the group icon for you) and use it to display, edit, and print graphics files.

When you save the graphic, you can choose from an incredible number of supported file formats. Figure 1.3 shows the shareware screen from Paint Shop Pro for Windows. Figure 1.4 shows the Paint Shop screen with the File menu open.

Figure 1.3:

The shareware notice screen from Paint Shop Pro for Windows.

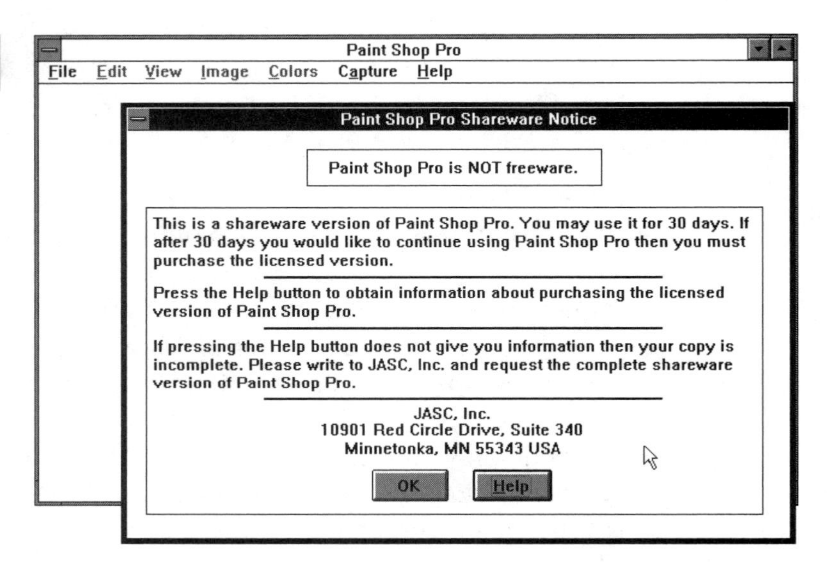

The other PC graphics editor included on the Graphics disk is the Graphic Workshop. The utility, also shareware, was created by Alchemy Mindworks in Ontario, Canada. GWS is a DOS program and supports a number of file conversion and editing tasks. Figure 1.5 shows a sample screen of GWS; figure 1.6 shows the shareware notice that appears after you exit the program by pressing Esc.

The final program available on the Graphics disk is GIFConverter, created by Kevin A. Mitchell. GIFConverter is a conversion and image editing utility for the Macintosh. This product also is shareware. Figure 1.7 shows the shareware notice for GIFConverter; figure 1.8 shows the basic screen with the Display menu opened.

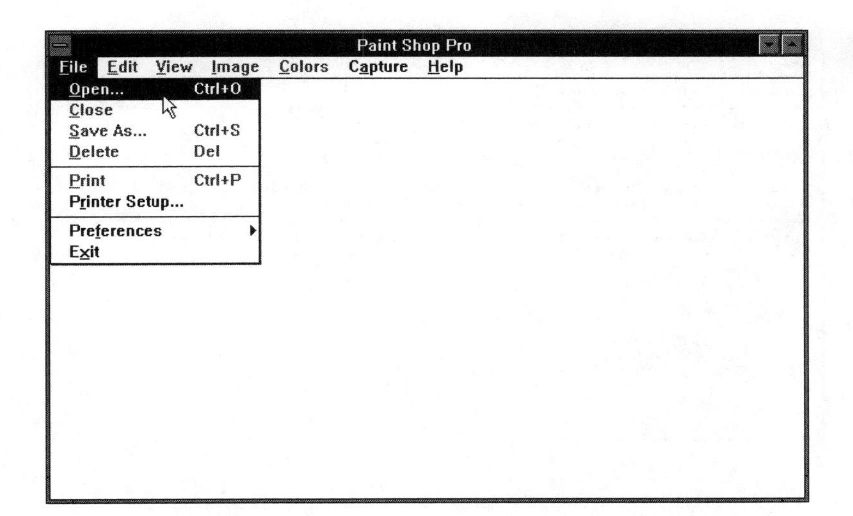

Figure 1.4:

A sample screen and menu of Paint Shop Pro.

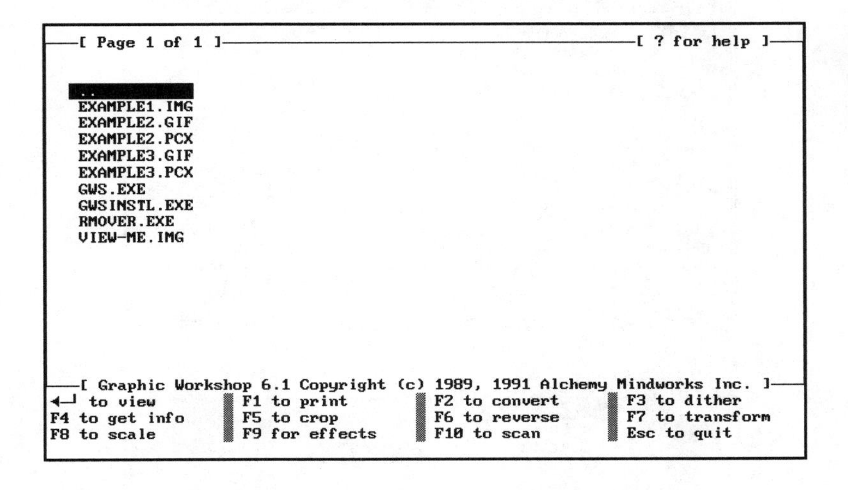

Figure 1.5:

A sample screen from Graphic Workshop.

Figure 1.6:

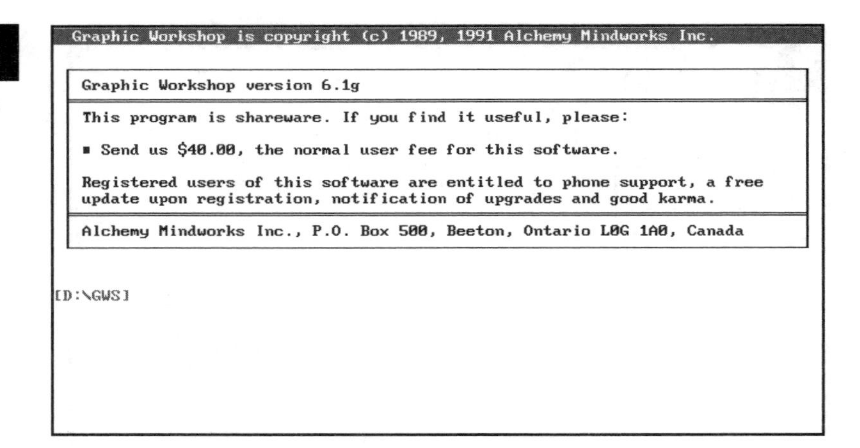

The shareware notice from Graphic Workshop.

Figure 1.7:

The shareware notice screen from GIFConverter.

Figure 1.8:

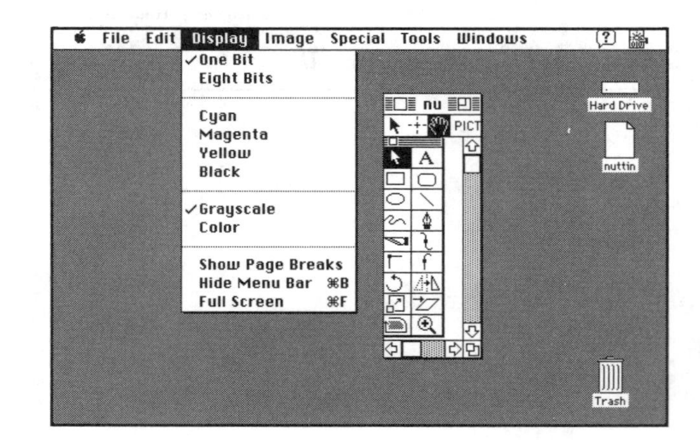

A sample GIFConverter screen with an open menu.

INSTANT REPLAY

This chapter has provided some basic graphics information, answered some fundamental questions, and explored common graphics verbiage. Specifically, you learned about the following topics:

INSTANT REPLAY

- ✔ What graphics are and why you should use them
- ✔ What types of hardware issues you need to worry about when creating graphics
- ✔ The types of graphics programs that are available
- ✔ The ins and outs of file conversion
- ✔ Understanding clip art
- ✔ Exploring the Graphics disk

WHY USE GRAPHICS?

Just a few short years ago personal computers were good for only one basic thing: capturing data. That data could appear as numbers or alphabetic characters, but anything beyond the standard alphanumeric character set was beyond the capabilities of the original PCs.

In this chapter, you learn the following aspects of graphics:

GAME PLAN

- ☐ How graphics fit into the way you communicate
- ☐ How can you use various tones to convey ideas
- ☐ How graphics enhance your documents and presentations
- ☐ How to choose the right look and feel for your message
- ☐ How to create effective graphics your first time out

In the evolution of PCs and Macs, things have become more graphics oriented. The first PCs were data-crunchers; but the new Macintosh brought a new standard—a user interface built on graphics— that enabled users to understand and use the Mac without struggling with arcane commands entered at an unfriendly system prompt.

The Macintosh brought with it on-screen art that opened the door for a previously untapped creative urge, something that had been lying dormant while users struggled with word processing and number crunching duties. The Mac set a standard for user interfaces that brought Windows to the PC. Tasks are no longer reliant on an unfriendly system prompt; you can use on-screen pictures called *icons* to find your way through applications.

With the PC and Mac families firmly established, the race for the best (fastest, coolest, easiest) software product is on. New programs emerge that help you create sleek publications and slicker spreadsheets. Programs now are available to help you make better presentations, organize your desktop, and be more productive. With the popularity of multimedia (the capability to mix sight and sound media), you can create even more with your computer. You can use your computer not only to perform specific tasks (to create complex financial analyses, crank out merge printed form letters effortlessly, and so on), but to create high-quality documents that were not possible in early days of computers.

Today, you can entertain, inform, enlighten, or challenge people with your computer. The computer can provide some talents that you do not have and help you make the best of the talents you do have so that you can do your job well. Graphics fit right into this niche.

The percentage of business people who are would-be artists is probably slim. Most people do not want to waste several hours learning a drawing program only to create artwork that looks

amateurish. Many graphics programs today include tutorials—either on-line or in the manual—that help users get up to speed with a minimum of practice. After you begin using graphics in your work, the benefits they bring to your documents and presentations make the learning curve seem less and less important. With the wealth of graphics programs available today—both through regular sales and shareware—people are adding that second dimension to their work more than ever before.

In this chapter, you learn how people use graphics in the age of visual media. You discover how the artwork you create and use fits into the way you communicate your ideas. You also discover the various tones you can convey, and learn how to choose the right "look and feel" for the messages in your publications and on-screen work.

UNDERSTANDING GRAPHICS

A *graphic* is any type of art that you create or use on your computer. People use graphics in many different ways to enhance the way they communicate. Chances are, you have seen many graphics elements today that you did not recognize as art. Many different items go into the overall design of a publication, presentation, or piece of art, including the following:

- ★ Lines, called *rules*, that set off text boundaries, surround articles, separate headers or footers, or call attention to a headline in the text (see fig. 2.1)
- ★ Charts, such as bar, pie, or line chart, that you create in a spreadsheet program
- ★ Borders that surround the entire page, a single item, table, article, headline, or banner
- ★ Bullet characters used in a bulleted list, such as the ones shown in the left margin here

Figure 2.1:

A rule to set off a header.

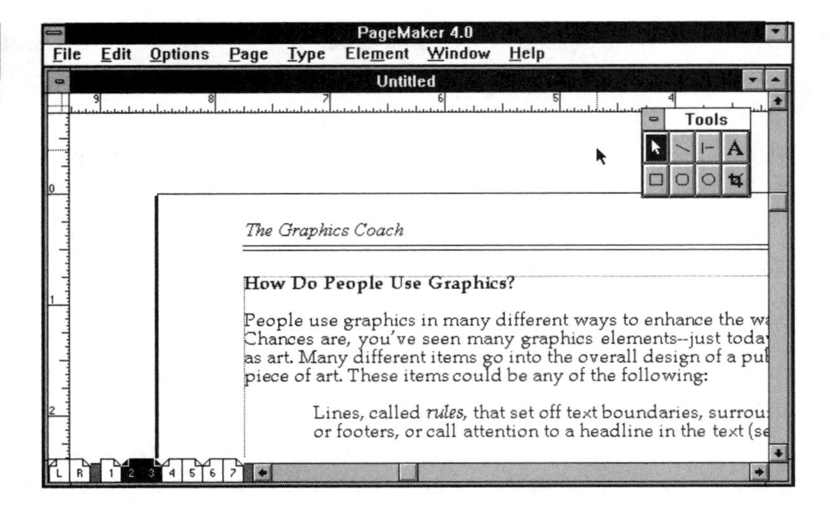

- ★ Company logos, for example, used at the top of business stationery or in the corner of presentation slides
- ★ Clip art, pieces of art created and sold by companies for use in publications, that you purchased from another company (see fig. 2.2)

Figure 2.2:

An example of clip art with Micrografx Designer.

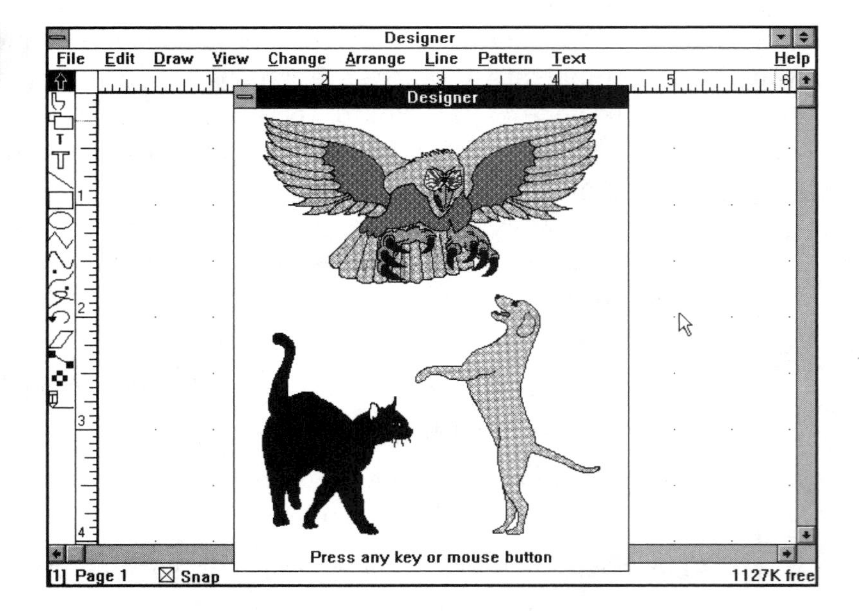

- ★ Original art that you create on your computer in a paint or draw program
- ★ Photographs you use in digitized form using a scanner
- ★ Charts, tables, borders, or symbols you create in a presentation graphics program (a program specifically designed to help you create on-screen presentations)
- ★ Organizational charts, schematics, and architectural plans that might be created in a CAD (computer-aided design) program

As you can see, there are many different types of uses for these things called graphics. Even text can be used as a graphic element, which you will see later in this chapter. Simple or complex, small or large, graphics add another dimension to your work that words alone cannot.

WHEN SHOULD YOU USE GRAPHICS?

You can use graphics for many different things and in many different ways. Even text can be used as a graphic element, which you will see later in this chapter. Graphics enhance your words, help reinforce your message, and pique the viewer's (or reader's) interest.

HOW WILL GRAPHICS BENEFIT YOU?

How should you use graphics in your work? Depending on the type of work you do, you may find yourself in one of the following situations:

- ★ You must create a corporate report that includes charts, a business logo, and scanned photos of a recent

sales conference. You also need to design a cover page that has an inviting design and highlights the corporate logo.

★ You must create a business newsletter. Although the tone is informal, you want to use clip art (and some original art) to spruce things up. You also need to design the overall layout of the publication and use the company logo. You also want to incorporate photographs in your work.

★ You must give the presentation at the board of director's meeting this month. As a member of the board, you have seen some presentations that were amateurish and some that really kept the audience awake. You want to create an on-screen presentation and offer handouts that make the most of presentation graphics technology. You also want to add a few multimedia effects. You want to use charts, background artwork, maps of various sales regions, and scanned photos of leading sales representatives to give the presentation you are envisioning.

★ You are training teachers in the Foreign Language department on new language software that they will use in the computer lab. You need to design and create a handbook that serves as a reference for the teachers when you are off-site. You want to include diagrams of "what to do next" and show the menus that users see on-screen. You need to use a *graphics capture program* (a utility that takes a picture of whatever is displayed on the screen) to take screen pictures and a regular graphics program to create the rest of the artwork.

★ You want to add life to your documents. Many word processors today have the capability to import and print graphics. You now can add a logo, a chart, a drawing, or a scanned image. Just two years ago such a possibilities were unthinkable.

No matter how simple or complex your involvement in the world of graphics will be, you need to start somewhere. Begin by exploring why graphics enhance the way you communicate with other people.

USING GRAPHICS TO COMMUNICATE

Graphics are the "facial expression" of your text. Remember the science teacher in sixth grade who said everything in a monotone voice? Sitting in that class was grueling; staying awake was almost impossible. What if that teacher had been animated, lively, jumping around, whistling, and standing on his head? He would get your attention.

The Coach Says...

Graphics add expression to words. Even a nice-looking piece of text with different sizes and styles seems to take itself too seriously until you show the intention of your message. Graphics help liven things up.

The document in figure 2.3, for example, shows how your presentation sets the tone for the reader. The simple two-column format and the choice of text used for the headline, subheads, and body text seem clean enough. If you received this flier in the mail, would you look at it? Knowing that in business, each piece of mail you receive competes for your attention, would you spend time reading through this advertisement? Probably not.

Figure 2.3:

A simple flier without graphics.

Three Reasons to Use MacAfee & Ryan As Your Consulting Firm:

At MacAfee and Ryan, learning about you is our first priority. What are your computer needs? Do you use your current system to its maximum potential? How can we best serve you in a consulting forum? There are three reasons why, in a recent survey, our clients listed us as the best consulting service in the midwest.

We Determine the Need.

Too often, new computer users purchase their systems and set them up to perform one task: payroll, accounts payable, word processing, whatever. They are so busy learning the routines necessary for their goals that they totally miss the extra advantages their computers can offer them.

Rather than just jumping in and taking over (perhaps even recommending our own products, as our competitors have been known to do), we listen. We explore your hardware and software to see if it's right for you. We analyze your data needs to see whether you're doing things as efficiently as possible. In business, we understand that getting your money's worth is extremely important. We assess your system thoroughly but in a cost-effective timeframe, and help you come up with that computer "wish list" that's been floating around in the back of your brain.

We Offer Solutions.

Once we've analyzed your computer situation, we sit down and draw out all your possible options; from most cost-effective to most elaborate. We provide a plan for implementing system changes and guarantee a minimum of downtime for employees. That saves you time, money, and headaches.

We've Got Experts.

The consultants who join our firm are industry-tested professionals; people who, like you, started out battling with program bugs and trying to set up workable systems. We've got specialists for any area you're questioning: programming, customizing, or just plain setting up a vanilla system that will--*wonder of wonders*--do what you want it to do.

For a free consultation interview or information on our specialty classes, please call our toll-free number Monday through Friday 7:30 am to 6:00 pm. Or contact:

MacAfee & Ryan, Inc.
4 Bainbridge Rd.
Newburyport, MA 01950
1-800-595-9000

© 1992 MacAfee & Ryan, Inc.

For contrast, look at the example in figure 2.4. This flier contains the same text, the same headline, subheads, and body text styles. Consider the impact just a few changes make. The text for the subheads appears reversed so that it contrasts against the dark color of the background boxes. This example uses the headline as a graphic element, with large type, a reversed out numeral leading into the headline, and graphics rules above and below the headline. The two pieces of artwork, of course, are clip art from Micrografx Designer, which is a draw program for PCs. The four-column layout, reversed-out subheads, and background color shades are elements that add to the "interest level" of the publication. If these two publications appeared side-by-side on your desk, you would be more likely to give the one with artwork a second glance.

3 Reasons We Win

© 1992 MacAfee & Ryan, Inc.

At MacAfee and Ryan, learning about you is our first priority. What are your computer needs? Do you use your current system to its maximum potential? How can we best serve you in a consulting forum? There are three reasons why, in a recent survey, our clients listed us as the best consulting service in the midwest.

1. We Determine the Need.

Too often, new computer users purchase their systems and set them up to perform one task: payroll, accounts payable, word processing, whatever. They are so busy learning the routines necessary for their goals that they totally miss the extra advantages their computers can offer them.

Rather than just jumping in and taking over (perhaps even recommending our own products, as our competitors have been known to do), we listen. We explore your hardware and software to see if it's right for you. We analyze your data needs to see whether you're doing things as efficiently as possible. In business, we understand that getting your money's worth is extremely important. We assess your system thoroughly but in a cost-effective timeframe, and help you come up with that computer "wish list" that's been floating around in the back of your brain.

2. We Offer Solutions.

Once we've analyzed your computer situation, we sit down and draw out all your possible options; from most cost-effective to most elaborate.

We provide a plan for implementing system changes and guarantee a minimum of downtime for employees. That saves you time, money, and headaches.

3. We've Got Experts.

The consultants who join our firm are industry-tested professionals; people who, like you, started out battling with program bugs and trying to set up workable systems. We've got specialists for any area you're questioning: programming, customizing, or just plain setting up a vanilla system that will--*wonder of wonders*--do what you want it to do.

For a free consultation interview or information on our specialty classes, please call our toll-free number Monday through Friday 7:30 am to 6:00 pm. Or contact:

4 Bainbridge Rd.
Newburyport, MA
01950
1-800-595-9000

MacAfee & Ryan, Inc.

Figure 2.4: The flier with graphic enhancements.

The press already understands the way your mind works. Today you need information quickly and want the presentation lively. The louder, the better. *USA Today* has capitalized on the quick-look visual format by feeding its readers bite-sized bits of text, striking colors, and multitudes of graphics. *USA Today* offers a totally different tone from the stressed-out, serious look of the *Wall Street Journal*.

Basically, the artwork you include in your presentations or publications can do one or more of the following things:

- ★ Inform
- ★ Persuade
- ★ Entertain

The following sections take a closer look at each of these graphics functions.

USING GRAPHICS TO INFORM

Most importantly, the graphics you use in your publications and presentations must have a reason to be there. That is, they must be functional to some degree. Putting a picture of a palm tree in the middle of an annual report for no apparent reason is not an effective use of graphics. Putting the palm tree in a brochure advertising an escape to a Caribbean island for winners of the spring sales competition, however, serves its purpose.

The art you choose can inform your audience of several different types of things. On one level, the graphics tell your viewers or readers something about you. Are you serious about your message? Is your tone formal or informal? Are you attempting a professional or artsy look? Readers can determine at a glance whether you are interested in portraying a dry or lighthearted tone. Depending on the data you present and the forum in which you present it, readers may either tune in or turn off to your work based on their first impression.

You can use some of the following graphics in your publication or presentation to inform readers:

- ★ Charts to show the sales percentages of new employees
- ★ Graphs to show the increased net sales for the first quarter
- ★ Organizational charts to explain the restructuring of your department (see fig.2.5)
- ★ Icons to call readers' attention to new company benefits in the corporate handbook

EarthTones Landscaping

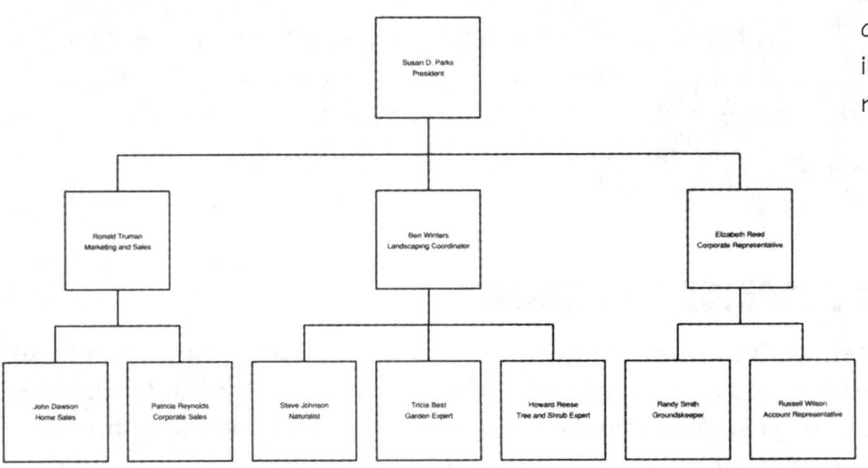

Figure 2.5: An organizational chart used to illustrate restructuring.

- ★ Scanned photographs to show readers what the top managers look like
- ★ Maps to introduce new salespeople to an unexplored region
- ★ The use of borders that call readers' attention to exercise sections in an instructional manual

Your business probably has its own informative graphics uses; these are just examples of some common uses. Although you will not want to use graphics in place of text in a publication or in place of an explanation in a presentation, graphics can reinforce your message and provide readers with another perspective to your ideas.

The Coach Says...

Another offshoot of informing is inspiring. More than a few sales meetings are organized around the idea of "pumping you up," helping you enhance your sales ability, and teaching you ways to harness your energy and channel it into mega-constructive tasks. Graphics can inspire, enthuse, excite, and motivate.

USING GRAPHICS TO PERSUADE

Often, an important decision rests on your ability to communicate. Perhaps you need to convince the board that you need funding for another year. You may be arguing for new staff members in your programming group or heading up an environmentalist group that relies on its ability to persuade the public to be more responsible about ecological issues.

In such cases, you can use graphics to further your message by evoking some feeling of response. If you are publishing a newsletter about homelessness in Chicago, for example, using scanned pictures of homeless people along with charts that illustrate the rise in homelessness over the last 12 months is more persuasive than presenting charts alone. Pictures truly speak louder than words. The emotional response you can achieve with a picture is something words rarely accomplish.

Figure 2.6 shows a sample flier of an environmentalist group. Notice the picture with the gun-sight is the focus of the entire piece. Without the graphic, this flier would lose its potential to persuade the audience to think twice about this ecological issue.

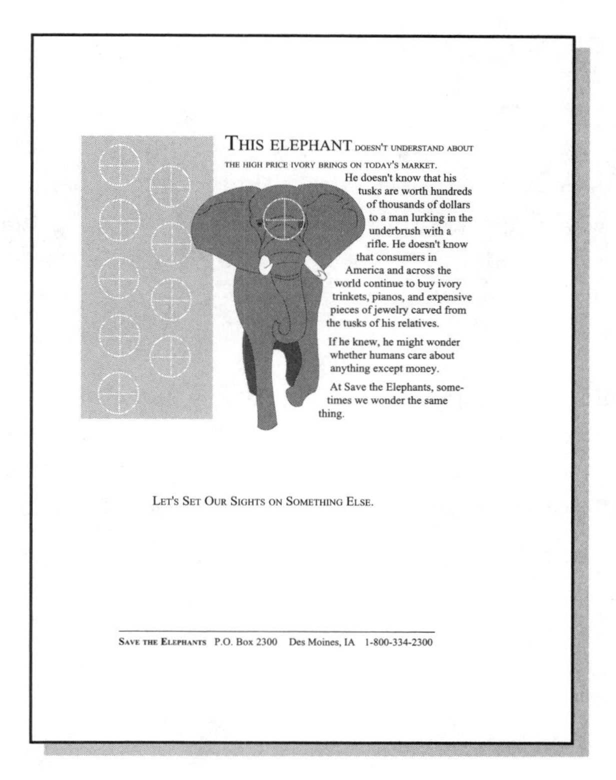

Figure 2.6: Graphics used to persuade.

USING GRAPHICS TO ENTERTAIN

Graphics have a certain degree of entertainment value. Nothing wrong with that. Most people prefer documents with entertaining graphics above all others. You get tired of being inspired, motivated, and informed. You see so much dry, factual stuff everyday that it is nice to encounter something lighthearted once in a while. In fact, when you do see something with a bit of humor, it catches your attention.

The Coach Says...

If you glance through a popular magazine, you can see examples of entertaining graphics that are used to sell products. Humor helps us communicate easily with a receptive audience. Humor—whether outrageous, knee-slapping, or slow-smile kind of humor—helps us communicate easily with a receptive audience.

You can tell from the pictures in figure 2.7 that this flier is more interested in entertaining than persuading. The graphics are lighthearted, almost cartoon-like, and the text resembles handwriting—a much looser style than traditional typeset characters.

Figure 2.7:

A flier with pictures for entertainment value.

Even the most entertaining communication generally does more than entertain; it usually informs or persuades (unless you are talking about comic books or *Mad* magazine). The difference is in the delivery; the information or the persuasion becomes the less-important point behind the entertainment. Romantic Adventures wants you to like what you see, and then perhaps call them for your next travel itinerary. Save the Elephants, on the other hand, wants you to dislike what you see. In fact, they would like to make you uncomfortable enough to resist buying any ivory.

GENERAL GRAPHICS GUIDELINES

Throughout the rest of this book, you learn practical information about different graphics types. You learn how to choose graphics programs, how to work with the programs you have, and how to understand and convert various graphics file types.

In this section you learn what makes a graphic good, how you can best use graphics in your publications or presentations, and how you can say a lot with very little effort.

Choose art that matches the tone of your publication. This might seem logical, but it is easy to miss. Remember that the overall publication or presentation is communicating a certain tone or personality. If you are publishing a document about new statistics in heart disease, cartoon illustrations cannot accurately convey your tone. On the other hand, using serious illustrations in a humorous article about passing midterms might confuse readers. Be as consistent with the tone you are presenting as possible.

Use clip art. Many people who use graphics for the first time are hesitant to rely on clip art. You might worry about copyright laws because you did not create the

artwork. If you paid for it, however, it is yours. Clip art is published specifically with the understanding that purchasers will use it in their own documents. What good would clip art be if you could only use it for nonprofessional purposes? Clip art was created by professional graphic artists to provide ready-made artwork for those who cannot create artwork themselves. Do not be afraid to use the expertise of others, and remember that how you use the art is still up to you.

Choose colors carefully. A piece of artwork that is too dark for a layout detracts from your document. Remember that your artwork may appear differently on-screen than it does in print—particularly if you are using a color monitor and printing in black and white. If you plan to print in color, be careful to choose colors that correspond to other colors in your publication or presentation. Do not introduce new off-the-wall colors in a single illustration.

Be consistent. Professional designers urge you to choose an overall theme for your document. A typical newsletter, for example, might include a logo enclosed in a square, boxes for figures captions, squares to enclose the figures, and squares (or rules) for text callouts. A logical choice of graphic elements would play off the square. This might sound as if you are using too many squares, but do not forget the range of options available in design these days. You can use many different colors, borders, patterns, photos, and text styles to make the squares unique and still follow the overall theme.

Do not overdo it. The urge to use every graphic tool available to create your document is almost overwhelming. Finally, someone hooked up your scanner and it is

working right. You can hardly resist scanning everything. That new package of clip art arrived. You are putting tigers and dolphins on every memo you write. Remember as you create your publications or presentations that a little art goes a long way.

The Coach Says...

Everything on the page competes for a reader's attention; do not drown your graphics by adding too many. Choose a few selective pieces—no more than three small or two medium pieces per page—and place them strategically to help the overall design.

Use white space as a design element. White space, as any good designer will tell you, is as important as the text or graphics in your document. White space is used to give the reader's eye a rest, help organize the rest of the page, and draw the reader's eye to the important elements in the document. A document overflowing with text and graphics probably will never get any serious attention. Cluttered publications are just too much trouble. You want something easy to understand and easy to read.

The Coach Says...

White space—the area of the page that is not used—is sometimes hard to come by. You may have 1,000 words and two pictures that need to fit on one page. How are you going to build in room for the eye to rest? It is not easy, but it is necessary; white space provides a much-needed service for the reader and adds a great deal to the design of your page. Consider, for

continues

continued

example, this page you are reading right now. If the text ran all the way to the edge of the page and inward to the gutter, the text—and even the concepts—presented here would be much more difficult to understand.

Use text as graphics. Earlier you learned that anything that was not text could be graphics. But text can be used as a graphic if it is used in the right way. In some cases, text is meant to add to the overall design of a page not to communicate a text-based message. You can use an artsy-looking font, for example, and then twist it, turn it, rotate it, or curve it into an attention-getting logo, a special headline, an icon, a text marker, or a number of other things (see fig. 2.8). As you plan the design and placement of your graphics, also think about ways to use the text as a graphical design tool.

Figure 2.8: Curving text as part of a logo.

Do not fill the entire page. In school, that may have been the objective (write big so it looks like you have written more), but in the professional world, you want everything neat and compact. A page that runs to the edges with text and includes graphics with no borders is a turn off. You can tell at a glance that there is just

too much reading to do. Your graphics will not even get a chance.

The Coach Says...

Leave comfortable margins around your graphics (unless, as part of the design, you run the text up to the art on purpose). Place text strategically around the graphics but do not let the text swallow them up.

Choose the placement of graphic elements carefully. Chances are, a reader will scan the title of your document and then glance through the graphics before settling in to read the text. Grouping all the graphics together in one spot distracts the reader. You should place graphics at points on the page that help lead the eye through the document. As a general rule, try to balance the overall page. You should think about placing text in blocks and consider how much space is required for each graphic element before you add it to the page.

Be subtle. Remember that you do not need to shout at your audience. Overuse of capitals, graphics that are too large or too domineering, and exaggerated head size underrates the intelligence of your audience.When in doubt, it is better to be subtle with the selection and placement of graphics and conservative with the sizes and styles of your text. You can always liven things up later, if you get a green light for unleashing those MTV-like creative urges.

The Coach Says...

Remember that a little goes a long way. It is a general rule in life: people hear better when you whisper than they do when you shout (which you learn especially well if you have a preadolescent daughter).

A BEGINNER'S GUIDE TO PAGE DESIGN

Organization is the key to a lot of things, in business and in life. If you have a plan, you know where you are going. If you start a project with no clue as to what you hope to end up with, your project could turn out to be a rather hodge-podge collection of ideas and pictures (it also could be an invention of sheer genius, but you would still be taking a risk).

The Coach Says...

Keep a folder of layout styles you like or things you would like to emulate in the future (emulate, not steal). If you run across a magazine layout that piques your interest, cut out the pages and save them in a design file. If a certain type of graphic catches your eye, save it so that you can refer to it later. Then, when you go to design your own publications, refer to your design file for ideas.

When you are preparing a page layout, rely on the following steps:

1. Sketch the page the way you want it to look.
2. Prepare a grid for the page layout. (If you are using a desktop publishing program, there is a command that

enables you to do this. If you are doing it manually, divide the page into the number of columns you want to use by folding it or marking off columns.) Figure 2.9 shows a page setup in Aldus PageMaker, a desktop publishing program available for PCs and Macs.

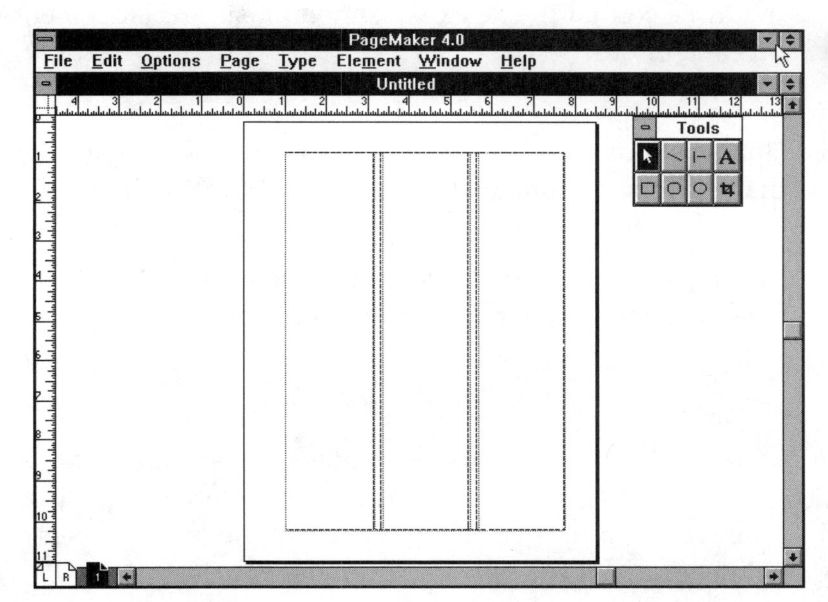

Figure 2.9: Setting up the page in Aldus PageMaker.

3. Mark off the area for the banner.

> **The Coach Says...**
>
> The *banner* of your publication is the title of the piece that typically appears at the top of the first page. Other names for the banner include masthead (which really is not accurate) and title.

4. Consider how many graphics you plan to use and how they can be placed most effectively on the page.

The Coach Says...

Arrange graphics so that they help the reader's eye move easily from picture to picture. If you use photographs of people (called *mug shots*), crop the pictures so that the faces are similar in size or placement in each photo.

5. Finally, choose a typeface and style for the body text that reflects the tone you want your publication to communicate.
6. Group pictures and text together in the center of the page with white space more toward the outside.

The Coach Says...

White space, used effectively, is as important as the other elements on the page. Do not leave big clumps of white space in the center of the page. Use extra white space on the outside of the page to draw the reader's eye inward, toward the content of the document.

INSTANT REPLAY

In this chapter, you learned the following principles about using graphics in your documents and presentations:

INSTANT REPLAY

- ✔ How graphics fit into the way you communicate
- ✔ How can you use various tones to convey ideas
- ✔ How graphics enhance your documents and presentations
- ✔ How to choose the right look and feel for your message
- ✔ How to create effective graphics your first time out

GRAPHICS PROGRAMS

So now we get down to the real issue. You know you want to use graphics, and you probably have an idea of how—specifically—you can enhance the work you already do by adding a few artistic touches. The next logical questions are "What do I need?" and "Where do I get it?"

This chapter focuses on the different types of graphics programs you can use to let your creativity loose. Specifically, this chapter explores the following topics:

GAME PLAN

- What is a paint program?
- What is a draw program?
- What are some procedures common to paint programs?
- What kind of operations do draw programs share?
- Which paint and draw programs are currently popular?

GRAPHICS...THE BIG PICTURE

Chances are, you will start your graphics experience with whatever is handy. If you use Windows, for example, you have a built-in paint program—Windows Paintbrush—right at the end of your mouse pointer. If you use a Macintosh, you can pick up MacPaint or MacDraw for a palatable price. For DOS users, there are a number of popular programs—like PC Paintbrush—available at a reasonable cost. If your tastes are more outside the mainstream retail offerings, many different shareware programs are available that can help you learn the basics of graphics without dipping too deeply into your pocket.

As your experience with graphics grows, you may want to raise your head and look around at all the other options on the graphics horizon. What types of programs are out there? You will find offerings ranging from a few bucks to several hundred, edging up toward a thousand. How do these programs differ and which ones do you need? That is what this chapter is all about.

The examples in this chapter explore the differences between paint and draw programs and illustrate some of the basic procedures you will find with each program type. Because of the number of programs available today—for both the PC and the Mac—and the sweeping variety of features, not all are discussed. This chapter provides a broad-brush look at the features of both paint and draw programs. That way, when the time comes, you can make an informed decision about the type of graphics program that best suits your needs.

INTRODUCTION TO GRAPHICS

Chapter 1 established that there are two different types of graphics programs: paint programs and draw programs. Each of these

programs produces a different type of graphics. Paint programs produce bit-mapped graphics, and draw programs produce object-oriented graphics. If the terminology is confusing you, don't worry: after you use a paint program, you will know exactly what a bit map is. Similarly, after you play around with a draw program, you will understand the differences involved in working with object-oriented graphics.

Concepts are never as easy to explain as they are to illustrate (which may be the very reason you are learning about graphics). Table 3.1 gives you a quick look at the various terms used to describe these two types of graphics.

Table 3.1
Making Sense of Graphics Terminology

Graphics Term	*What you might hear it called*	*What it really is*
paint program	raster graphics	A graphics program image painter or editor program that stores images as a pattern of dots called *pixels*
draw program	vector graphics object-oriented	A graphics illustration program that stores design program images as formulas program that create shapes

Table 3.1
Continued

Graphics Term	*What you might hear it called*	*What it really is*
bit-mapped graphic	bit map paint graphic raster image scanned image pixel-based art	The type of graphic you create in a paint program
object-oriented graphic	vector image draw graphic	type of graphic you create in a draw program

The sections that follow introduce you to each of these graphics types and set you up for some in-depth exploration of the differences these two graphics types offer.

A BIT MAP BY ANY OTHER NAME

Put simply, *a bit-mapped graphic* is a map of bits displayed on the screen or in print. Paint programs and scanners produce bit-mapped files. The bit-mapped graphic is actually a pattern of dots that you can see if you magnify the view.

The Coach Says...

A scanner is a device you can use to turn hard-copy photos, drawings, and even text into electronic files usable by your computer. For more about scanners, see Chapter 7.

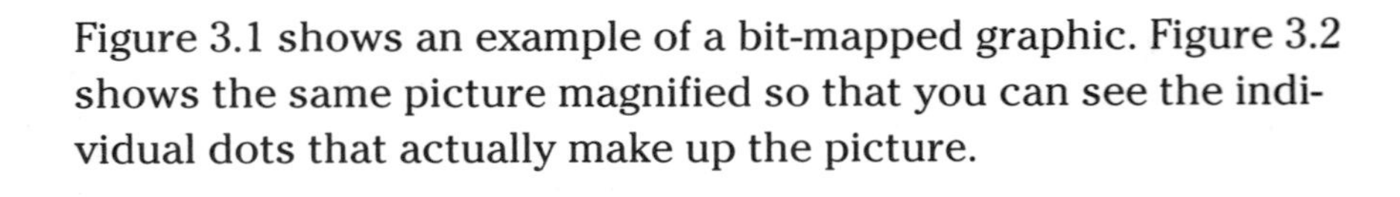

Figure 3.1 shows an example of a bit-mapped graphic. Figure 3.2 shows the same picture magnified so that you can see the individual dots that actually make up the picture.

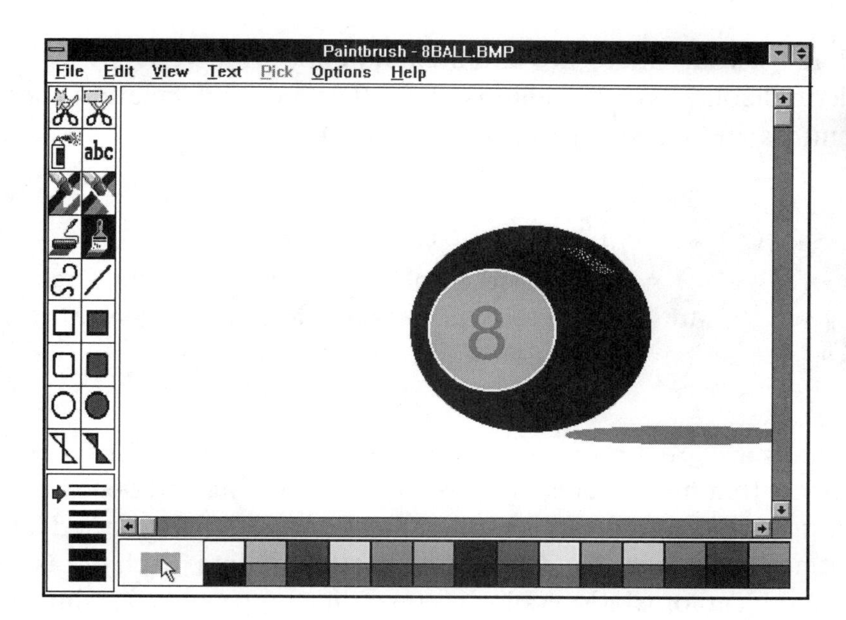

Figure 3.1: An example of bitmapped graphic.

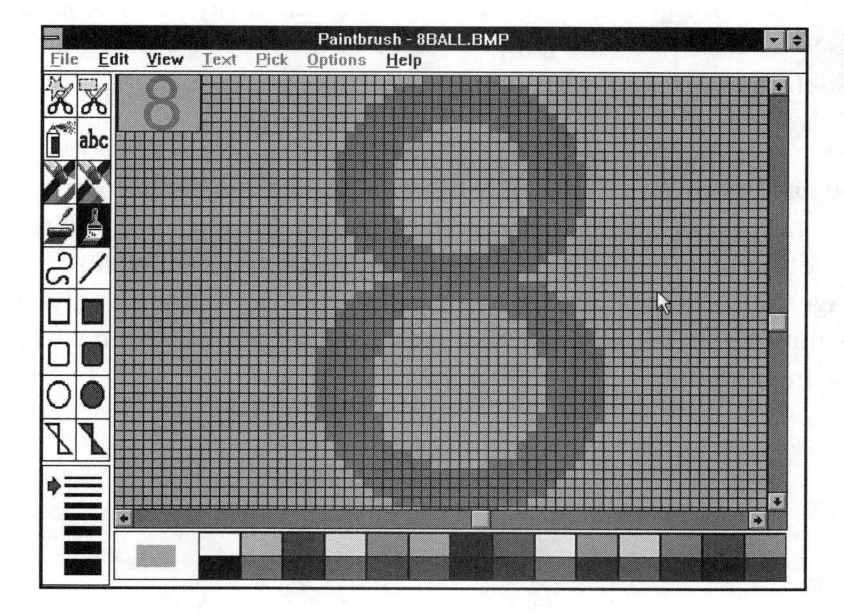

Figure 3.2: The bit-mapped graphic magnified.

Each dot on-screen is called a *pixel*. On a black-and-white mono-chrome monitor, the pixels are either black or white. On color monitors, the pixels can be assigned an overwhelming number of

colors—if your video card and memory support it, you may be able to display over 16 million colors. (For more information about monitors and video cards, see Chapter 6.)

The Coach Says...

A bit-mapped graphic is a pattern of dots. Each individual dot, or *pixel* (short for *picture element*), is assigned a color or shade.

Bit maps are great for scanned photos and for many other types of projects that make significant use of color shading and delicate editing. For example, once you scan a photograph, it is turned into a bitmapped image. The bitmap is a pattern of dots. Each dot is assigned a color (if it's a color scanned image) or a black, white, or gray value (for gray-scale scanning). You can easily edit the image you've scanned by changing the color or grayness level of individual dots; you can also smooth out the edges by turning stray pixels white around the outer edge of the image.

The downside of working with bit-map graphics is a syndrome known as the "jaggies"; because bit-mapped graphics are, at best, a collection of dots, the dots are always there. You cannot resize the image without some loss of quality. If you enlarge the image, you are bound to see the pixels that make up the graphic. Even without resizing, the dots are usually pretty easy to see.

The Coach Says...

Armed with the right software, you can change a bit-mapped graphic into an object-oriented graphic, curing a runaway case of the jaggies. Many draw programs have autotrace features that can trace the edges of a bit-mapped graphic, turning it into an

object-oriented image. If your drawing program does not have this feature, you may want to invest in a stand-alone program that serves this purpose, such as Adobe Streamline.

OBJECT-ORIENTED BY ANY OTHER NAME

An *object-oriented graphic* is a different kind of animal entirely. Only draw programs—also called *illustration programs*—create object-oriented graphics. The image you see in a draw program is not a pattern of dots on the screen; rather, the image is produced based on a mathematical definition.

Angles, circles, squares, and various other shapes are defined in the program as calculations, so when you choose to use a particular tool, the program uses its mathematical definition of the shape, and, responding to the way you move the mouse or write on the graphics tablet, calculates the way the image appears on-screen. You can resize these graphics with no loss of quality because the calculations are performed each time the object is moved, resized, or modified in any way. You will not see a stray jaggie in the bunch.

Figure 3.3 shows an image that was resized several times. (The original shape was drawn with the polygon tool.) As you can see, there's no loss of quality between any of these images.

Now that you know the basic differences between bit-mapped and object-oriented graphics, take a closer look at the programs that create each of these graphics types.

Figure 3.3:

A resized object-oriented graphic.

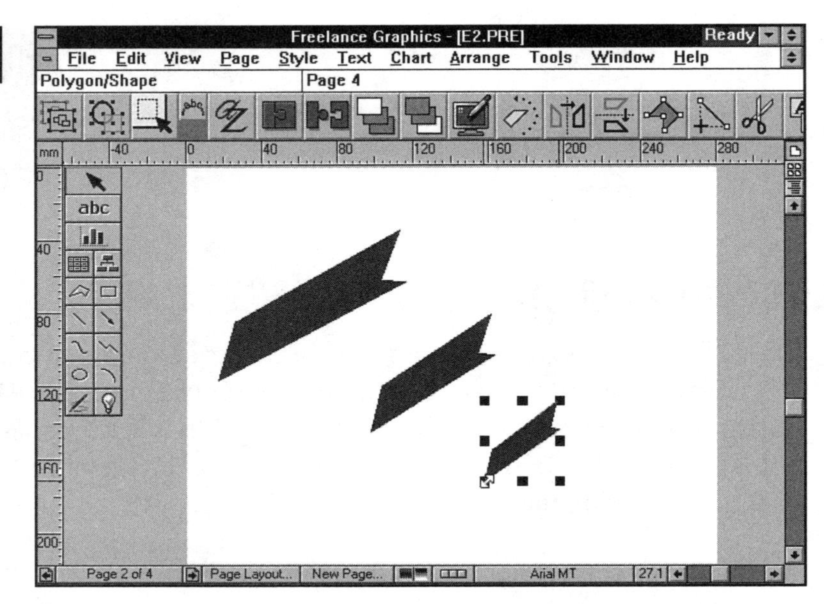

UNDERSTANDING PAINT PROGRAMS

As you learned in an earlier section, paint programs produce bit-mapped graphics. With this type of graphic, each picture is actually a pattern of dots on the screen or page. Paint programs generally offer a range of painting tools, a color palette, and a similar range of menus that provide you with commands for creating and editing the pictures you create. Figure 3.4 shows the screen area of Windows Paintbrush, a popular paint program included with Microsoft Windows at no extra cost.

You will find that some of the commands—but not many of the tools—are similar in both paint and draw programs. In most programs, the File menu houses commands you can use to setup the printer and make page specifications, as well as start new files, open existing files, and save the files you created. The Edit menu—where you find some similarities—enables you to cut, copy, and

paste your work and undo changes you've recently made. The View menu is another menu that may have similar commands but shows you different things. Depending on the program you are using, you may see Zoom In or Magnify commands that enable you to display the graphic at pixel level.

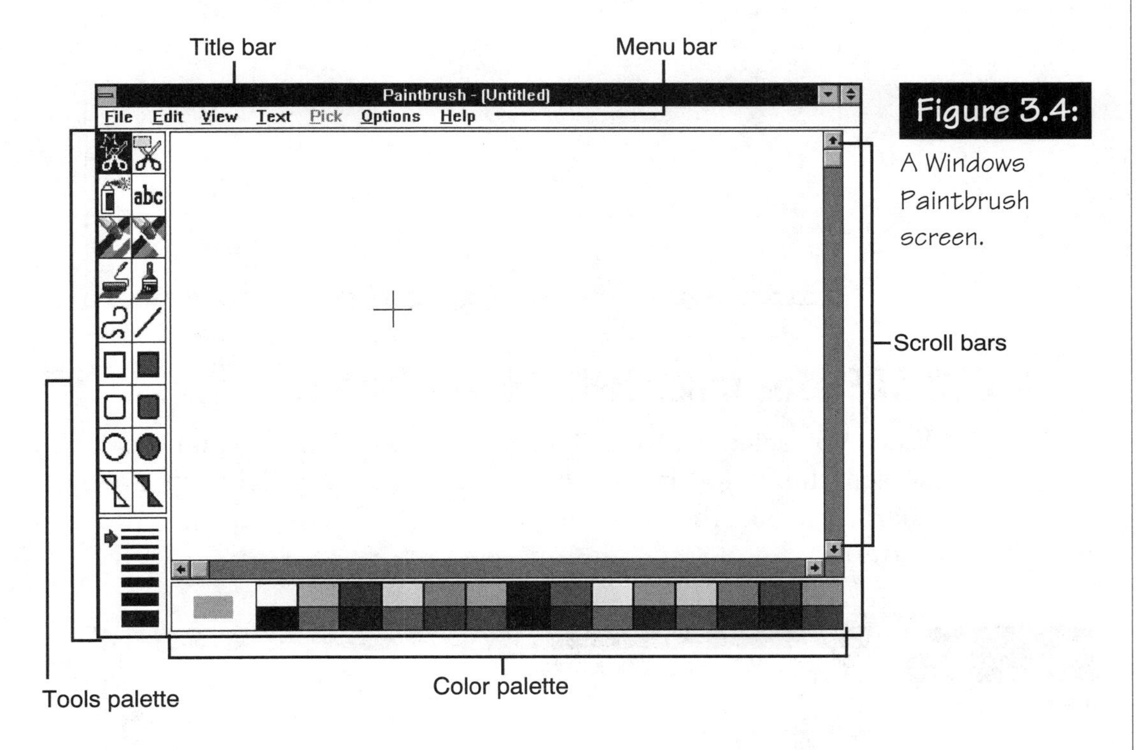

Figure 3.4: A Windows Paintbrush screen.

Figure 3.5 shows a paint program popular with Macintosh users, Fractal Design's Painter. Painter is a terrific paint program that gives you all sorts of options for painting on-screen. You can control the stroke of the brush, making it look like thin-line paint, broad strokes, charcoal sketching, or any number of special effects. Painter includes a familiar tool box but houses many of its other options in menus that are unique to this program.

Figure 3.5:

The tool box in Fractal Design's Painter.

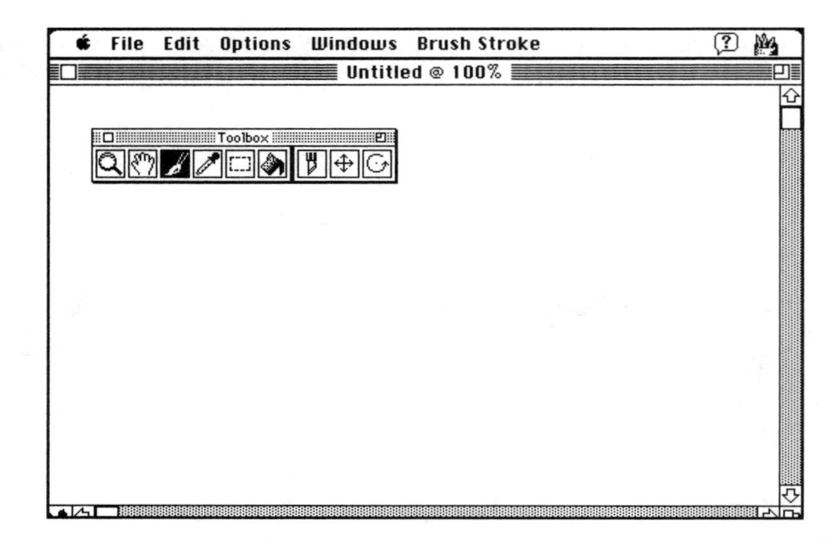

HOW DOES THE COMPUTER SEE THE IMAGE?

When you select a tool and a color and begin painting on the screen, the "paint" is spread in a pattern of dots. Even alphabetic characters, like the ones shown in figure 3.6, are really just dot patterns.

Figure 3.6:

Text characters in a paint program.

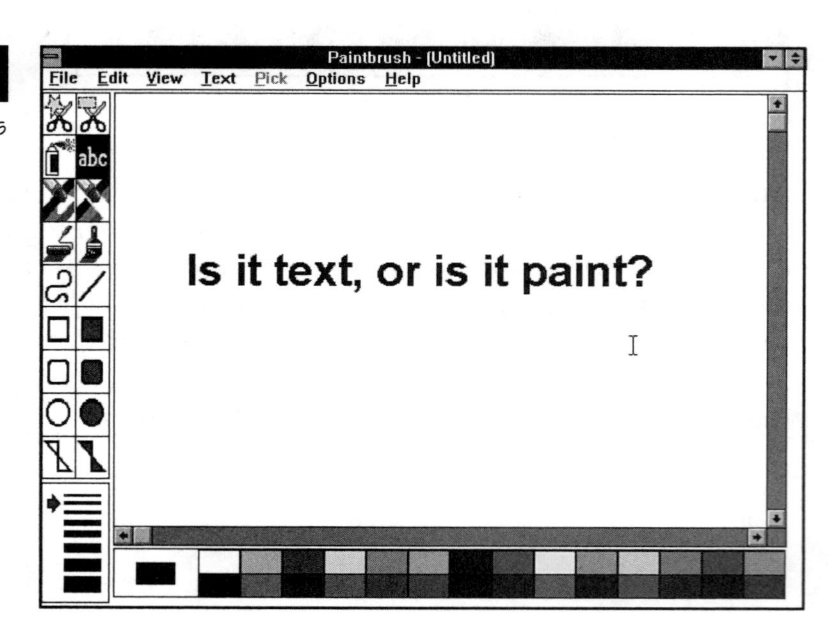

The Coach Says...

You can add text in all paint programs. After you add the text, however, it becomes a pattern of dots like everything else in the graphic. You cannot highlight the text and change the font, style, or size of text added to a paint graphic. Instead, you must erase it like you would any pixel on the screen and retype it after making the necessary text selections.

When you zoom in on the characters, the pattern of dots is easily discernible (see fig. 3.7). If you want to edit the characters you entered, you must erase them as you would any other graphic "dot" on the page.

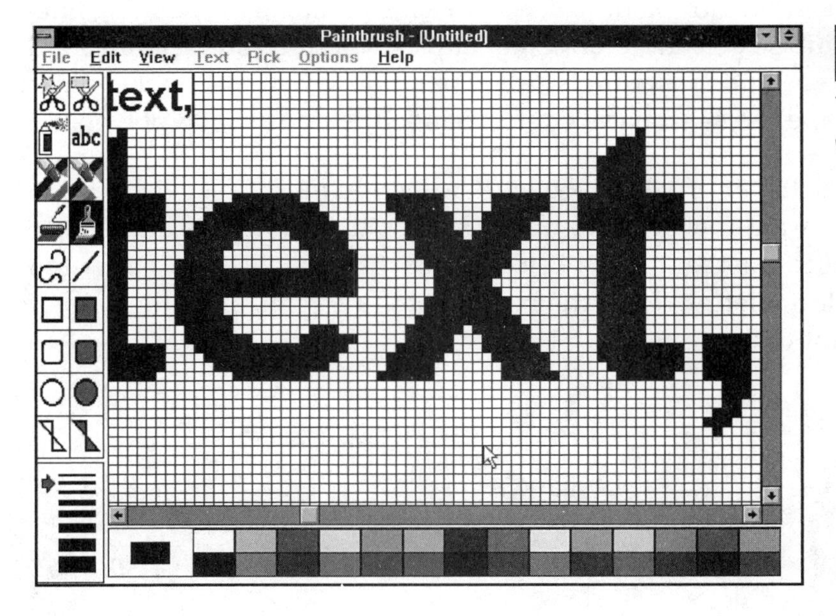

Figure 3.7:
The text in pixel view.

When you save the picture you created in a paint program, the file is written as-is in memory. That is, when you save the file, the graphic is represented as a map of bits in your computer's storage space. When you re-open the file, the program paints the graphic

on the screen by reading the map of dots in memory and recreating the image you produced earlier. Similarly, when you print a bit-mapped image, the graphic is sent to the printer as it is read in your computer's memory.

ON-SCREEN PAINTING

Painting on the screen is as simple as clicking on a tool, clicking on a color, and painting away. The variety of tools available in a paint program give you options for creating your pictures; the process is similar to using a paint set like the one you used in kindergarten (but less messy).

Both PC and Mac paint programs include a standard set of tools: something for painting large areas, something for painting fine-points, a selection tool that enables you to "grab" sections of the image, and eraser tools. Some paint programs also include a set of shape tools—square, circle, rounded rectangle, and polygon.

Whichever program you work with, you must first select the tool you want to work with by clicking on it. That tool is darkened, indicating that it has been selected. Then move the pointer to the color palette area at the bottom of the screen. Click the color you want to use.

The Coach Says...

Not all paint programs display the color palette automatically at the bottom of the screen. Some programs, such as Painter on the Mac, keep the color palette tucked away in a menu. To display the palette in Painter, open the Window menu and choose Color Palette.

When you move the pointer to the work area in the center of the screen, the pointer may change to a different shape, depending on the tool you selected and the program you are using. To paint, simply hold the mouse button down and drag the mouse. The invisible pixels are painted the color you specified.

Figure 3.8 shows the effects of using the spray paint tool in Windows Paintbrush. As you can see, the density of the paint is thicker in the upper portion of the "sprayed" area than it is in the lower area. Because the spray paint tool functions similarly to a real can of spray paint, holding the mouse in a certain area for a longer period of time adds more paint to that area, making it darker. On pixel level, this translates to adding more colored pixels in a smaller area (see fig. 3.9).

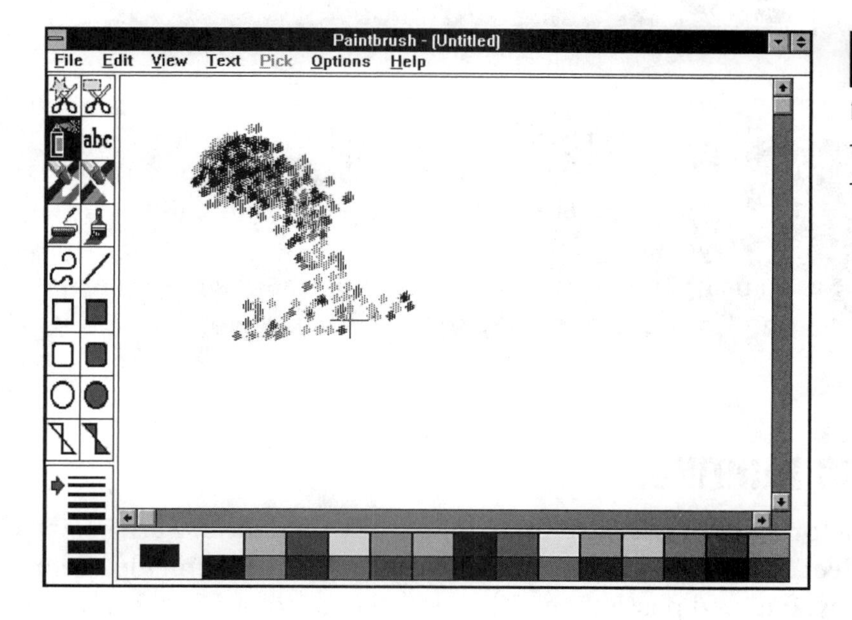

Figure 3.8:

Painting with the spray paint tool.

When you use one of the shape tools, the program helps you draw an image, but the assistance stops there. After the image is drawn, you cannot resize the image or change its shape. You can, however, move, copy, cut, paste, or change the color of the item.

Figure 3.9:

The spray paint effect at pixel level.

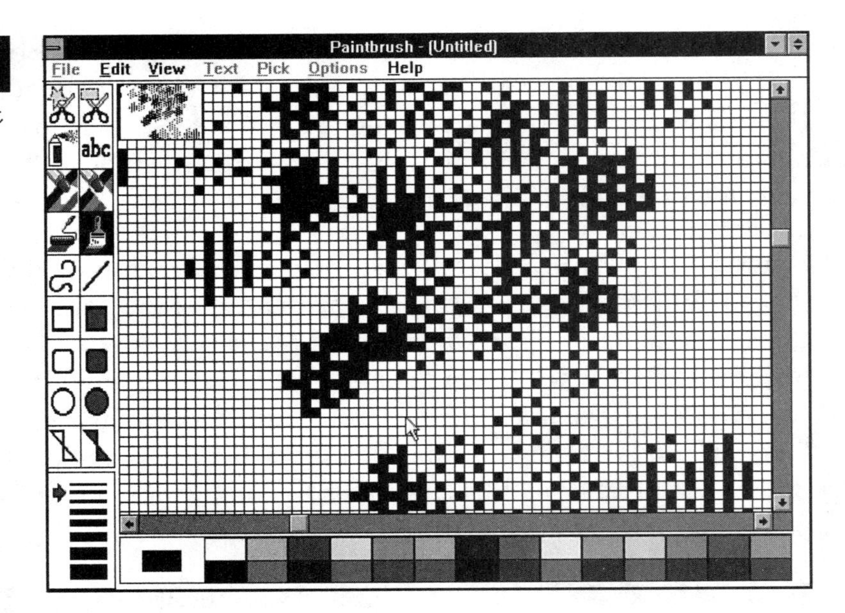

The Coach Says...

This chapter serves only to whet your palette (no pun intended) for working with the different types of graphics programs. For specific instructions on using the tools in these programs and hands-on examples you can try yourself, see Chapter 10.

EDITING PAINTINGS

The process of editing a bit map is really straightforward. You can select images (or portions of images) and move them, flip them, copy, cut, and paste them. You can change colors; you can erase elements you do not like. You are always somewhat limited, however, by the fact that you are copying and pasting pixels—so be ready to see some dots before your eyes.

USING THE ERASER TOOL

All paint programs provide a kind of eraser tool that, as you might expect, erases the pixels you painted, returning them to white. Some programs, like Windows Paintbrush, have a top-level eraser, which erases only the most recent item you added to the picture. If you spraypainted a patch of blue and then added an overlapping patch of yellow, for example, you can use the top-level eraser tool to erase only the yellow. If you select the traditional eraser, both levels are erased.

> **The Coach Says...**
>
> If your paint program does not have a top-level eraser (and many of them don't), look for the Undo command in the Edit menu. Undo reverses the last action, so if you just added that splotch of yellow, you can remove it by selecting Undo.

PIXEL-LEVEL EDITING

Additionally, all paint programs offer you the capability to zoom in and explore pixel level. Not all programs enable you to *edit* in magnified mode, however. (Check your program's manual for details.)

> **The Coach Says...**
>
> *Pixel level* is a technical sounding term for the screen displayed when you zoom in, displaying the individual pixels in your bit-mapped graphic. This also is called *magnified mode*, because the actual image is magnified.

If you can edit in magnified mode, you can change the color of individual pixels by clicking on the color you want (in the color palette) and then clicking on the pixel you want to change. Usually, the paint tool is chosen by default when you work in pixel mode. The paint bucket, which spreads paint over large areas, also may be available. Other tools are restricted and you cannot select them.

Suppose, for example, that you want to change the 8 in the eight-ball displayed earlier from gray to black . First, in Windows Paintbrush, you would change to pixel mode by opening the **View** menu and choosing **Zoom** In. The pointer changes to a large box. Move the box to the area you want to see (in this case, the 8), and click the mouse button. The area you selected is displayed on the screen, and the paint tool is selected by default.

Then move the pointer to the palette and click on black, if it is not already selected. (The color you used most recently is the selected color.) Finally, move the pointer to the area you want to change and click on a pixel. The pixel changes from gray to black. Figure 3.10 shows the screen after only a few pixels have been edited. Notice that the small view window, in the upper left corner of the work area, reflects the editing changes being made.

The Coach Says...

If you use a different paint program, the steps you follow to display the picture in magnified view and edit individual pixels may be slightly different. In Painter (the Mac draw program), for example, you magnify the view by clicking on the magnifying glass tool and then clicking on the area you want to magnify.

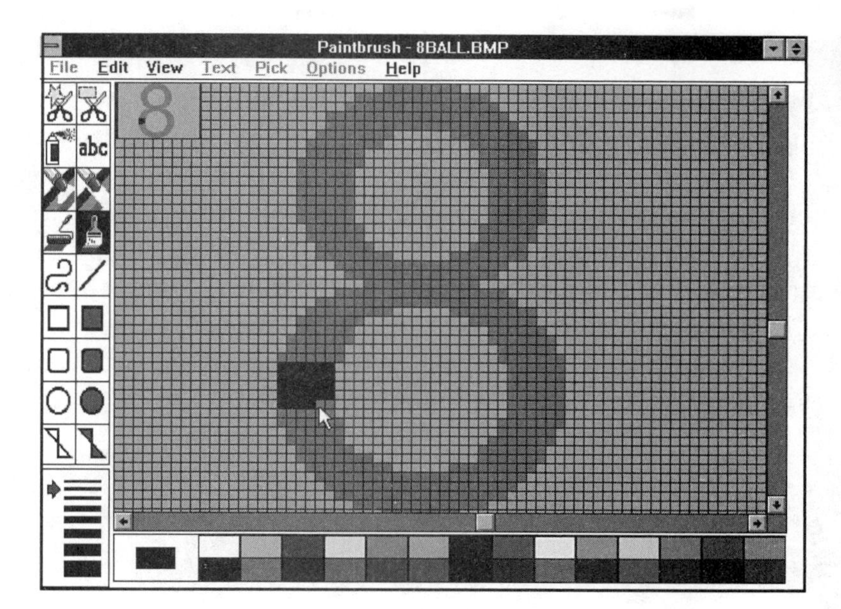

Figure 3.10:

Editing in pixel mode.

SELECTION EDITING

You use another type of editing when you want to do anything that involves selecting, moving, copying, cutting, and pasting areas of the picture. Suppose, for example, that you want to create another eight-ball. You can do this by making a copy of the original eight-ball and then modifying the copied image. Your first challenge is to select the area you want to copy.

The Coach Says...

Selection editing is any kind of graphics editing that requires that you select an item first. Before you can copy an image, for example, you need to select the image in order to tell the program what you want to copy. Depending on the paint program you are using, your selection tool may look like a pair of scissors, a dotted rectangle, a hand, or an arrow.

SELECTING GRAPHICS

Windows Paintbrush offers two different selection tools (the cutout selection tool and the rectangle selection tool), but most programs only give you one. When you want to select an area of the screen, click on the selection tool, position the pointer in an area above and to the left of the area you want to select, and press the mouse button while dragging the mouse down and to the right. A flashing rectangle expands as you drag the mouse, enclosing the area you want to select. When you have selected what you want, release the mouse button. The image is selected.

> **The Coach Says...**
>
> If you use Windows Paintbrush, you can use the cutout selection tool (the scissors with the star cutout) to select a specific image without enclosing the surrounding space. Some Mac programs have a comparable tool called the *lasso tool.* The rectangle selection tool encloses a rectangular area on the screen.

Figure 3.11 shows the eight-ball after the image has been selected using the cutout selection tool in Windows Paintbrush.

CUTTING AND COPYING GRAPHICS

You then can use one of the commands in the Edit menu to cut or copy the image. Although you do not really see anything happen, the program takes a second to write the area you selected to a reserved portion of memory. If you select Cut, the selected area is removed from the page; if you choose Copy, the selected graphic remains on the page while a copy is placed in memory.

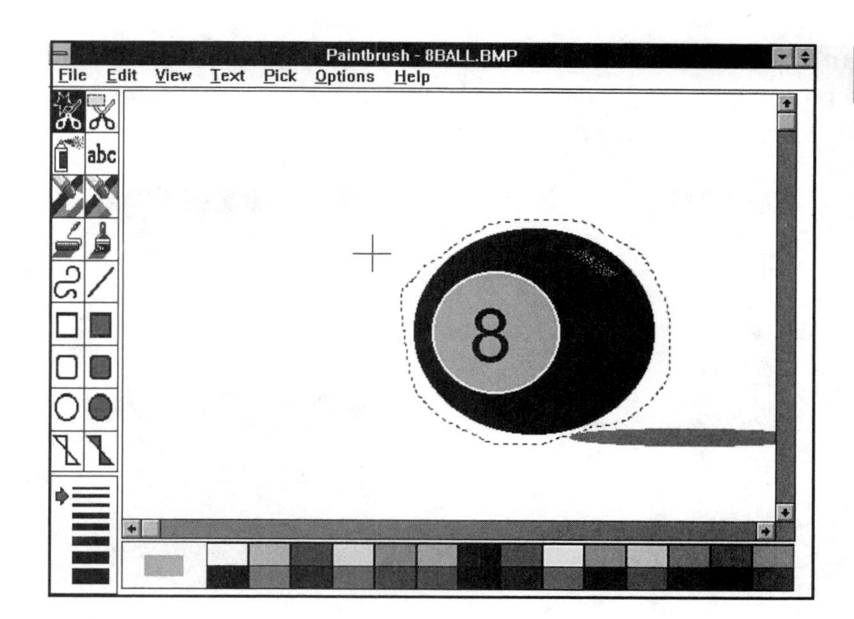

Figure 3.11:
Selecting a portion of a paint graphic.

The Coach Says...

Depending on the paint program you use, you may be able to use short-cut keys to carry out simple commands like Cut and Paste. In Windows Paintbrush, press Ctrl-C to copy and Ctrl-V to Paste. In Painter (on the Mac), press ⌘-C to copy and ⌘-V to paste. As you can see, the short-cut keys are similar.

PASTING GRAPHICS

You use the **P**aste command, also available in the **E**dit menu of most programs, to place the copied or cut image on the page. You can move the pasted portion to the position on-screen you want it; then click outside the area to remove the highlighted area and place the item in the picture.

Figure 3.12 shows the image after it has been copied and pasted in the picture. After placement, you changed the color of the pool ball (to red) and turned the 8 into a 3.

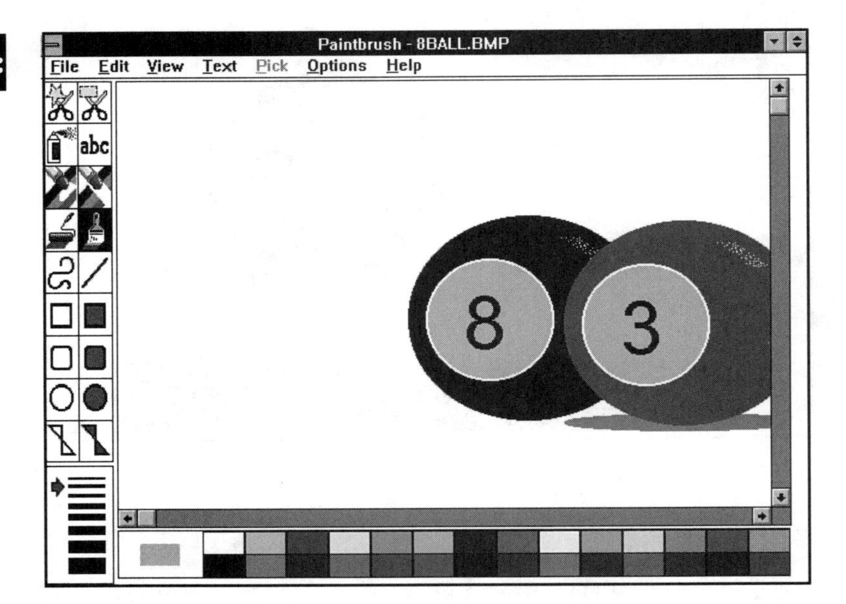

Figure 3.12: The changed, pasted eight-ball.

The Coach Says...
For more information and hands-on practice working with various paint editing procedures, see Chapter 11.

SAVING PAINT PROGRAM FILES

The process of saving paint program files is similar to saving any type of file. Look for the **S**ave command in the **F**ile menu. When you choose the **S**ave command, a dialog box appears, asking for the name of the file and, in some programs, the graphics file format in which you want to save the file. The Save As dialog box in Windows Paintbrush, for example, asks you for the name of the file, the file type, and the drive and directory in which you want to save the file (see fig. 3.13).

The Coach Says...

In Windows Paintbrush, you can choose the file type you want from PCX, BMP (16-color bitmap), 24-color bitmap, or a 256-color bitmap. Mac programs often give you the option of saving files in PICT or MacPaint format.

Figure 3.13: The Save As dialog box.

After you enter a file name (you don't need to enter the extension; the program will do that for you, according to the file type you choose), click on OK. The program then saves the file in the format you specified.

The Coach Says...

After you save the file, you may want to use it in other programs. If the file type in which the picture is created is not compatible with the program you want to use, you can use a conversion utility to change the image into a format usable by the other program. *The Graphics Coach* bonus disk contains three shareware conversion utilities (one for DOS, one for Windows, and one for the Macintosh). See Chapter 13 for more information about file conversion.

POPULAR PAINT PROGRAMS

Thus far, you have seen examples of one of the most popular—and easily accessible—PC paint programs: Windows Paintbrush. Paint programs are available from a variety of sources, including retail, shareware, and bundled software.

Retail is, of course, the shrink-wrapped version of the program you buy either mail order or off the shelf in the computer store. Shareware is often available on-line or directly from the designer. Bundled software is a program that is included with another item. When I purchased my Logitech mouse, for example, a version of Logitech Paint was included at no extra charge.

The Coach Says...

Shareware, as you may know, is not freeware (you cannot have it free), but rather software based on a trust-your-neighbor concept: if you like it and use it, pay for it. Many shareware programs ask that you purchase the full version of the program after a certain period of time—perhaps 15 or 30 days.

This section highlights some of the more popular paint programs available for Windows, DOS, and Macintosh users. Before you begin, a distinction should be made here: Windows Paintbrush, and most of the paint programs mentioned in this section, are known as *entry-level* paint programs. They do not do incredibly sophisticated things. Other types of paint programs, known as *professional-level*, or 24-bit paint programs, are used for high-end applications and are capable of providing a range of features not available in their smaller counterparts. Programs, such as CA-Cricket Paint (for Windows), Tempra Pro (for DOS), or SuperPaint (for the Mac), enable you to bring in video clips, digitized images, and work with both bitmapped and object-oriented files easily.

If the work you do needs the highest resolution possible, a wide variety of input sources, the capability to work with both paint and draw graphics, and an almost baffling range of special effects, such as brush styles, paper types, and unique shape controls, a professional-level paint program may be what you need. This level also comes with a higher level price tag, however: from $400 to more than $700 is the average cash outlay.

ZSOFT'S PC PAINTBRUSH

One of the most popular lower-end paint programs currently available is PC Paintbrush 5+. Published by ZSoft Corp., this program is the newest version in a string of mega-popular revisions. PC Paintbrush's popularity has been in part due to its user-friendly interface and easy-to-figure-out commands and tools.

PC Paintbrush brings out in its newest release additional support for color editing, a special effects mode that allows you to do easy 3-D modeling on the fly, and a number of color filters that help you improve gray-scale or color scans you've imported.

PC Paintbrush 5+ runs on only 640K (something most programs cannot say) and will work efficiently on a decidedly low-end PC. Built-in autotrace features help you bring in scanned images and clean them up easily.

The Coach Says...

PC Paintbrush 5+ works with all popular file formats, including PCX, BMP, TIFF, and GIF. The cost of the program is a nominal $149.

FRACTAL DESIGN'S PAINTER

One company that is fine-tuning its focus to the needs of graphics users is Fractal Design Corporation. Painter is available for both Macs and PCs.

Their PC version of Painter is a high-end 24-bit-color paint program that runs under both Windows 3.0 and 3.1. The version available for the Mac won *Personal Business Publishing* magazine's Paint Program of the Year award.

Painter gives you those extra perks most basic paint programs cannot offer: brush textures, pen stroke special effects, and paper typing. One feature that is available only with high-end paint programs is the ability to use special fonts: Adobe Type 1 and TrueType fonts are supported. The costs? Somewhere around $279 retail.

> **The Coach Says...**
>
> Another program from Fractal is Sketcher, which is a gray-scale paint program for users with monochrome monitors. Sketcher includes a full library of tools, including utensils such as pencils, airbrushes, calligraphy pens, crayons, and oil and water paints.

MACPAINT

MacPaint was the original painting program for the Mac. Although considered a low-end paint program, MacPaint still covers a large portion of the paint market. With on-screen palettes that can easily be displayed or hidden, MacPaint makes the process of creating paint graphics easy and fun.

The standard menus offer a variety of simple editing commands, and you also have the ability to change font, size, and style. Separate color and pattern, tool and line width, and measurement palettes keep you organized while you work but provide everything you need within mouse reach.

> **The Coach Says...**
>
> MacPaint saves files in MAC format, which can be converted to other formats in some popular Windows programs.

THE BENEFITS OF PAINT PROGRAMS

Although many paint programs are less expensive than their draw counterparts, it does not hold true that the less expensive programs are always low-end offerings. Paint programs have certain uses; they offer a type of art creation and editing not available in draw programs. If you want to do any of the following types of graphics work, for example, a paint program is what you need:

- ★ Creating a piece of art in which the brush stroke or pen style is important
- ★ Creating paintings that have a variety of custom blends that can only be achieved through pixel editing
- ★ Importing a photo by using a scanner and preparing it for final publication
- ★ Creating art based on an photograph or other scanned image

UNDERSTANDING DRAW PROGRAMS

Draw programs, as you learned earlier in this chapter, offer a different approach to art generation and editing. Unlike paint programs, which create images that are composed of individual dots on the screen, draw programs work with shapes instead of pixels. When you select the rectangle tool and draw a square, for example, that square is not represented by a pattern of dots on the screen; rather, the square is an object that can be moved, resized, flipped, rotated, and otherwise modified as a whole. You can make all these changes without any loss of clarity or the onset of jaggies that plague paint program users.

Figure 3.14 shows a screen from a popular PC draw program, Micrografx Designer. Similar to the example of the paint program you saw earlier, this screen has a title bar, a menu bar, and a tools row.

Figure 3.14: The screen in Micrografx Designer.

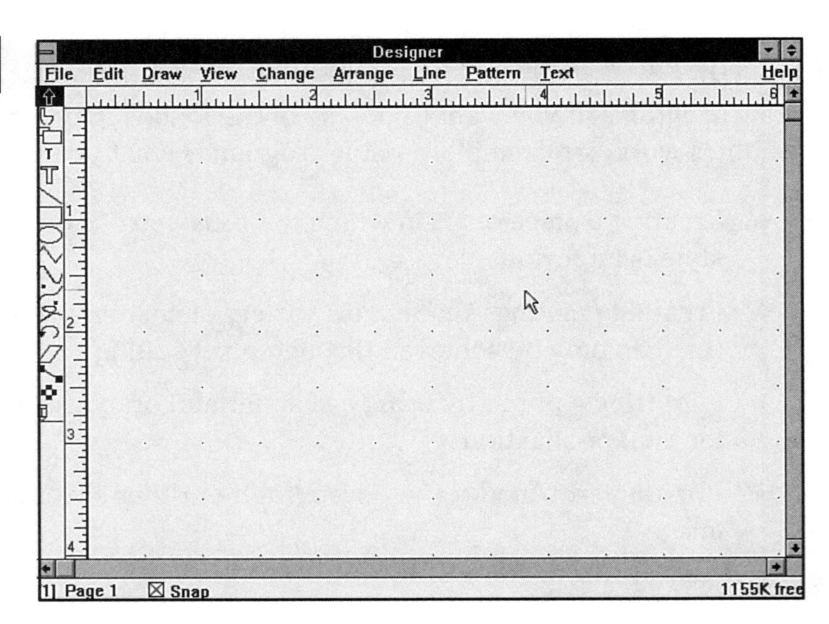

As you can see, many of the tools available in the tools row look much different from those in paint programs. A wide variety of shapes, lines, and odd-looking symbols comprise this row. Additionally, no color palette is present (although you can set color choices from within the Pattern menu).

The menus, at the top of the screen, also are different from those offered by paint programs. The **F**ile, **E**dit, and **V**iew menus house similar commands, allowing you to open, save, and enter settings for files; copy, cut, paste, and make other editing changes; and change the way the screen is displayed. Beyond those similarities, however, the program types differ greatly. The Change and **A**rrange menus help you work with layers and placement of the objects on the screen. The Pattern menu houses the commands you need to set and control the pattern you choose for filling shapes you create. Finally, the Text menu contains a wide variety of text commands for working with text fonts, sizes, styles, and special effects like curved text and text fills.

Figure 3.15 shows a screen from Adobe Illustrator on the Mac. Here you see another set of tools and different menus stretching across the top of the screen. The **F**ile, **E**dit, and **V**iew menus contain the commands you'd expect them to; the Arrange menu helps you control the placement of items; Paint includes commands for setting colors and patterns; Type controls text; Window includes commands for displaying and hiding on-screen palettes; and Graph enables you to import and work with graphs.

Drawing programs offer you the precision that a hit-or-miss paint program cannot. For technical drawings or line art, the accuracy offered by a drawing program is far superior than trying to achieve similar results with a paint program. If you plan to work with text in a graphics environment—perhaps creating artsy logos, curving or filling text, or working with a wide variety of fonts—a draw program will also offer you text capabilities a paint program cannot.

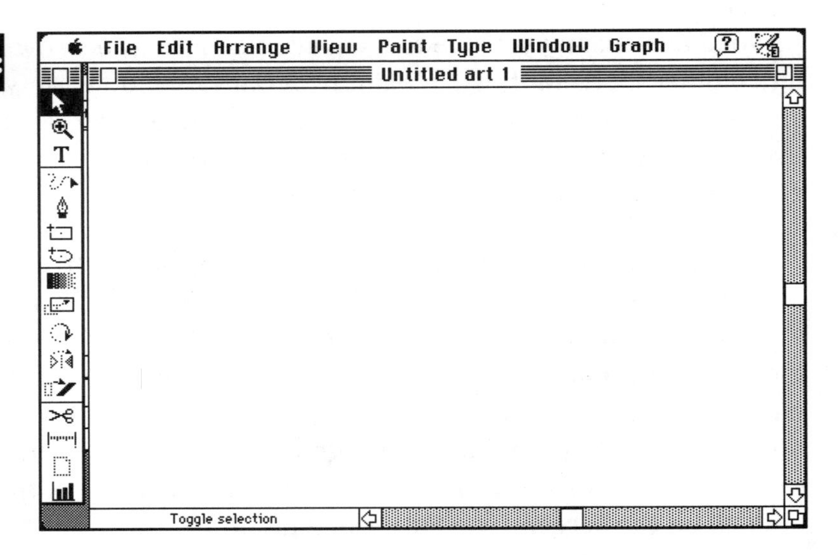

Figure 3.15: A screen from Adobe Illustrator for the Mac.

HOW DOES THE COMPUTER SEE THE IMAGE?

As you learned earlier in this chapter, a draw program creates an object-oriented graphic. This piece of art is not the sum total of a series of dots; rather it is an object created based on a mathematical equation that is refigured each time the object is moved, resized, or redrawn. Because the curves or angles of the object are recalculated with every change and the lines are drawn to fit the calculation, drawing programs give you perfectly drawn objects every time. No stray pixels floating out there in the white space—just complete, accurate images and curves.

Working with a draw program can be more challenging, at first, than playing around with a paint program. After all, the paint programs follow the way we think; you have been painting, more or less, since kindergarten or earlier. But draw programs bring a more avant garde style to art production. Rather than drawing freehand—as the name draw program might suggest—a draw program requires that you think in layers as you create an image. You might combine several shapes—each placed on top of the others—to create the desired effect.

Yet there are tools from kindergarten we can bring to draw programs, as well. Remember when you studied shapes? The teacher (Mrs. Pickles with the bouffant hair) brought around stencils to trace on a piece of manila paper. We drew around the shapes, overlapping them, and coloring them in to make some kind of picture. Put two triangles on top of a circle and you've got a kitty's face. A big square with four little squares inside it becomes a window. With draw programs, you layer shapes to create a desired effect. The draw program remembers all these shapes and lets you to layer them as necessary, rearranging them, changing their color, controlling the inside pattern, making them transparent or opaque. Still and all, the program sees them as shapes—or, perhaps more accurately—as mathematical calculations that *define* the shapes you see on-screen.

When you print the object, the program sends the file—in a special object-oriented language—to the printer. PostScript printers, which understand this type of language, print graphics files beautifully. Other printers may have to convert the information being sent from the program, which may result in a slight loss of quality.

When you save the file, the program saves the file in the object-oriented description language. When you re-open the file at a later time, the program reads all the necessary calculations and redraws the image for you with lightning speed.

DRAWING OBJECTS

After you understand the basic philosophy of drawing programs, actually creating the image is not much more difficult than painting on the screen. Select a tool from the tools row, position it in the work area, and draw the shape you want. You may have to spend some time experimenting with individual tools; some may not behave the way you expect them to. (The polygon tool often takes some practice.) Some draw programs offer freehand tools, which let you create a drawing without relying solely on shapes and lines.

Figure 3.16, for example, shows the Designer screen after the circle tool has been selected and a circle has been drawn on the screen. Notice the pointer shape, indicating that a drawing tool is selected. The grid dots in the work area, the horizontal and vertical rulers, and the object measurement in the status line at the bottom of the screen all help you ensure that you're creating an object just the size you need it

Figure 3.16:

Drawing a circle in a draw program.

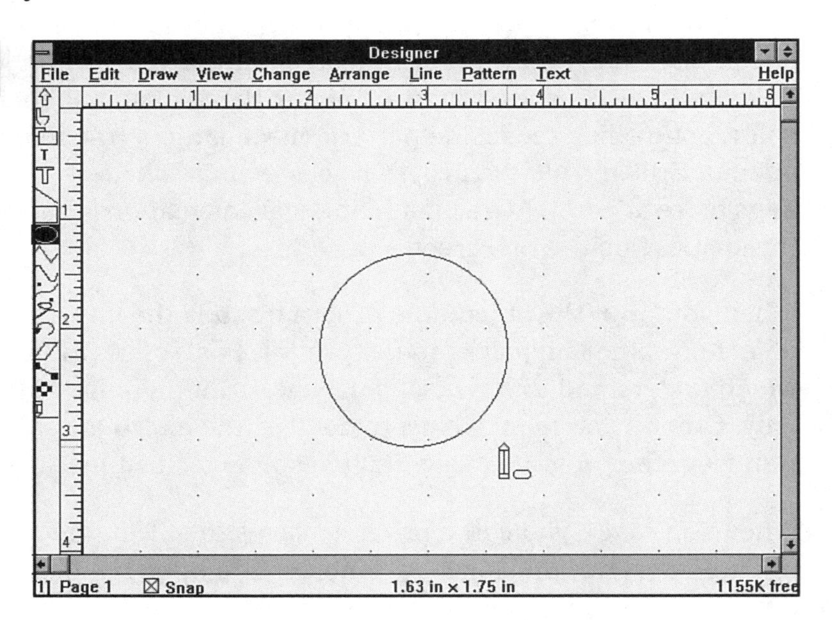

Obviously, this is a simplification of the basic drawing process. You can make many selections before you draw, including fill color (so the circle will be colored in), outer line color, or internal pattern. You can also control line thickness and determine whether you want the shape to be an oval or a round circle.

EDITING OBJECTS

Editing in a draw program is much different from editing in a paint program. Because there are no pixels to show, there is no pixel

mode. You can display the screen in different views by opening the View menu and choosing the display you want.

SELECTING OBJECTS

In every case, you must select the object you want to work with before you can edit it. You select an item by clicking on it. When you do so, little black handles appear around the outside edge of the item. You can then perform one of the following editing operations on the item:

- ★ Change the color of the object
- ★ Specify a pattern instead of a color
- ★ Change the line color or width of the outer border
- ★ Rotate the object
- ★ Change the layer of the object
- ★ Modify individual points on the object
- ★ Change the shading of an object
- ★ Cut, copy, or paste the object
- ★ Add or modify text

> **The Coach Says...**
>
> Remember that the draw program looks at the object in layers, so if you have a multiple layer object—perhaps a shape with several more overlapping it—the draw program will select the topmost layer. You can cycle through the layers by continuing to click the mouse button or by using one of the commands in the Arrange menu (this menu may be different in your program).

CHANGING OBJECT COLOR

Figure 3.17 shows the circle after the first circle is changed to black and another circle—this one white—is added. To change the first circle, you clicked on the selection tool (the top arrow in the tools row) and clicked on the circle. Handles appeared surrounding the shape. Then, you opened the Pattern menu and selected the Colors command. A small popup box appeared, offering different color choices. After clicking on black and clicking OK, the circle was changed to black.

Figure 3.17:

Editing a draw object.

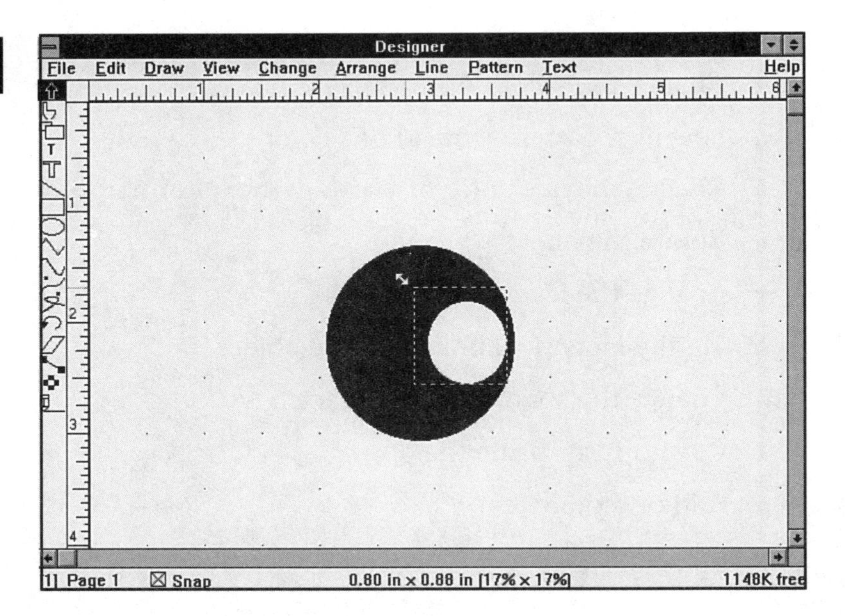

DRAWING THE OBJECT

Drawing the circle was a simple process. This time, you set the color to white before drawing. You selected the circle tool, then opened the Pattern menu and chose Colors. After selecting white and clicking OK, you drew the circle on top of the black circle. Because it is opaque, it covers that portion of the black circle, although the entire black circle is still intact of the layer beneath the white one.

You see something else in figure 3.17, as well. A dotted outline surrounds the white circle, and a double-headed arrow is positioned above and to the left of the dotted rectangle. This figure was captured while the white circle was being resized, another editing operation.

RESIZING AN OBJECT

To resize an object, position the mouse pointer on the object you want; then click and hold the mouse button while dragging the mouse in the direction you want to resize the object. In this case, you are making the white circle bigger by moving the mouse up and to the left. When the circle is the size you want, release the mouse button.

WORKING WITH TEXT

One major benefit of working with a drawing program is the font manipulation ability of most object-oriented programs. With programs like Micrografx Designer, you can choose the font you want to work with and make a number of choices including color, style, size, placement, and other more specialized options.

The Coach Says...

Most paint programs enable you to add text, but after you select the font and add the characters, the text becomes pixels like everything else in the painting. Not so with a draw program. The text is an object of its own, on its own layer, so you can highlight text you've already added and change it in any way necessary.

Other variations among different programs may enable you to trace objects, convert images from one type of image to another, import and export objects, and perform a wide range of other functions. For specific instruction on using the various editing and maintenance commands with your program, consult your program's documentation. For more hands-on examples you can try with your own draw program, see Chapter 11.

SEEING IN LAYERS

As mentioned earlier, draw programs look at the objects you create in terms of what layer they occupy. If you cover up a circle with a square, for example, the circle is still under there whether you can see it or not. With Micrografx Designer (and also with Adobe Illustrator), you can use one of the commands in the **A**rrange menu to change the order in which the objects are placed. Figure 3.18 shows the contents of Designer's **A**rrange menu, which contains the commands used to move objects through the layers in the drawing.

Two commands in this menu that are currently disabled are important ones after you finish changing the drawing. When you are happy with the image, you may want to combine all the objects—in this case, that's the bottom circle, the top circle, and the text item—into one object. This enables you to copy, cut, and paste the object easily. You also can import the item into another program easily if the objects have first been combined. As you can guess, the command in Designer for doing this is the Combine command. Later, if you need to edit an individual item that is part of the entire object, you can use the Break Apart command to separate the object into its elements.

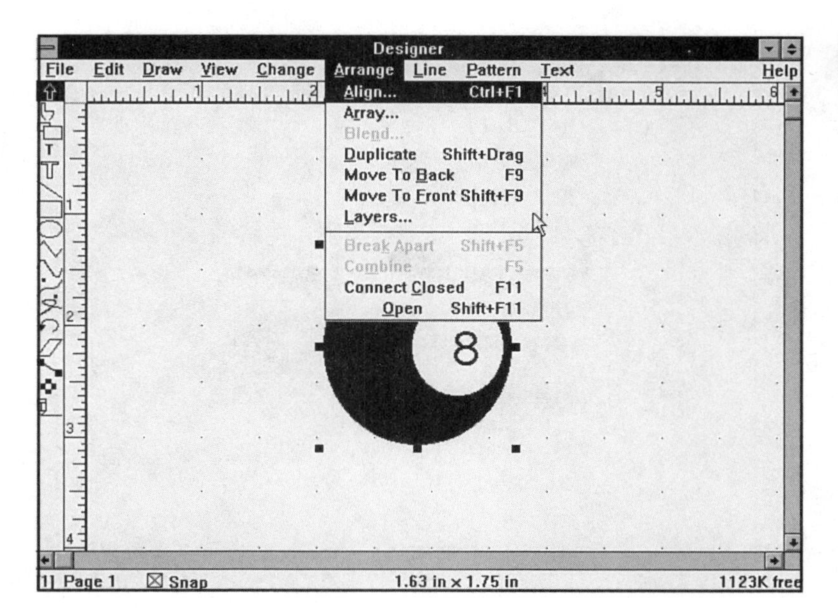

Figure 3.18: The contents of Designer's Arrange menu.

The Coach Says...

All draw programs provide you with some method of grouping items. The command might be called Group, while the command the separates the items might be called Ungroup (this is the case with Adobe Illustrator). Look for these commands in the program's Arrange menu.

SAVING DRAW PROGRAM FILES

When you are ready to save the file you created in the draw program, look in the **F**ile menu for the command you need. Chances are, the command appears as either **S**ave or Save **A**s. In Designer, when you choose Save from the File menu, the Save dialog box appears, as shown in figure 3.19. In Adobe Illustrator, the command is the same.

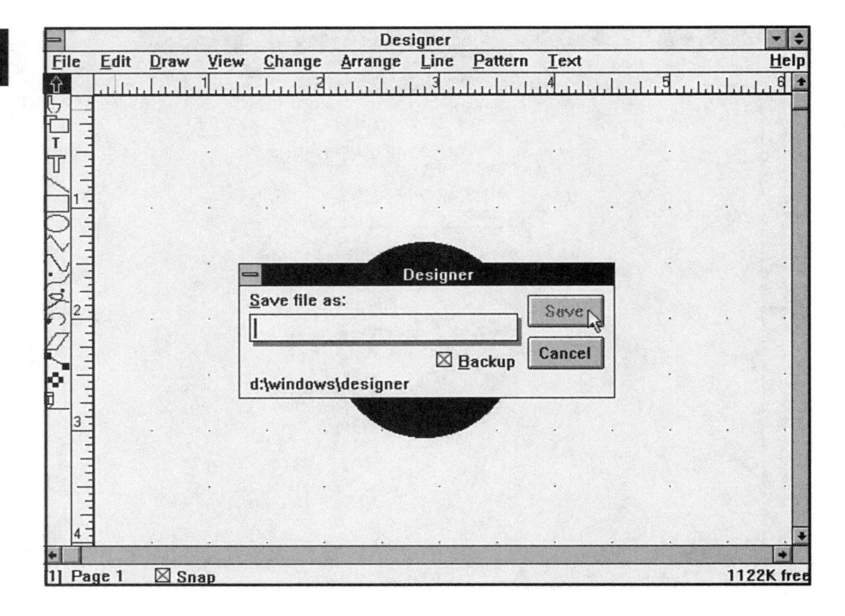

Figure 3.19: Saving the drawing file.

You can type the file name, but you do not need to enter the extension. The program adds the necessary extension for you. (This procedure differs, depending on the type of drawing program you are using.)

> **The Coach Says...**
>
> Like some other draw programs, Micrografx Designer enables you to use many other file types and export (or save) Designer files in other formats, as well. You use the Import and Export commands, in the File menu, to work with other file types.

POPULAR DRAW PROGRAMS

This section highlights some of the draw programs currently used for today's high-end graphics work. In general, you will find the offerings in the draw category more expensive than paint

programs, but they also do more. Another consideration is the amount of storage space required by most high-end draw programs; you may need from 2M to 10M to fully install some draw programs with all available clip art.

MICROGRAFX DESIGNER

Up to this point, you have seen several examples of one draw program—Micrografx Designer, which runs under Windows 3.0 or Windows 3.1. Designer is touted by its manufacturer as the highest-possible quality precision graphics tool currently available for Windows. The hefty price tag ($695) shows the weight of available features. Designer offers all the basic features and more, although it may be a bit "old world" in its user friendliness.

The Coach Says...

Micrografx includes hundreds of pieces of clip art and offers additional art packages for a cost of $249. Micrografx can import and export files in most common file types, including PCX, TIF, and EPS.

ADOBE ILLUSTRATOR

Other popular draw programs include Adobe Illustrator, one of the first standard high-end graphics programs available. Illustrator was originally available only for the Mac, but enjoyed such enormous success that it soon was made available for the PC.

Illustrator supports a wide range of file formats and, in addition to its many draw features, makes it easy for you to add custom-drawn graphs to your illustrations. Bit maps you open in Adobe can be automatically traced, which essentially turns the image into object-oriented art during the conversion process. You can customize this program to a great extreme by making your own colors, patterns, and special effects.

The Coach Says...

Illustrator outputs to all high-end devices, including PostScript printers and imagesetters. The cost weighs in at a whopping $695 (retail), the same as major PC competitor Designer.

CORELDRAW!

Another popular high-end drawing program that runs under Windows is CorelDRAW!. Corel Systems, the manufacturer, came up with a new area of graphics when this program introduced high-powered text manipulation features. You can do almost anything with letters you can envision; stretch them, rotate them, squash them, fill them with color (or other characters), bend them, turn them into something else. The possibilities are endless.

CorelDRAW! also offers standard drawing tools, complete with Bezier curves, tools for freehand drawing, an autotrace feature, and a large library of clip art images. In addition to all this, CorelDRAW! is one of the only PC graphics packages that allows you to do real bitmap editing, giving you a paint and draw program in one. Like Illustrator and Designer, CorelDRAW! does very well with PostScript output and runs in the ballpark of $595 (retail).

The Coach Says...

The newest version of CorelDRAW!, version 3.0, is available with a CD-ROM storing over 14,000 clip art images and 250 fonts.

ALDUS FREEHAND

Another popular drawing program available for both the PC and the Mac is Aldus Freehand. Designed as a seamless drawing

companion for people using Aldus PageMaker, the desktop publishing program, Freehand offers artists tools that feel familiar. By enabling you to create objects in the way that seems most comfortable for you—whether that means building an image layer by layer or drawing the image freehand on a graphics tablet—the flexibility of the program enables you to master computer drawing with a minimum of trouble.

Additionally, Freehand supports the usual slew of fonts and outputs in all popular formats. The easy integration between PC and Mac environments is a big plus. Also, Freehand offers a pressure-sensitive feature for graphics tablet users that changes the thickness or heaviness of a line on-screen when you press the stylus harder on the tablet.

OTHER GRAPHICS PROGRAMS

This chapter has not covered all the graphics programs available—or even a small percentage of them. Remember that in addition to retail paint and draw programs, there are almost uncountable freeware, shareware, and bundled software programs available. Additionally, besides the basic paint and draw types, there are other types of graphics programs, as well. Not only do you have graphics manipulation programs, like file converters, image processors, and photo cleaner-uppers, you still have several different graphics categories from which to choose: presentation graphics, multimedia, and CAD programs.

PRESENTATION GRAPHICS

Presentation graphics program are rather large-scale (and large-memory-hog) programs that are designed specifically for those of us who are forced to give presentations—for managers, for clients, for the PTA, for whoever.

Most people are not too keen on creating a presentation of any type, and more often than not, business people have little more than a few minutes to devote to a last-minute presentation. Several popular presentation graphics programs, which allow you to create on-screen charts, bulleted lists, title pages, and incorporate original art and clip art, have recently made a big splash in the graphics applications market.

One of the most popular of these programs is Freelance Graphics for Windows, another creation of Lotus Development Corporation, that makes the whole process of creating presentations incredibly painless and even fun (see fig. 3.20). Freelance is available for DOS and Windows (the newest version, 2.0, is a Windows version) and includes full drawing capabilities. Other popular presentation graphics programs include Harvard Graphics, Aldus Persuasion, and Microsoft PowerPoint.

Figure 3.20:

A sample screen from Freelance Graphics for Windows.

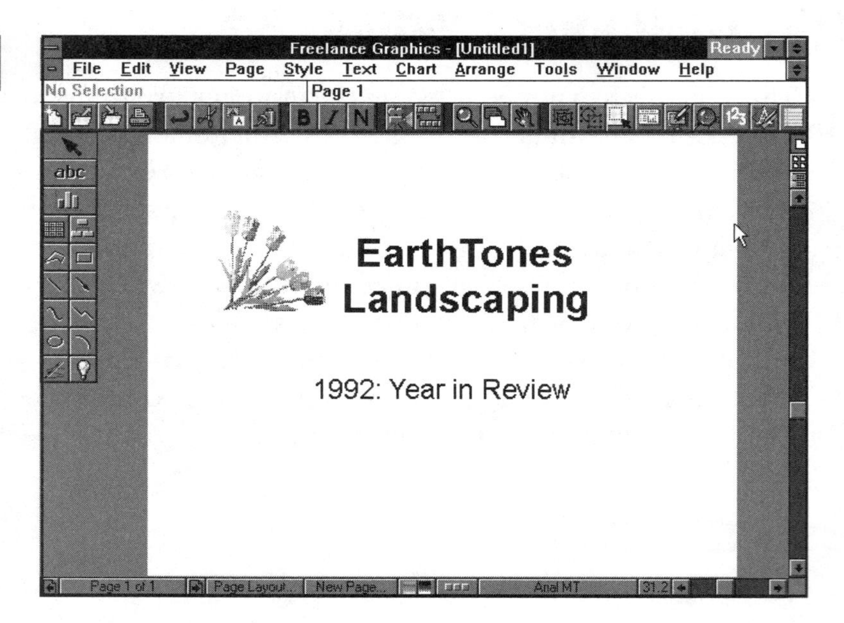

MULTIMEDIA PROGRAMS

Multimedia programs are not so much graphics programs as they are video and sound integration programs. Many multimedia programs include full-scale graphics capabilities as well as the ability to import files from a variety of formats. Popular multimedia programs include MacroMind Director, Animation Works Interactive, MediaBlitz, Adobe Premier, and Diva VideoShop.

> **The Coach Says...**
>
> Several presentation graphics programs, which also include slide show features for on-screen display, now incorporate multimedia features.

CAD PROGRAMS

A final type of graphics program this chapter will discuss here is CAD, or computer-aided design. CAD applications are ordinarily used for highly specialized, technical illustrations. Need to do the floorplan for the new offices? A CAD program gives you the tools and the accuracy you need. Popular CAD programs include the ever-popular AutoCAD, Generic CAD, and MiniCAD (for the Mac).

THE BENEFITS OF DRAW PROGRAMS

Draw programs are not for everyone. They often carry with them a pretty substantial learning curve and the requirement that you learn to think in terms of shapes and objects instead of freehand art tools. You must also consider the price tag—which, in some cases, many be many times higher than a paint program. As a trade-off for these more negative aspects, however, the following are big pluses:

★ Draw programs offer higher quality output than paint programs

★ Draw programs enable you to create an incredible range of special text effects

★ Draw programs give you precision control over the placement, creation, rotation, and modification of objects

★ Draw programs often support a large number of graphics file formats and enable you to import and autotrace bitmap files

★ Draw programs often come equipped with a library of clip art you can use in your own work

★ Some draw programs—and especially presentation graphics programs—are beginning to implement multimedia features, allowing you to mix video and sound output for dazzling effect

★ The support for draw programs often exceeds that available for paint programs (although this varies greatly from program to program)

WHAT TYPE OF GRAPHICS PROGRAM DO YOU NEED? (A CHECKLIST)

No doubt, you have seen yourself and some of the graphics tasks you need to accomplish somewhere in this chapter. What type of graphics program will you be shopping for? Do you have the time to play around with the closest program or will you have to invest real money (yours or the company's)? Table 3.2 helps you review the various considerations involved in purchasing a graphics program.

Table 3.2
What Type of Program Do You Need?

Feature	*Paint program*	*Draw program*
Paint tools		✔
Object fill		✔
Ability to rotate, layer, and resize objects	✔	
Ability to flip items horizontally and vertically	✔	✔
Low cost		✔
Low data storage requirements (for program)		✔
Lower data storage (for files)	✔	
Capability to change color on pixel level	✔	
Capability to import and export most popular file formats		✔
Pixel editing for scanned images	✔	
Autotrace for imported images		✔
Special text effects		✔
Object alignment		✔
Print PostScript output		✔

INSTANT REPLAY

In this chapter, you learned quite a bit about the different graphics programs available today and explored some of the features that may be important to you. Specifically, you learned the following:

INSTANT REPLAY

- ✔ What a paint program offers you
- ✔ What you can do with a draw program
- ✔ Procedures common to paint programs
- ✔ Operations in most PC and Mac draw programs
- ✔ Popular paint and draw programs

GRAPHICS FILE FORMATS

If you read any literature that has anything to do with graphics, chances are it mentions file formats. You have seen the benefits of graphics and found out about the differences between graphic program types, but what is all the fuss about a difference in file names?

This chapter introduces you to the different file formats you see used for both PC and Macintosh graphics files. Specifically, this chapter discusses the following topics:

GAME PLAN

- The formats currently used
- Where all these formats came from
- The file formats used for bit-mapped files
- Common object-oriented file formats
- Working with the conversion utilities on *The Graphics Coach* bonus disk

Unfortunately, working with computers is, at best, complicated. You cannot just sit down at a stand-alone system and pump out all the art, publications, documents, and spreadsheets your job demands of you. You need software that works with your computer to do that, and each piece of software has its own program code, its own look and feel, and its own hardware requirements. In many cases, each program also saves files in its own way.

PCs are notorious for this "hunt-and-patch" method of putting things together. You might use three of four different programs to produce one newsletter. Suppose, for example, that you work on a 386 PC with Windows 3.1, Microsoft Word, and Aldus PageMaker. You already are using three programs and you still have not chosen a graphics program. If all you need is a low-end paint program, you can use Windows Paintbrush (which is included with Windows). Paintbrush saves files in BMP graphics format. Microsoft Word saves your documents in DOC format, and PageMaker saves publication files in PM4 format.

If you decide to purchase a different graphics program, you must make sure that PageMaker recognizes the file type created by the new program. If PageMaker does not recognize the file type, you must find a conversion utility to change your graphics files from one format to another. Does this sound complicated? It gets worse.

Suppose, for example, that memory on your computer is a problem. You need to save your graphics files in TIFF format (written TIF), but each TIF file takes up almost 800K of storage space. If you are creating illustrations for a book such as this one, you may have a few illustrations or a few hundred.

Someone tells you that PCX files take up less space, so you think about converting all your TIF files to PCX files. Someone else gives you a data compression utility that turns large files into smaller

ones. All you want to do is get up to speed and create your own graphics. Now you are forced to become a graphics file wizard.

On the Mac, this baffling array of graphics file types is not an issue. The Macintosh was designed to be more logical in its approach to sister applications. Everything designed for the Mac looks like the Mac, with the familiar interface, similar commands, and a general look and feel that help you become comfortable with new programs right away.

The Coach Says...

Although you can find different Macintosh graphics formats—MAC for MacPaint, PICT for MacDraw II, and PICT2 for color Mac format—you do not have the overwhelming number of choices that you do with PC graphics file formats.

If you use a Mac, the trouble with graphics file types begins when you need to export graphics to or import graphics from PCs. If you create a graphics file on a Mac, you must find a PC program that accepts the format of the file you created. If you create a graphics file on a PC and want to use it on the Mac, you must have a special DOS board that enables you to read and write in DOS formats.

The Coach Says...

Windows is bringing the same user-friendly approach to PC applications that the Mac has provided for years. Today, programs written for Windows all have a similar look and feel, use the same menu structures, and have achieved some amount of compatibility with other Windows applications.

This chapter discusses the variety of different graphics file formats available and investigates solutions for using them together in your work. The three graphics file conversion and maintenance utilities included on *The Graphics Coach* bonus disk also will help.

DIVERSITY OR COMPATIBILITY?

For a moment, stop thinking about files and think instead about computers. This book deals with two different kinds: PC and Macintosh.

When the first PC appeared on the market many years ago, it was met with enthusiasm that spawned a barrage of similar-but-different computers. Few of these computers were truly compatible with each other. You could not easily swap files among the different computer types even if they claimed to be IBM-compatible. Today, the hardware available and the software used to run it is much different, and in a world of diversity, compatibility is extremely important. Hundreds of PC clones are popular in the market today.

The Coach Says...

A PC clone is basically any IBM-type computer that is not a "real" IBM. Literally hundreds of PC clones are manufactured and sold at a fraction of the IBM brand name price.

Graphics file formats started out in the same direction as the original PC clones—each format forging its own technology based on a different precept and independent of other formats. In some cases, the graphics program that saved files in a particular format (such as PC Paintbrush) became so popular that the standard file type (PCX) became an accepted norm.

In other cases, it was the open architecture of a specific graphics type (such as TIFF, Tagged Image File Format) that enabled developers to come up with a hundred and one variations on the original theme. The original developers continue to update the format, which means software that supports the file type must have the new upgrade information.

Today many distinct graphics file formats are available some of which are offshoots or revisions of early file formats. Not only must you worry about whether your program supports these file types, but you also must consider whether the program has the most recent file format upgrade.

Suppose, for example, that you occasionally use an older version of PageMaker, version 3.0. When you try to open a graphics file created in a new graphics program, you get an error. Although PageMaker supports that graphics file type, the most recent version of the format information is not included with the older version of PageMaker. This makes the new graphics file incompatible with the older version of PageMaker.

The Coach Says...

To make sure you have the most recent version of graphics file formats for your particular software program, contact the manufacturer (in this case, Aldus) and find out whether an upgrade on that file format type is available. You should be able to get a copy of the new format for little or no cost if you are a registered user.

Graphics file formats seem to be moving toward some new standards in compatibility. High-end graphics programs generally accept a wide range of graphics file formats. (Windows programs are especially benevolent in this area.) File conversion utilities,

such as the ones you find on *The Graphics Coach* bonus disk, make working with a variety of graphics file formats less frustrating.

AN OVERVIEW OF POPULAR FILE FORMATS

File formats are not the most interesting subject in the world. You will find that file formats are a concern only after your first `Unable to read image file` error appears. Your program documentation may or may not offer any constructive advice. Hopefully this section will serve as your Ann Landers.

Before you try to import a graphics file into an application for the first time, do some research to make sure that format is supported. The program's help system should tell you something about supported file types if you look under a topic similar to the topic "importing files." If the format is supported, go ahead and try to import the graphics file.

If the format is not supported, take a minute and use one of the file conversion utilities on *The Graphics Coach* bonus disk to convert the format into something your program can use. Taking steps to avoid an error now is a lot less frustrating than messing around in the program and ending up with an `Unable to place` error.

This section describes the basic file formats you see as you begin working with graphics. Because this chapter discusses the two different graphics program types, it divides the file format discussion into similar categories: bit map and vector (or object-oriented) formats.

BIT MAP FORMATS

As you learned in the last chapter, a bit-mapped graphic is a piece of art that is stored as a pattern of dots, or pixels. As you might expect, this file is saved in a much different format from its counterpart, the object-oriented image. Bit maps are the creation of paint programs or scanners that produce digitized, bit-mapped files of art or photos run through a scanning device. Table 4.1 lists the various bit map formats you may see as you work with paint and image-editing programs.

Table 4.1
Common Bit Map Formats

Format	*Stands for*
BMP	Windows bitmap
DIB	Device-independent bitmaps
GIF	Graphics interchange format
IMG	Image (GEM environment)
JPG	Joint Photographic Experts Group
MSP	Microsoft Paintbrush
PCX	PC Paintbrush
PICT	Macintosh format
PNT	MacPaint—early version
MAC	MacPaint—current version
TGA	Targa
TIF	Tagged image file
WMF	Windows metafile
WPG	WordPerfect graphic

In Table 4.1, you can see how file extensions get their names. Do not be fooled, however. Just because a file type stands for a particular program (such as PCX for PC Paintbrush), the program shown is not necessarily the only program that accepts or works with that file type.

The most popular graphics file formats for bit-mapped images are TIF and PCX files. TIF, in fact, can be used with a wide variety of DOS, Windows, and Macintosh applications. Most major programs that accept graphics files accept both TIF and PCX formats. In addition, most file conversion utilities can change more unusual formats into TIF or PCX format. The following sections provide brief descriptions of each of these graphics file formats.

BMP FORMAT

If you use Windows and have played around with Windows wallpaper, you should recognize the BMP file type. This is a standard format for Windows bit-mapped files and is the type of file created by Windows Paintbrush. When you cut or copy an image to the Windows Clipboard, it is saved in BMP format. You will not have any trouble using BMP files in Windows applications, but most DOS-based programs probably will display an error if you try to use an unconverted BMP file.

DIB FORMAT

DIB which stands for Device Independent Bitmap, is the standard format used by OS/2 applications. Windows applications can read DIB files but cannot output them in the same format. DOS and Mac applications are both incompatible with the DIB format.

GIF FORMAT

The GIF file format, which stands for Graphics Interchange Format, is a format created by CompuServe. You find GIF files by the hundreds—perhaps thousands—on CompuServe. GIF files are stored in compressed format so that the time required to download the graphics files from bulletin boards is minimal, even for extremely large files. Almost no applications accept GIF files directly, but both PC and Mac users can work with GIF files. The shareware file conversion utilities on *The Graphics Coach* bonus disk can display these files for you.

IMG FORMAT

The IMG file type is more and more rare because it was created and used by Ventura Publisher and the GEM environment, produced by Digital Research. The only graphics program you may run into that saves files in IMG format is not a graphics programs at all but a desktop publishing program: Ventura Publisher. IMG saves files exclusively in gray-scales, and can store files of limitless size (if you have enough storage space to hold them). Most Windows applications cannot read IMG; if you plan to use Ventura graphics files in your Windows applications, you need to find a conversion utility that supports IMG.

JPG FORMAT

The JPG format creates a highly compressed data file by leaving out some of the data to create a more tightly compressed file. You control how much data is removed. This relatively new standard significantly reduces the need for massive disk storage but still maintains the quality and clarity of your pictures. Support for this format, however, may be limited because it is new. Check your program documentation or the formats supported by your file conversion utilities before you save a file in JPG.

PCX FORMAT

PCX format is actually the offshoot of one product: PC Paintbrush, by Zsoft. Years ago, PC Paintbrush was introduced in the DOS market and rapidly became an extremely popular graphics program. The format in which PC Paintbrush files were saved—PCX—was one of the first graphics formats available for the PC. In the years since the introduction of PC Paintbrush, the PCX format has spread until almost all PC applications that accept graphics files in any form can read PCX. PCX files are usually monochrome or 4- or 256-bit color, and tend to be rather large in size.

> **The Coach Says...**
>
> If you plan to save a large number of graphics files in the PCX format, the size of the files may be too much for your available disk storage. To get around this problem, use a file compression utility, such as PKZIP, to compress the files into a zipped file that is more memory-efficient.

PNT FORMAT

The PNT format is a Macintosh format used from the beginning with MacPaint, the popular paint program now in its second generation. Support for PNT files in the PC realm is fairly limited; only a few Windows programs support PNT files. Aldus PageMaker, a desktop publishing program available for both PCs and Macs, is one example of a program that will successfully import PNT files without conversion.

MAC FORMAT

Mac format is available for the new version of MacPaint. Mac format is supported more widely and is recognized as a conversion option by many graphics file conversion utilities for both PCs and Macs.

MSP FORMAT

Another file type common to Windows is the MSP file format. MSP is the original format that earlier versions of Windows Paintbrush used. MSP also is the format used by Microsoft Publisher, although Publisher can save graphics in other formats as well.

TGA FORMAT

TGA stands for Targa, which you may recognize from the Truevision Targa board, a hig-end industry standard in color video adapters. TGA format is used most often for extemely sophisticated RGB color work with image-editing software and with scanned images. Few Windows or word processing programs support the format at the present time.

TIFF FORMAT

The TIFF format, which stands for Tagged Image File Format, is one of the most widely supported graphics file formats available for both PC and Mac applications. Unlike the PCX format, TIFF was not originally designed to be the format of a specific software product. The format was created to be an independent standard, not reliant on any particular machine or graphics program. TIFF files are among the most widely supported formats today, and continuing revisions of the format ensure that the widest possible range of applications and technological advances are supported.

The Coach Says...

One downfall of TIFF files is their size; a TIFF file can be many times the size of the same image captured in PCX format. If you are saving many graphics files and your storage capacity is limited, consider either compressing the TIFF files or converting them to a file format, such as GIF, that takes less space on your hard drive.

WMF FORMAT

The WMF format stands for *Windows metafile*, which is the format Windows uses for storing its own graphics. You can store both bit-mapped and object-oriented graphics in a WMF file, but WMF is recognized by few programs outside of Windows. The WMF standard is of interest more to software developers than to the average end-user; one of the popular features of the format is the ease with which it is written in to software code. If you use Windows, chances are you have worked with WMF files without even noticing it; WMF is one of the formats in which Clipboard items are saved.

WPG FORMAT

WPG format is the only format supported by WordPerfect. Unlike all the other popular high-end word processing programs, WordPerfect does not support widely popular graphics file formats. Before you can use a PCX file in WordPerfect, for example, you have to convert the PCX file to a WPG format.

The Coach Says...

Although WPG files can contain both bitmapped and object-oriented graphics, many conversion utilities (including Graphic Workshop) recognize and work with only bitmapped WPG images.

OBJECT-ORIENTED FORMATS

As you might expect, many object-oriented formats are available, similar to the variety of their bitmapped counterparts. Vector files store data as image descriptions, or calculations, that enable the program to recreate the image on-screen as necessary. Many popular draw programs support vector formats from a variety of sources. Table 4.2 introduces you to popular vector formats.

Table 4.2
Common Vector Formats

Format	*Stands for*
CDR	CorelDRAW!
CGM	Computer graphics metafile
DRW	Micrografx Designer
DXF	Data Exchange Format
EPS	Encapsulated PostScript
GEM	GEM metafile
HPGL	Hewlett-Packard Graphics Language
PIC	Picture format
PICT	Macintosh format
WMF	Windows metafile

In the high-end scale of graphics programs, support for graphics files becomes a little less hazardous. Sophisticated programs such as Micrografx Designer are equipped with built-in filters that accept programs from a variety of other sources.

The major competitors in the draw program arena understand that keeping their format specifications to themselves does not help anyone. Micrografx, and more recently CorelDRAW! have opened up their format specifications so applications can be written that use their files directly. This cuts down on the hassle of proprietary graphics compatibility.

CDR FORMAT

The CDR format is a format used by only one program: CorelDRAW!. As of this writing, no other graphics or desktop publishing program currently imports CDR files. However, Corel Systems has recently opened the format specifications so that other applications can support the format. If you use CorelDRAW!, you have a library of other formats in which you can save your files; therfore working with CDR files is no problem.

CGM FORMAT

CGM format (the CGM stands for *Computer Graphics Metafile*) is currently the most widely used vector file format available—most popular draw programs (as well as most presentation graphics programs) support CGM files. Among the major software products that can import and export CGM files are CorelDRAW!, Lotus Freelance Graphics, Harvard Graphics, and Micrografx Designer.

DRW FORMAT

The DRW format is the graphics file format used by Micrografx Designer, the high-end draw program produced for the PC. Recently, the developers of DRW released the specifications for the format so that other developers could write applications to support the DRW format. Currently, programs including Word for Windows, Ami Pro, and PageMaker all support the DRW file format.

DXF FORMAT

The DXF, or Data Exchange Format, file type is used in AutoCAD and AutoCAD-compatible programs. This is the standard draw file created on a CAD system and does not offer the artistic qualities—such as color blending and shading—that most general graphics applications need. Most graphics and desktop publishing programs cannot import DXF files without conversion, although CorelDRAW! enables you to open DXF files and save them in a different format.

ENCAPSULATED POSTSCRIPT

EPS (Encapsulated PostScript) files are known for their enormous size and high quality. PostScript files can store both bitmapped and vector images, and EPS files can be used on both PC and Mac systems (you may see some difference between the two versions, however).

When EPS files are displayed, they may appear as standard vector images, or they may appear as grayed-in boxes with an identifier tag. If you see this box after importing an EPS graphic, don't panic: your program simply doesn't know how to interpret the PostScript language that makes up the image. When you print on a PostScript printer, the image will appear as expected.

The terms *PostScript* and *Encapsulated PostScript* are used in this book. Is there a difference? Basically, an Encapsulated Postscript, or EPS, file is a PostScript file that contains graphics. The only real difference between the two files is additional code added to the EPS file that tells the program receiving the file that the graphics file is about to be loaded.

GEM FORMAT

Another more specialized file type is the GEM format, created specifically for use with the GEM environment (from Digital Research). GEM is the object-oriented format for graphics files; IMG is the bitmapped format used by GEM programs such as Ventura Publisher. The GEM format has many limitations, including the total number of points allowed in an image and total number of shapes permitted. Most Windows applications do not support GEM, and this format cannot be used on the Mac.

HPGL FORMAT

HPGL, which stands for *Hewlett-Packard Graphics Language*, is a format used specifically for plotters. This format was first developed by Hewlett-Packard as a standard file format for plotter-output files. HPGL isn't right for your applications, unless you are producing only line art—it cannot handle color fills or shading within enclosed shapes. Letter formation, while possible, is primitive, at best. Many CAD programs output HPGL files, and several popular desktop publishing programs import them, but support is limited.

The Coach Says...

A *plotter* is a high-end output device often used to print large-scale output that requires a great deal of precision. The plotter receives output from the computer and uses several colored pens to plot coordinates on paper from a large roll. Plotters are often used to output blueprints, schematics, and other design-related products.

PIC FORMAT

Two different types of PIC files exist; one is a bitmap format, used with a paint program called Pictor (which used to be PC Paint). The second PIC format stores object-oriented files from Lotus 1-2-3 in the form of charts from the spreadsheet graphing feature of the program. The process of importing 1-2-3 charts into reports, manuals, and newsletters is a big deal. If you've been using 1-2-3 for your number-crunching, compatibility with other programs enhances your work and makes life easier.

Support for the PIC file type (from Lotus) is as widespread as suppor for CGM or TIFF images; virtually all popular programs can import the 1-2-3 charts.

PICT FORMAT

PICT is the "chosen" format for the Macintosh. Most Mac applications have the capability to save screen shots and graphics files in PICT format. Both bitmapped and object-oriented graphics can be stored in PICT format. Virtually all applications that read graphics files on the Mac can read PICT format. This is not a format available to PC users because the way in which the PICT file is opened requires decoding by the Mac's operating system.

The Coach Says...

PICT2 is a newer version of the Macintosh PICT format. This version stores object-oriented graphics in full color.

UNDERSTANDING CONVERSION UTILITIES

A whole generation of software has evolved to make sense of file compatibility. All users want to do is sit down and create the images they see dancing around in our heads, and they instead spend countless hours frustrated about changing one file type to another in an effort to integrate powerful but independent programs. How hard would it be, with the combined brainpower of all the independent developers, to develop a few tools that make graphics easier to work with?

On *The Graphics Coach* bonus disk, you find three types of salvation. Paint Shop Pro is a Windows program that enables you to view, edit, convert, and print a variety of bitmapped images. Graphic Workshop is a DOS-based shareware program that enables you to view, edit, convert bitmaps and scan images. Finally, GIFConverter is a Mac program that helps you view, modify, print, and convert paint images in Macintosh format. The following sections explain each of these programs in more detail.

Table 4.3
Programs on the Bonus Disk

Program	*Used with*	*Features*
Paint Shop Pro for Windows	PC—Windows	Easy to use Range of views Image editing Color manipulation Shading control Flip and rotate Printing File conversion
Graphic Workshop	PC—DOS	Easy to install and use Works with wide range of programs Special effects Printing Scanning Rotation options Dithering choices File conversion
GIFConverter	Macintosh	Easy to start Support for nine different file types Sophisticated color controls Blending and shading options Rotation options Customizable file conversion

> **The Coach Says...**
> For step-by-step instructions on converting and managing graphics files, see Chapter 13.

PAINT SHOP PRO FOR WINDOWS

Paint Shop Pro for Windows is an extremely popular program that is available in both shareware and retail versions. Paint Shop Pro is described as a graphics utility that helps you view, convert, modify, and print graphics images. Paint Shop Pro also includes a screen capture utility, a program that enables you to take a picture of whatever's displayed on your computer screen. With Paint Shop Pro, you can convert your bitmapped files *from* one of the following formats *to* one of the following formats:

BMP	MAC
DIB	MSP
GIF	PCX
IMG	PIC
JAS	TGA
WPG	TIF

Paint Shop Pro for Windows has celebrated some acclaim in recent months, winning the 1992 Shareware Industry Award for Best Graphics Application. With its ease of use and flexible conversion formats, Paint Shop Pro takes conversion headaches away from any Windows user. Figure 4.1 shows the File Open dialog box.

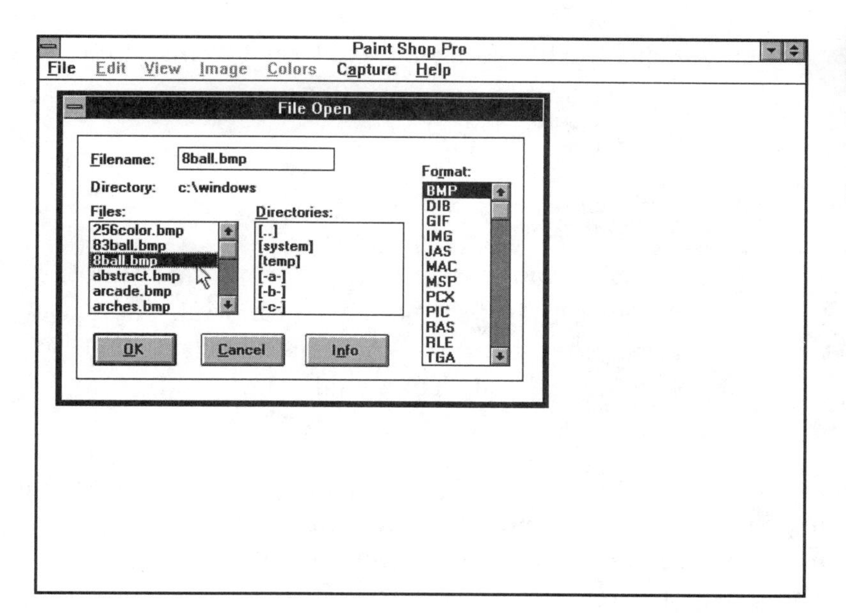

Figure 4.1:

Opening a file to be used in Paint Shop Pro.

OPENING A FILE

To open a file in Paint Shop Pro, follow these steps:

1. When the File Open dialog box is displayed, choose the file type you want from the Format list box.
2. Click on the directory in which you want to look for the file. If necessary, change the drive designation.

> **The Coach Says...**
> If you do not see the file you're looking for, you may need to scroll through the displayed list of files. Simply position the mouse pointer on the down-arrow in the scroll bar to the right of the Files list. When you click on the mouse button, other files scroll up into the displayed list.

3. When you see the file you want, click on it to highlight it.
4. Click on OK to open the file.

The Coach Says...

If you want to see some information about the file before you open it (such as the width, height, maximum number of colors, and file size), click on the Info button in the File Open dialog box.

When the file is open on-screen, you can use any of the commands in the program's seven menus to work with the image.
For more information about working with Paint Shop Pro for Windows, see Chapter 12.

GRAPHIC WORKSHOP

Graphic Workshop is a file conversion and screen capture utility that runs under DOS. With Graphic Workshop, you can perform a variety of editing and manipulation functions, including change scale, display file statistics; print to a LaserJet or PostScript printer; add special effects such as smudge, soften, or sharpen; change color intensity; and rotate and flip graphics.

Graphic Workshop is capable of converting your file to a number of popular graphics file formats, including the following:

MAC	GEM/IMG
GIF	BMP
IFF/LBM (Amiga)	TGA
MSP	WPG

PIC	TIFF
EXE	TXT
EPS	CUT (Halo)

The menu system is easy to understand and use, and files in the current directory are displayed in the area at the top of the screen. Figure 4.2 shows a sample Graphic Workshop screen.

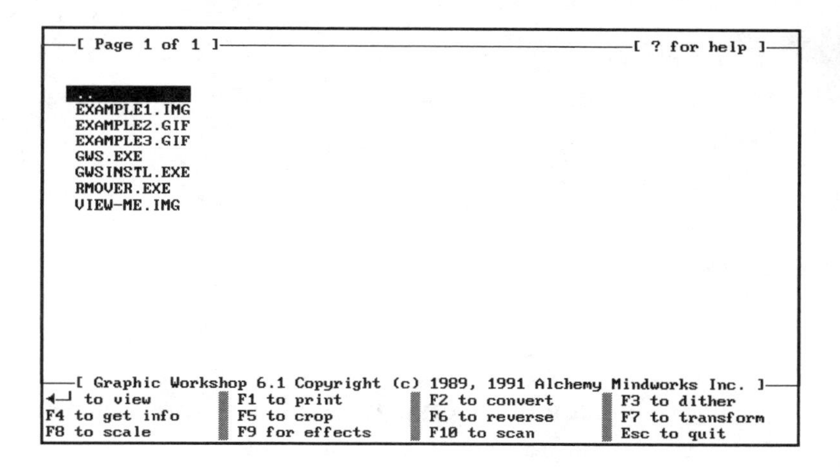

Figure 4.2: A sample Graphic Workshop screen.

The Coach Says...

Graphic Workshop has no mouse support in this program; all commands are assigned to function keys and arrow keys to highlight the options you want.

One benefit of Graphic Workshop is the large number of file formats the program is capable of converting. In addition, Graphic Workshop can convert batches of files rather than individual files one at a time. For example, if you want to convert a directory-full of TIFF files into PCX files, you can tag all the files you want to change and have Graphic Workshop convert them all in one sweep. For more information about working with Graphic Workshop, see Chapter 13.

The Coach Says...

Graphic Workshop also allows you to scan images, if you've already hooked up your scanner and installed scanning software. You can scan an image and look at it immediately by viewing it in Graphic Workshop.

GIFCONVERTER

GIFConverter is a Macintosh shareware graphics utility that allows you to work with a variety of paint images or scanned files. GIF files are found on most online services, such as CompuServe and GEnie, and can be used on almost any computer, which dramatically enhances their popularity. As mentioned earlier in the chapter, GIF files are not directly supported by most applications and require conversion into a more widely accepted bitmap, although conversion programs support the widespread use of the GIF format.

GIFConverter, developed by Kevin A. Mitchell, provides you with an incredible range of image manipulation options. You can edit images by moving, stretching, scaling, rotating, and cropping them. You can fine-tune picture resolution and color configurations, output to several different printer types, and customize file options for formats you often use. All these features, combined with a well-written manual for registered users, provide you with all the power you need to convert GIF images on the Mac.

GIFConverter can change your GIF files into one of nine different formats, among these the TIFF format popular in PC applications. Later in this book, you learn through hands-on practice how to work with each of these graphics file conversion utilities (Chapter 13).

> **The Coach Says...**
>
> In addition to the file conversion utilities included on the Graphics disk, you'll find many other popular graphics conversion utilities available today. Among these are Hijaak for Windows, Conversion Artist, WinGIF, WinJPEG, and PictureEze.

INSTANT REPLAY

In this chapter, you learned the ins and outs of graphics file formats. Specifically, you examined the following topics:

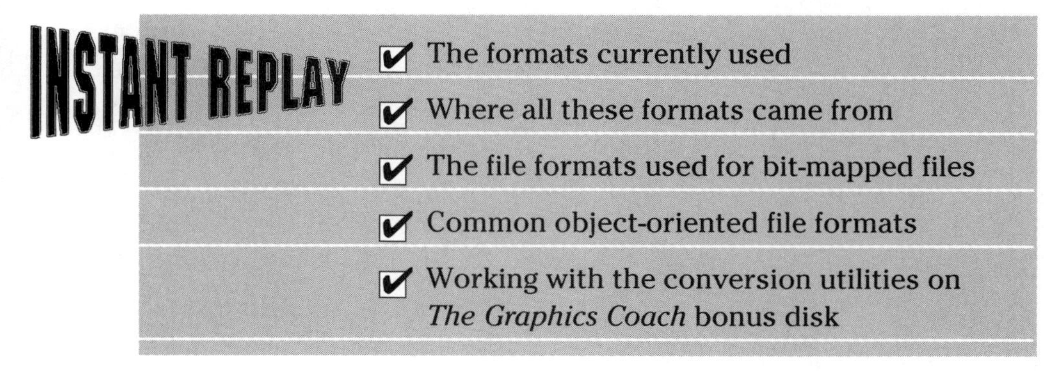

- ✔ The formats currently used
- ✔ Where all these formats came from
- ✔ The file formats used for bit-mapped files
- ✔ Common object-oriented file formats
- ✔ Working with the conversion utilities on *The Graphics Coach* bonus disk

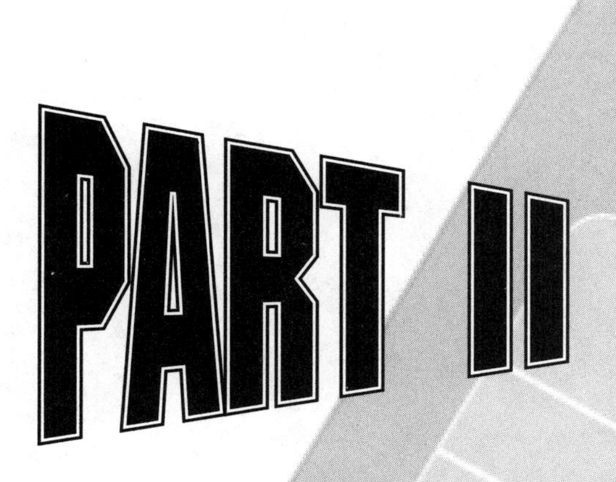

PART II

GRAPHICS NUTS-AND-BOLTS

UNDERSTANDING BASIC HARDWARE

If you, like many others, have been bounced off technology and are being whirled around through a maze of hardware and software choices, this chapter is for you. This chapter gives you an overview of the products available and helps you determine which products best suit your needs.

In this chapter, you also learn the ways that different system elements affect the type of graphics work you do. Specifically, you learn the following:

GAME PLAN

- Parts of the system unit
- The microprocessor
- Upgrading your current system
- RAM versus ROM
- The hard disk
- The floppy disk

A CLOSE LOOK AT THE SYSTEM UNIT

The differences in system units exist for a reason. The variety of models and features available will make your head swim. Just as the features of individual systems vary, so do the needs of users. Some users get more upset about slower processing speed than they do about limited disk storage. Some applications require only a basic, solid workhorse of a machine, while others (including graphics) need an animal with more speed and finesse. What can you do when you realize that you need a thoroughbred and you are sitting in front of a saggy farm horse?

All computer systems have a system unit that houses the all-important microprocessor, the computer's memory, disk drives, and other life-support systems such as the power supply and cooling fan, and the internal hardware needed for connecting other outside devices like the printer and the mouse. Since the introduction of the first IBM PC in 1981, more than a generation of evolution' worth has taken place inside that tan, rectangular box.

By contrast, the first Macs were system-unit-and-monitor-in-one contraptions, saving users from cluttering their already busy work areas with unnecessary computer girth. Although many new Macs have been developed in the last several years, some Macs, such as the Macintosh Classic, are still available in the original chassis.

Today, in addition to these widely used desktop models, there are computers ranging in size from portables to laptops or notebooks to palmtops. As the computers get smaller in size, so do their system units. Although the system units are small, they are in the computers, processing information, updating the screen, and connecting external devices. Without the system unit, there would be no computer.

But even if the outsides of system units are completely different, the inner parts function in much the same way. Each system unit, no matter which model you use, contains the following elements:

- ★ Microprocessor
- ★ Motherboard
- ★ Computer memory (RAM)
- ★ Chips that control the internal processing of the system (ROM)
- ★ A power supply
- ★ Expansion slots
- ★ Disk drives

Figure 5.1 shows the various parts in a typical system unit. Whether your system unit includes a hard disk or not (and any system you consider for graphics work will need, at the very least, a pretty hefty hard disk), the items discussed in the following section are inside, working silently. Also, depending on the type of system you use, the amount of memory you have available, and several other considerations, these elements will enhance—or limit—your graphics experience.

THE MICROPROCESSOR

It's a cliche, but it's true; the microprocessor is the brain of your computer. Without that single chip, which is about the size of the end of your thumb, your computer cannot even turn on. The microprocessor is one lone IC (an acronym for *integrated circuit*) that packs enough power to control all the internal workings, calculations, and data transmissions that take place—sight unseen—beneath the cover of your system unit.

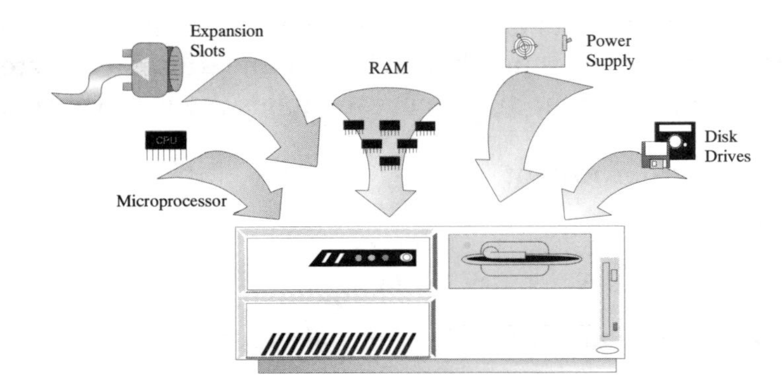

Figure 5.1:

A typical system unit.

Every computer has a microprocessor (also called a *CPU* or central processing unit). Computers in the PC realm often are named for the microprocessor they use. You probably see ads or hear computer enthusiasts refer to 286, 386, and 486 machines. The numbers are actually a short form for the longer number of the CPU chip itself. The microprocessor in a 386, for example, is actually an 80386. People tend to drop the "80" because all PC microprocessors begin with the same two characters. Macintoshes are built on a different microprocessor, the 68000 series. Currently, Macs use the 68030 or 68040 chip made by Motorola, Inc.

The Coach Says...

The original Intel microprocessors from the first PCs—the 8088 and the 8086—got left back in the 80s with other slow-moving and cumbersome software and hardware products. Today's microprocessors must be lightning fast and simple to use.

Different microprocessors offer different processing speeds. The lower the number, the slower the chip. The 68000 CPU in the Macintosh Classic, for example, is a significantly less powerful chip than the 68040 used in the new Macintosh Quadras. The 80286

available in the early PC ATs is much slower than today's standard 80486.

The microprocessor's speed is measured in *megahertz*, written as MHz. Some microprocessors in the PC world include the speed as an added part of the chip name. You may see an add for a 486/33 machine, for example. The 33 is the speed in megahertz of the 486 chip. Other versions of the 486 chip are available in different speeds of 20 and 25 MHz, as well. Table 5.1 lists the differences in the speeds of the Intel and Motorola microprocessors.

Table 5.1
Differences in CPU Speeds

Manufacturer	*CPU*	*Speed (MHz)*
Intel	8086	8
	80286	10 or 20
	80386	20 or 25
	80486	20, 25, 33
Motorola	68000	7
	68030	16 or 25
	68040	33

You pay more to get the faster processing power. 486 machines are more expensive than 386 machines, and 286 machines are hard to find for sale. With some educated shopping, you can find 486 systems at 386 prices. As technology evolves, things keep getting faster and smaller. The PC's 80586 chip is currently under construction, as are OverDrive chips that increase the speed of the microprocessor. As a general rule, buy the system with the highest microprocessor you can afford.

The Coach Says...

When you shop for computer equipment, you often can find better deals through direct mail order and wholesale club businesses. If you shop retail, you may pay an inflated price.

In the Macintosh realm, pricing is more fixed because of the lack of competition. If you are set on a high-end Macintosh, be prepared to pay top dollar from an authorized dealer. The up side, however, is that you get a top-of-the-line machine that has the power to produce any graphics you may be envisioning.

HOW DOES THE MICROPROCESSOR AFFECT YOUR GRAPHICS?

Some programs will not run on systems that have outdated microprocessors. Other programs run but are painfully slow and not worth the wait (see fig. 5.2). Check the hardware and software requirements of any graphics program you plan to use before you try to install the software. Usually manufacturers include a list of required hardware and software items (such as CPU, RAM, hard disk storage space, and operating system version) on the outside of the shrink-wrapped software package.

The CPU also affects how fast the way graphics are redrawn on your screen. Each time you modify a piece of art or change the view—whether you work with bit-mapped or object-oriented graphics—the program you are using updates the screen. The speed or slowness with which your computer updates the screen has to do with both the CPU speed and the memory and speed of your video adaptor.

Figure 5.2:

The screen-update wait.

The Coach Says...

For more information on video adapters, see Chapter 6.

UPGRADING YOUR SYSTEM

What happens when you realize that you need a more powerful system and you are stuck with an old, outdated PC? It is possible to upgrade older systems, but the process is not for the faint-hearted. Depending on the limitations of the system you are using, you may need to replace the motherboard, update memory, and perhaps even change the power supply.

> **The Coach Says...**
>
> Do not take it upon yourself to mix and match hardware elements—especially when it involves sliding the cover off the system unit. Things rarely go back together the way you expect them to. To be safe and cost-effective, consult technical support or the manufacturer for information on upgrading your system.

AVAILABLE RAM

RAM is another computer acronym, short for *random-access memory*. Your computer stores the program you currently are working with—and any data files you create—in RAM. On most systems, this memory is expandable—you can add to it to increase your computer's RAM size.

> **The Coach Says...**
>
> ROM, or *read-only memory*, is another type of memory that is housed inside the system unit. ROM chips store information that was burned onto the chip at the time the computer was created and cannot be erased or written over. ROM stores the instructions your computer needs to power up and perform basic functions. RAM, on the other hand, is erasable memory that is blanked each time you turn off the computer or reboot.

WHAT IS RAM?

Many new users confuse RAM with disk storage space. They read something in an advertisement that says 160M hard disk and,

when asked, they reply that they have 160M of RAM. It is an easy mistake to make because in both cases you are talking about storing programs and data, right?

The biggest difference between RAM space and storage space is that RAM holds information temporarily—only while the computer is on or until you reboot. Your computer looks to RAM when it searches for program instructions and data information. To help you understand RAM, consider the following example.

You turn on the computer and start Microsoft Windows. When you type **WIN** and press Enter, the light on your hard disk flashes on, and the inside of the system unit churns a bit before the Program Manager appears.

What just happened? The WIN command sent the computer to look for the program. It then copied what it needs of the program into RAM. If you turn off your computer (which you should never do without exiting properly), the Windows files do not remain on your computer because anything stored in RAM is erased. The next time you turn on the computer, you start back at the DOS prompt.

When you work on a file, such as an illustration in Windows Paintbrush, it is stored in RAM—it temporarily sits there while you work with it. You must remember, however, that the file is only temporarily stored in RAM and not saved anywhere in your computer. To save the file, you must issue the Save command and enter a file name. Otherwise, a poorly timed trip over the power cord might squelch the power to your computer and—POOF!—the file is gone.

HOW IS RAM MEASURED?

RAM is measured, for the most part, in megabytes. A *megabyte* (M) is one million bytes of information (a byte is equal to

approximately one text character). Another term you see in relation to computer memory is kilobytes (K). A *kilobyte* is equal to one thousand bytes of information. Most systems today come equipped with 2M or 4M of RAM—a pretty big jump from the 64K RAM reserves of the earliest PCs.

Why the change? In most cases, applications today, such as Microsoft Windows, require more RAM to function efficiently. Other applications—especially graphics and multimedia applications—take up so much room that it is difficult to work with large files unless you have the memory to support them.

> **The Coach Says...**
>
> How much difference does RAM size make? In recent tests, increasing a computer's RAM from 2M to 4M increased the average processing speed of Microsoft Windows over 100 percent.

WHAT TYPES OF RAM MEMORY ARE USED?

If you are unsure of how much memory your system has, you can always look through your sales literature or call technical support. On second thought, don't bother them; there's an easier way. If you use a Macintosh, you can find out how much memory your system has available by opening the Apple menu and selecting About the Finder. If you use a PC equipped with DOS 5.0, go to the DOS prompt, type **MEM**, and then press Enter.

> **The Coach Says...**
>
> In Windows, select the Help menu and then About Program Manager. The About Program Manager window tells you the amount of memory you have, including virtual memory.

In computer advertising you see terms such as expanded, extended, and virtual memory. What are these kinds of memory, and how do you know if you need them?

Each of these terms is used to explain a technological twist that "tricks" the computer into using more RAM than DOS limits allow. This enables your applications to work faster, and helps you manipulate larger files.

Extended memory is RAM above the 1M mark (the maximum recognized by DOS) that can be used only by certain programs. Check the program documentation for information on whether extended memory is supported.

Expanded memory uses a "windowing" technique to peek through a certain segment of memory to look beyond the 1M barrier and use memory in higher addresses.

Virtual memory has been used in the PC camp for some time and recently was added to the newer Macs. Virtual memory uses part of the hard disk RAM space—which really is storage space—as a part of RAM. Figure 5.3 illustrates these different RAM-expansion technologies.

HOW MUCH RAM IS ENOUGH?

As you peruse computer magazines, fantasizing about the ideal system, keep in mind that graphics files often take up quite a chunk of your computer's memory. You know that programs work faster when more RAM is available. You also know that some programs will not run without a sufficient amount of RAM. Other programs leave you sitting long past the point of cold coffee, waiting on molasses-like screen updates and even slower internal processing. The more complex your graphics files, the larger the memory requirement. If you plan to create sophisticated graphics in a high-end draw program, be sure to give yourself enough RAM room to keep things comfortable.

Figure 5.3:

Expanded, virtual, and extended memory.

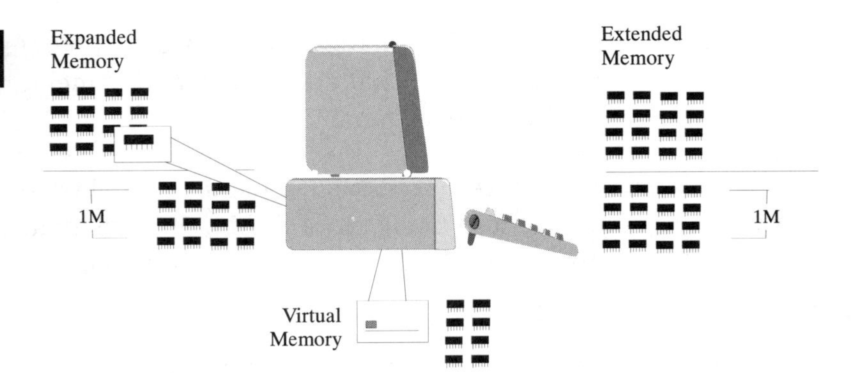

The Coach Says...

Anytime you work with EPS files, the drain on your computer's RAM is going to be large. PCX files tend to be small, but TIFF files can be weighty. It is better to invest a few hundred dollars to get a system—or expand to a system—that meets your graphics needs.

Now the big question: If you know you want to add to the RAM in your system, is it something you can do yourself? Some people will tell you "Sure go ahead; there's nothing to it." Others turn green around the gills and shudder at the thought of exposing the system unit. As a general rule, you should get someone else—some technically savvy person—to add memory for you.

Although adding memory is a simple procedure (provided you have the room on the memory board and do not have to add a memory card), any number of things can go wrong including the following:

- ★ You could break one of the little pin leggies off, rendering the chip useless
- ★ You could get all the legs in the socket except one or two, which would cause a major short circuit after the power started rushing through

★ You could turn the chip around backwards and zap a few innocents

★ You could fail to get the chips seated properly (that is, pushed in all the way), and your system will not work

★ The static electricity from your body could zap one of the components on the motherboard

> **The Coach Says...**
>
> Another consideration, especially for Mac owners: if you work with a new system still under warranty, you may be violating your service agreement by opening the system unit. Keep the technical support number handy, and whenever possible, fight the urge to be "Joe Cool Fixit Person." A good rule of thumb is: "When in Doubt, Don't."

ROOM FOR EXPANSION

Inside most computers sold today, in addition to all the gadgets that help your system function properly, are possibilities for the future. These possibilities are known as *expansion slots* or empty plug-in places on your computer's main board (known as the *motherboard*) for adding items, such as a printer, mouse, modem, graphics tablet, mixer...no, wait, wrong book.

Early cheapie computers often were sold with no, or almost no, expansion slots. You purchased the system, and you were stuck with it. Virtually all computer manufacturers today recognize that in order to be successful, computers must grow with the needs of their users. You may not need a modem today, but what happens when you become a famous graphic artist and people all over the country want your artwork? Installing a modem and sending graphics files via Ma Bell is faster and much less expensive than

Federal Express. (If your computer does not have an available expansion slot, you cannot add a modem.)

As you add devices, plug-in boards are added to the motherboard, filling the expansion slots. When you add a mouse, a board is plugged in, filling a slot. One portion of the board has another kind of plug-in receptacle, called a *port*. The port sticks out of the back of your computer. You plug the mouse cable into the port, and, voila! you have a mouse. When you use the mouse, the movement sensors inside the mouse relate information through the cable, through the port, to the board. The board sends the data through the necessary channels in the system unit, and you see the results of the mouse operation on the screen. All of this, of course, takes place faster than you can blink. The expansion slots serve as a liaison between the peripheral device (big word for "other computer things") and the CPU.

So how do you know whether your system has room for expansion? Consult your user manual. If you lost the manual or used it to line the bird cage, check the backside of your system unit. If you see several metal strips (you will not see ports unless you already have boards installed in the expansion slots), you can assume you have room for a few additional devices. Most popular computers sold today have between two and eight available slots.

The following are just a few ideas of how a graphics user might use expansion slots:

★ A graphics tablet

★ A flatbed scanner

★ A modem

★ A plotter, for schematic or architectural work

★ A printer (of course)

- ★ A fax
- ★ A tape backup system

Depending on your needs for input (getting the art in there) and output (printing, plotting, or faxing your files), the number of additional components, and therefore your need for expansion slots, may be more limited. Remember, however, that as you become more comfortable with graphics, you may want to experiment with new avenues. Do not limit yourself now by purchasing a system that does not give you—or your creative initiative—room to grow.

STORAGE CONSIDERATIONS

This chapter started by explaining the difference between RAM and storage space. RAM stores programs and data temporarily; only while power is surging through your computer. When you turn off the power, anything stored in RAM disappears.

Unlike RAM, the storage space available on your hard disk or floppy disks retains the information you put there until you delete it or cover it up with something else. This type of storage device enables you to save important files for as long as necessary and also gives you the option to delete unnecessary data and use the storage space for something else.

If you have done any research, you have seen programs now available on CD-ROM. CD-ROMs offer an overwhelming amount of storage space—much more than the average hard disk—and are capable of retrieving files with lightning speed. CD-ROMs look like the music CDs you put in a CD player, but they store data in compressed and read-only form.

> **The Coach Says...**
>
> Read-only means that the information stored on the device—in this case, a CD-ROM—cannot be erased or written over. The data is burned into the surface of the disk so that you can read it over and over again, but you cannot write information to it.

Although you can retrieve multimedia or graphics files from a CD, you still, for the most part, cannot write your information back to a CD. This feature is coming, however, and probably sooner than you expect. For now CDs are used as a type of storage device, but not for *your* storage needs. Programs, such as CorelDRAW!, use CDs to provide you with an incredible library of clip art that you can load and use in your own graphics work.

This section discusses the type of storage device you will use to store your graphics files. The necessary cables and boards for connecting your hard disk drive or floppy drives are located in the system unit. No matter which type of system you purchase, the cables and boards already are hooked up for you. Today, a *hard disk*—a nonremoveable disk housed inside a case in the system unit—is a necessity for most popular applications because of the need for larger storage capacity. Disk drives—in 5 1/4-inch mini-floppy or 3 1/2-inch micro-floppy size—are used most often for copying files to and from the computer's hard disk.

WHAT IS A HARD DISK?

A *hard disk* is a small platter stored inside some kind of housing. The platter itself resembles a CD. The housing may be a box that fits into the system unit. The entire ensemble—platter, recording heads, and housing—is called a *hard disk drive*. The disk might be enclosed within a cartridge that can be removed from the system unit (as is the case with removable hard disks). Additionally,

another kind of hard disk—known as an external hard disk—connects to your computer through an expansion port.

The most common type of hard disk drive is the type that is housed in the system unit. A hard disk access light is the only thing you can see to indicate that there is a hard disk (although you may occasionally hear some chunking and grinding sounds). The light flashes red (or perhaps yellow) when the CPU is reading information from or writing information to the hard disk.

Hard disks are available in an incredible range of storage capacities. When hard disks were first made available—with the original IBM PC XT—a hard disk capacity of 10M was considered terrific. Users were thrilled; they had something else to use besides floppy disks. In the decade that followed, technology evolved and so did expectations. Today, by most standards, hard disks with 60M are considered small and capacities of 160M, 210M, or even 1.6G (gigabytes) are common.

The following reasons describe why hard disks are so popular:

- ★ Hard disks can store an incredible amount of information
- ★ Hard disks, unlike floppy disks, are enclosed in a housing and therefore not susceptible to coffee spills, dust, cat hair, and melted M&Ms
- ★ Hard disks load and save files much faster than floppy disks
- ★ Hard disks are easier to organize and use than floppy disk boxes
- ★ You might misplace a file on a hard disk temporarily, but you know it is in there; using a floppy, you can lose or damage the disk at any time

★ Most applications work better and faster installed on a hard disk; many popular programs today cannot be run on floppy-based systems

As a graphics person, storage capacities will concern you sooner or later. Graphics files eat up quite a bit of storage space, and depending on the type of graphics you create, they may do so faster than you expect. By the time you install the graphics program and create all the files you need (plus add any other necessary applications, such as file managers, conversion utilities, word processors, desktop publishing software, and so on), megabytes are gobbled up like Halloween candy.

The Coach Says...

Many high-end programs, such as MicroGrafx Designer, require between 10M and 20M just to store the program files, templates, and clip art files. Freelance Graphics for Windows eats up a hearty 19M for full installation (but it's fun).

Even if you think you are working with small files—but lots of them—the storage space will trickle away. If you create a zillion PCX files for book illustrations, chances are you will come up against one of those unfriendly `Unable to save file` errors that can really botch things up.

The Coach Says...

Storage space is just like income—no matter how much you have, your needs expand until you use all of it. Even if you purchase a 160M hard disk, someday the time will come when you are blinking at the screen as the computer struggles to save a file. To cut

down on the fat in your disk storage practices, routinely back up necessary files and delete those you no longer use. Use data compression utilities, such as PKZIP, to group and compress similar data files. Doing so on a regular basis keeps you in touch with the amount of storage still available on your system and teaches you important maintenance procedures, as well.

So, best advice: size does make a difference when you talk about hard disks. Purchase the largest amount of storage you can afford. If you need more room, consider upgrading to a larger hard disk (the process is relatively easy and inexpensive) or add a second hard disk to your existing system.

WHAT ARE FLOPPY DISKS?

Okay, so maybe it's a stupid question. Everybody knows what a floppy disk is. Some people call it a disk, a minifloppy, or a microfloppy. Whatever you call it, most people know that you are referring to those small square things you stick in a disk drive.

Floppy disks have been around since the first generation of PCs, way back in 1981. Like hard disks, floppy disks are available in different storage capacities, although the options are limited. Two primary types of floppy disks are available. A 5 1/4-inch disk is made of a plastic mylar recording surface covered by a black, bendable cardboard-like material. It's 3 1/2-inch counterpart (not really called a "floppy" at all) is enclosed in a hard plastic case.

Figure 5.4 shows a minifloppy (the 5 1/4-inch black disk) and a microfloppy. The minifloppy is more vulnerable to outside elements. Dust, spilled Coke, cigarette ash, and other hazardous wastes can stick to the recording surface that is exposed through the jacket holes. The microfloppy (3 1/2-inch disk) enclosed in a

plastic case is more sturdy. The recording surface of the disk is exposed only when the disk is inside the disk drive.

Figure 5.4:

A minifloppy and microfloppy disk.

How do disk drives concern you when you work with graphics files? In several ways. When you purchase a new program, it comes on disks. Usually you can choose between 5 1/4-inch or 3 1/2-inch disks, so be sure to request the size you need if you have only one size disk drive on your computer. (Most systems today are sold with one drive of each size.) You must insert the disks into the appropriate drive to install the program on your hard disk.

You will probably use disks to keep copies of graphics files you need to safeguard. Saving files to a disk and putting the disk away somewhere safe—beyond the reaching fingers of a Frisbee-hunting preschooler—is a suggestion that cannot be overemphasized. As your graphics needs grow, you may look into purchasing a tape backup system or a removable hard disk so that you can save important files on a regular basis. For most of us, the starting place for our backup disciplines is the floppy disk.

If you trade files with coworkers or print on other machines, you need some way of transferring the files from one system to another. A floppy disk is a simple way. You need to send a set of files to a publisher on the East Coast and you have not yet figured out your modem? Get a copy of *The Modem Coach* and in the meantime, send your files on disk (packaged in a special cardboard disk pack).

One important consideration beyond the type of disk drives you have and the size of the disk: storage capacity. The original 5 1/4-inch disks store only 360K, which is not a lot of data. Today's minifloppies can store either 360K or 1.2M (called *high-density*), depending on the type of disk you buy. Microfloppies, on the other hand, have higher storage capacities; 720K or 1.44M. A new type of microfloppy, known as the extra-density (or ED) disk, can store 2.88M.

When you purchase a system or think about upgrading, remember the following points:

★ Minifloppies and microfloppies are great for saving files and putting them away someplace safe; but do not use these disks for your day-in-day-out work.

★ Disks can fail at one time or another. The failure rate of mini- and microfloppies is many times greater than that of hard disks. In any case, be prepared. Make copies of your important files on a daily or weekly basis.

★ If you plan to print files on one system that you created on another, make sure the disk drives are compatible. Do not try to read a 1.44M disk in a 720K drive.

★ Consider using a compression utility, such as PKZIP or Stuffit!, to shrink the size of your graphics files before you save them to disk.

★ If you work with a large number of graphics files, keep your eyes open for good tape backup deals. Saving everything out to floppy gets old and is less reliable than having a good backup unit.

A SYSTEM CHECKLIST

As you review the mysterious system unit elements in this chapter, chances are you have been asking yourself which parts of your system are good enough and which need some improving. The answers you are looking for will be found, no doubt, somewhere between your dream list and your checkbook. Table 5.2 reviews some of the system unit issues that are important for graphics work.

Table 5.2
System Unit Elements and Graphics Needs

Feature	*Considerations:*
System unit	
	Do you need the fastest processing speed possible?
	Will you be working with complicated graphics files?
	Will the programs you use require new CPUs?
RAM	
	Would upgrading the amount of RAM in your system dramatically increase its speed?
	Do the programs you use require large amounts of RAM?

Feature	***Considerations:***
	Will you work with Microsoft Windows or another type of application manager that eats up RAM space?
	Can you increase the RAM in your system, or are you maxed out?
	Is it possible to add virtual memory, extended memory, or expanded memory to your system?
	Will your graphics programs support these alternative memory forms?
Expansion Slots	
	Does your system have room for expansion?
	How many add-ons are you using now? (Include any device that is plugged into the back of your computer.)
	How many add-ons do you plan to add in the future?
	Is there any way to change things around in your system in order to free up expansion slots that are currently used?
Storage Capacity	
	Do you have a hard disk?
	What is the maximum capacity of your hard disk?
	What is the average size of your typical graphics file?

continues

Table 5.2
Continued

Feature	*Considerations:*
	Will you need a hard disk with smaller capacity or a mega-memory hard drive?
	What types of disk drives (type and capacity) do you now have?
	Will the storage capacities of these drives be sufficient?
	Would you benefit from using a tape backup unit?

INSTANT REPLAY

In this chapter, you learned ways that different elements in your system unit affect the type of graphics work you do. Speed and storage considerations are the two biggest issues in this chapter—things that slow you down, frustrate you, and perhaps rob you of your files. Specifically, you learned the following:

INSTANT REPLAY

- ✔ Parts of the system unit
- ✔ The microprocessor
- ✔ Updating your current system
- ✔ RAM versus ROM
- ✔ The hard disk
- ✔ The floppy disk

UNDERSTANDING MONITORS AND VIDEO CARDS

If you already use a computer system, you are familiar with your monitor: the squarish-looking display that may enable you to control contrast and brightness. Perhaps you are happy with it—the text looks clean and crisp, everything seems fast enough. Then you try working with sophisticated graphics. Suddenly, the same monitor that did passably well with text doesn't look so good.

In this chapter you learn how the various elements of your video display system affect the way you work with graphics. Specifically, this chapter covers the following:

GAME PLAN

- Understanding monitors and video cards
- Investigating screen size and resolution
- Understanding interlacing and refresh rate
- Exploring color capabilities

If you plan to upgrade your system to add a monitor and graphics card capable of supporting your new graphics tablet, you will find the basic "how to" in this chapter. If you are stuck with the system you have, you will become more aware of what goes into a good graphics system than you had when you started out.

One warning, however: Sometimes you are happier with the hardware you have until you realize what you are missing. After you discover the new and evolving technologies available for graphics display, you may look at your monitor differently.

EXPLORING YOUR VIDEO SYSTEM

Obviously, the monitor is a necessity—not something optional that you can add later if you choose to. Although you do have the option of purchasing an inexpensive monitor and then upgrading to a better monitor later on, doing so only lowers your standards. You may find yourself paying for that cheap monitor in ways you did not expect—such as extra bottles of aspirin and trips to the optometrist.

What is so important about the monitor and why you should spend some extra cash to get a good one? Lots of things. In this section, you learn about the various differences in monitors and display adapters and see how the important factors—besides the price tag—affect the way you work with graphics.

DISPLAY BASICS

How does the picture get on the screen in the first place? No item in your video display system can work by itself: the CPU cannot display without the monitor, and the monitor cannot display

anything without instructions from the graphics card. The sections that follow look at each of these items more closely.

THE DISPLAY ADAPTER

The monitor is actually a component that cannot do anything without its counterpart, the graphics card.

Chapter 5 explained expansion slots. Expansion slots provide the means to add peripheral devices—things outside the computer's system unit. When you add another piece to your system, an accompanying card (the small piece of hardware adorned with various chips and capacitors) plugs into the expansion slot.

A *graphics card* is one of those items that occupies an expansion slot. The card's function is to turn the signals it receives from the computer's CPU into an electronic form that can be displayed on the monitor screen. Suppose, for example, that you are using a paint program. As you move the mouse, electronic pulses are transmitted through the mouse cord to the CPU. The CPU, in turn, sends the signals to the graphics card, which turns the information into the line you see drawn on the screen.

> **The Coach Says...**
> A monitor is only as good as its graphics card. Be sure to find a graphics card that offers the features you want (support for the number of colors you need, refresh rate, and resolution) and then purchase a monitor that makes the best use of those features. Remember that the "talent" you see on-screen cannot be attributed to the monitor alone.

Figure 6.1 illustrates how graphics information flows from the CPU to the graphics card and, finally, to the monitor.

Figure 6.1:

The progression of graphics data.

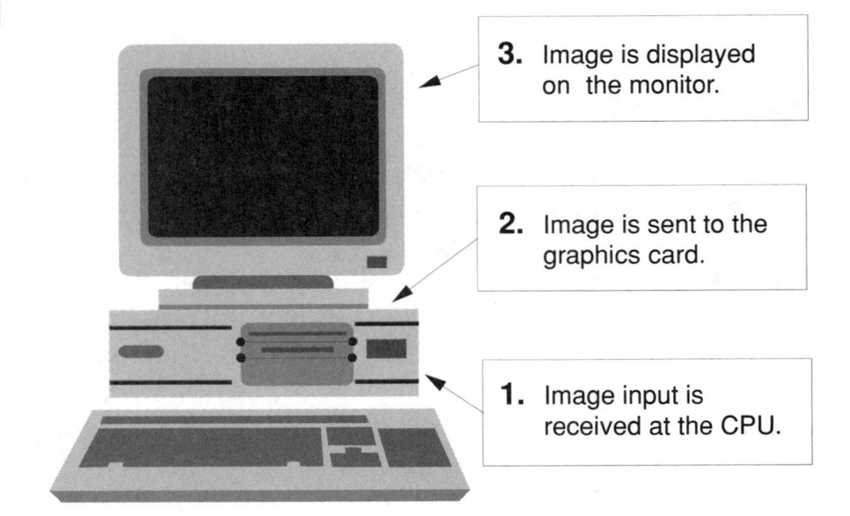

Some newer computers today are sold with the graphics card already included on the same board with the CPU or in plug-in slots on the motherboard that provide the graphics card with direct access to the CPU. This technology is known as *local bus video*. It offers much faster screen updates and general all-around computing power that its predecessor, the traditional AT data bus. A *data bus* is a rather cryptic-sounding term for the data path along which information flows to and from the CPU.

When you create or modify graphics, the CPU receives input, then sends data to the graphics card and the card sends data to the screen. When you move the mouse or alter a graphic, input goes to the CPU, and so on.

The primary difference between the older technology and the local data bus is in the processing speed of the card and the width of

the data path along which data travels. The local data bus paths have been increased (16-bit for the local bus compared to 8-bit for the traditional data bus), allowing data to get to its destination faster and freeing up more CPU power. Figure 6.2 illustrates the differences in the data buses.

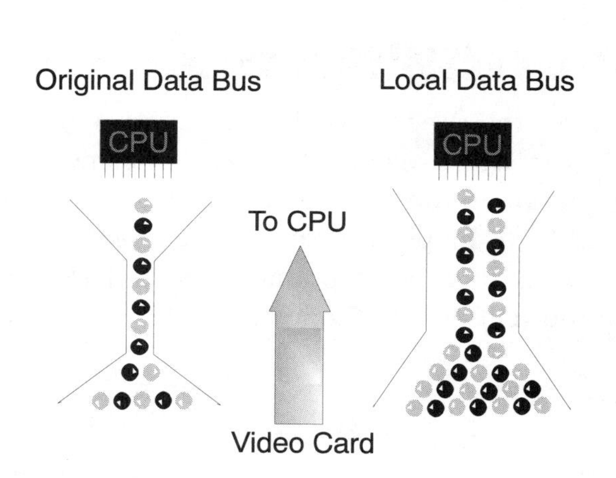

Figure 6.2: Understanding data paths.

For the fastest possible processing time, you may want to look into the new local bus designs in newer computer systems. Because this is a major design issue built right onto the motherboard, you cannot upgrade a computer system with a regular data bus to a local data bus design. You must purchase a system that supports the new design.

WHAT DOES THE MONITOR DO?

After the graphics adapter translates the data into a form that can be used by the monitor, the monitor receives the data through a cable that connects it with the graphics card. Then, a device inside

the monitor, called an *electron gun*, paints the inside of the screen electronically, causing the phosphors on the screen to glow. If you have a color monitor, these phosphors glow in red, green, or blue (or on some monitors, up to 16 million combinations of these colors).

IMPORTANT VIDEO CONSIDERATIONS

Many things affect the speed and clarity of information displayed on-screen. Whether you are considering purchasing a new monitor or trying to understand the monitor you have, knowing the ins and outs of these features helps you understand what separates the good monitors from their less-suitable cousins. These items are the subject of the sections that follow.

RESOLUTION

If you have spent any time surveying the computer world, you have heard the word resolution. *Resolution*—both on-screen and in print—refers to the clarity with which your images are displayed or printed.

What controls the resolution of the display? High-resolution is, of course, preferable over low-resolution (sounds logical). The higher the screen resolution, the clearer the picture. The resolution of the display is controlled by the capability of your graphics card, which determines how many dots are displayed per screen. The greater the number of dots used to make up a character or image, the greater the clarity of the image.

The size of the dots (measured in millimeters) displayed on-screen is referred to as the *dot pitch*. The smaller the size of the dot, the clearer the picture. For smaller monitors, a dot pitch of .28mm provides good quality; for larger monitors, you should not use anything over .31mm in size.

The Coach Says...

It is not only important that you choose a good, solid resolution (such as 800x600 or 1260x768), but that you invest in a monitor capable of displaying small dot pitch.

What resolutions are available? The earliest PCs offered horrible resolutions, but users were thrilled anyway because they had nothing to compare them to. The resolution offered by the CGA (color graphics adapter) was big and clunky. The characters on-screen looked choppy, and color was limited to the primaries. EGA (enhance graphics adapter) technology offered improved screen quality but still at a lower resolution.

What you can expect from a monitor/graphics card combination today you could not dream of several years ago. Today's standards are VGA, Super VGA, and Extended VGA. Table 6.1 lists the screen resolutions of today's popular displays.

Table 6.1
Today's Resolution Standards

Display adapter	*Resolution*
VGA	640 X 480
Super VGA	800 X 600
Extended VGA	1024 X 768
Ultra VGA	1280 X 1024

The top three resolutions—Super VGA, Extended VGA, and Ultra VGA—are so new that their names have not been standardized. You may see all three of these resolutions referred to as Super VGA.

You can find the first three screen resolutions available in a variety of products; both graphics cards and monitors

offer a number of choices for graphics display. Likewise, most popular programs support at least VGA and Super VGA resolutions and a fair number support the higher ends, as well. Windows and Mac applications are capable of adjusting their displays to the hardware capabilities being used. The top-of-the-line resolution, 1280x1024, is the newest standard. It currently is supported by few popular programs, but like everything else in the computer industry, that should change soon.

> **The Coach Says...**
>
> If you purchase a new monitor and graphics card, do not purchase more than you need. If you select a smaller monitor, for example, a 14-inch monitor (screens are measured diagonally), you do not need to shell out the extra money for an Extended or high-end VGA adapter. If you only have a 14-inch display area, why cram 1280x1024 dots into that small area? The result is small, scrunched characters and perhaps disproportionate graphics. If you use a large-screen monitor, on the other hand, the added resolution significantly enhances the quality of your display.

MONITOR SIZE

What does the size of the monitor have to do with the quality of the display? If you are talking about the monitor all by itself—nothing. The graphics card actually controls the quality of the display: the monitor is simply the vehicle on which the image is shown. The monitor does have to support the resolution displayed by the card, but that has nothing to do with size.

Monitor size is clearly a personal preference issue. Common sense tells you that the more you have to look at, the better. But if you remember the clunky quality of the first big-screen TVs, you know

that a larger display area does not guarantee a better picture. Flaws you might overlook in a small screen you are more likely to see in a larger screen's display.

Most monitors are capable of producing screens at several resolutions. Be sure to choose a monitor that it is capable of displaying screens in the resolution you want. Not all monitors can display in Super VGA or Extended VGA and only a few can reach the highest 1280x1024 resolution.

Some people prefer smaller monitors, such as the 13-inch Apple monitor available with Macintosh IIsi; the 15-inch NEC; or the smaller PS/2 monitors. Larger monitors include the Apple Portrait monitor, which offers full-page display; the 17-inch ViewSonic, the 19-inch Sony, or the 21-inch Mitsubishi.

The Coach Says...

Other types of monitors that are popular for specialized publishing applications include the full-page monitor and the two-page monitor. The full-page monitor, also called a portrait display, is taller than it is wide, enabling you to display a full document page within the screen area. The two-page monitor is a large wide monitor capable of displaying two pages on the screen at once.

When you try to choose which monitor to buy (if you have a choice), consider the type of work you will be doing. Would you benefit from a full-page monitor, or will a standard display do? Do you have room on your desktop for a larger monitor, or would you be better off conserving some space with a smaller monitor? (For more ideas about monitor decisions, see "A Video Checklist" later in this chapter.)

REFRESH RATE

The refresh rate of the display is another factor you should consider when evaluating monitor capabilities. The monitor displays the image you see on-screen by painting the picture on the inside of the screen with an electron gun. The gun moves back and forth across the screen causing the phosphors on-screen to glow. The phosphors glow only briefly and then fade; then the gun quickly repaints them so that no on-screen wavering or flickering appears to the user. The rate at which the gun moves to repaint the screen is known as the *refresh rate*.

The rate at which the gun moves from left to right is known as the *horizontal scan rate*. The rate at which the gun moves from the top of the screen to the bottom is known as the *vertical refresh rate* (see fig. 6.3).

Figure 6.3:

Horizontal and vertical scan rates.

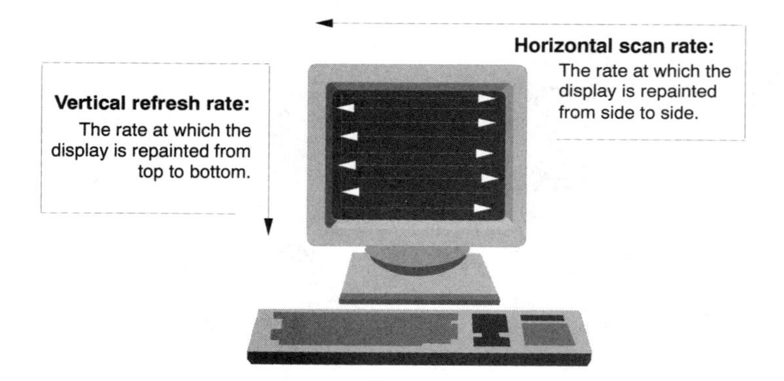

The refresh rate is measured in hertz, written as Hz. When you shop for a suitable refresh rate, look for a refresh rate of 72Hz, or 72 passes of the electron gun each second. When you purchase a monitor, the specifications tell you the refresh rate. Most ads show a range of vertical refresh rates from 50Hz to 120Hz. The range of refresh rates is due to different display resolutions; an image displayed in higher resolution, for example, would have a lower refresh rate (because there are more dots to repaint).

Refresh rate is an important consideration—especially important for highly detailed graphics work. When you stare intently at the screen for long periods of time, a lax refresh rate, which enables the phosphors to dim and causes the display to waver in intensity, can give you headaches or cause eye strain.

INTERLACING

In addition to offering a wide range of refresh rates available at different resolutions, some monitors and cards rely on interlacing to help hasten screen refreshes in larger monitors. *Interlacing* is a technical word for "slipping every other row" in the repaint passes. To speed up screen repainting, for example, the electron gun repaints lines 1, 3, 5, 7, 9, and so on, the first time through. Then, it moves back to the top of the screen and paints lines 2, 4, 6, 8, and so forth.

Interlacing is hard on the eyes over a long period of time. Although generally more expensive, noninterlaced monitors are worth the investment. Some manufacturers resort to interlacing only at higher screen resolutions, which you might want to consider if your display needs are taken care of by typical VGA or Super VGA displays.

COLOR CAPABILITIES

When you purchase a monitor, you must choose between color and monochrome. As you learned earlier in this chapter, the electron gun is responsible for repainting the screen. If you work with a color monitor, the phosphors on the screen glow in red, green, or blue (or a combination of those colors). If you work with a monochrome (single color) monitor, the phosphors glow in only one color—perhaps green, amber, or white.

How important is color? Users line up on both sides of this issue. Some adamantly claim working in black-and-white provides better resolution and a crisper, cleaner image that puts less strain on the eye. Others feel that color is as important as any other issue related to video display and the more colors your monitor displays, the better.

> **The Coach Says...**
>
> As the owner of both black-and-white and high-resolution color monitors, I prefer using a monochrome monitor when working with text and a color monitor when working with graphics. It is not because of screen clarity or resolution, however; it has something to do with graphics work being the more "visually creative" of the two tasks.

Today's color technology provides a puzzle to decipher. You will find 4-bit color, 8-bit color, 16-bit color, and 24-bit color. What is the difference, and which do you need?

The 4-bit color graphics cards provide a maximum of 16 different colors on-screen, although these hues can be mixed to create blends of those colors. 4-bit (also called 16-color mode) is popular because of its fast screen updates and low price tag.

The next mode is known as *pseudo color* and can provide up to 256 shades of color. This affordable mode gives you the option of a relatively fast screen display and enough color variety for most applications.

High color is the name for the color mode displaying over 32,000 different colors. These 16-bit color graphics cards are terrific for high-end applications requiring sophisticated colors, such as detailed graphics work, retouching and editing scanned images, and desktop publishing applications.

The highest standard, known as *true color*, can display over 16 million colors making it the highest possible quality color display. The downside of the new 24-bit color technology, however, is that it can be extremely expensive and requires more processing power (24-bit boards include their own coprocessor).

Windows and Macs can support just about any capabilities your system can offer, but before DOS programs can use the technology, they must be written to support that particular graphics card.

The Coach Says...

Even color capability is affected by the resolution of the screen. Now, graphics cards are capable of providing the maximum number of colors at the highest screen resolution. For most applications, this will not bother you. However, if your work requires up-close work with fine color detail, you may be frustrated by a system with limited color capabilities.

A VIDEO CHECKLIST

You have seen throughout this chapter a long stream of considerations that are important whether you are purchasing a new video system or assessing the one you already have. Chances are, you are not the one responsible for assembling a system from the ground up—system unit, graphics card, monitor, and so on. Most computer dealers put together a system for you, with an adequate (if not supercharged) graphics card and a monitor (or at least support for a wide range of popular monitors).

Whether you are simply exploring your options for a future wish list or researching your choices for an upcoming buy, consider the following items in Table 6.2 as you look through the computer ads.

Table 6.2
Video System Considerations

Feature	*Considerations:*
Video basics	
	Does your system come with a graphics card and monitor included?
	Do you need more power than your system's graphics card offers?
	Is the graphics card included in an expansion slot or does the system have a local data bus design?
Resolution	
	How important is screen resolution to your graphics work?
	What resolution does your monitor offer now?

Feature	Considerations:
	What is the dot pitch of your current (or intended) monitor?
	What type of screen resolution—VGA, Super VGA, Extended VGA, or Ultra VGA—does your monitor deserve? (Remember, larger monitors need higher resolution, but do not waste a high-resolution card on a small screen.)
Monitor Size	
	What is the current size of your display?
	Would your graphics work benefit from a larger screen?
	If you do publishing work, would a full-page monitor be better than a traditional monitor?
	Do you need a two-page monitor? (Remember, not many applications support this type of display.)
	Are you working with a minimum of desk space?
Refresh Rate	
	What is the vertical refresh rate of your current monitor (or the monitor you are considering)?
	What is the horizontal scan rate?
	Can you get a suitable refresh rate at the resolution you want to use?

continues

Table 6.2
Video System Considerations

Feature	*Considerations:*
	Does your screen have a noticeable flicker? (You can tell by looking ten inches to the right or left of your monitor; the flicker will appear in your peripheral vision.)
Interlacing	
	Does your monitor or the monitor you are considering interlace screen repaints?
	Does the interlacing happen only at high resolution?
	If so, will you be working at a lower resolution, or will your screen quality be affected by the interlacing?
Color	
	Is color an important consideration for your graphics applications?
	How many colors do you need?
	How many colors are supported by your graphics adapter?
	Do the applications you work with recognize high- or true-color modes?
	Do you prefer working in black-and-white or color?

INSTANT REPLAY

This chapter discussed the importance of the various elements in your video display system. It also discussed the wide range of options available to you if you are shopping for a new monitor and graphics card. In the next chapter, you explore the various methods of getting your graphics into the computer—whether you draw with a pen on a graphics tablet or use a mouse or scanner.

Specifically this chapter covers the following:

INSTANT REPLAY

- ✔ Understanding monitors and video cards
- ✔ Screen size and resolution
- ✔ Interlacing and refresh rate
- ✔ Color capabilities

UNDERSTANDING ART TOOLS

The items introduced in this chapter can be loosely lumped into the category *input devices*. As you learned in the last chapter, the CPU receives the data as you create and modify graphics and then sends it to the graphics card and finally to the monitor. This chapter introduces those "somethings" you use to send the input to the CPU in the first place.

This chapter introduces many of the art tools you may use in computer graphics. Specifically, you learn about the following topics:

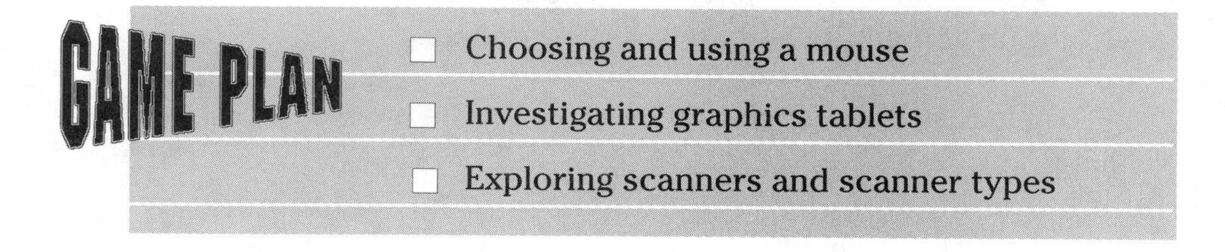

Whether you use a PC or Macintosh system, you are familiar with the mouse. The mouse is the most common—and still the most popular—input tool used in addition to the keyboard. Used in virtually every type of computer application, the mouse is no stranger to graphics work. In fact, graphics without a mouse or some other kind of graphics input tool can be totally exasperating, especially when you try to draw circles, create polygons, control fills, and draw freehand. Keys on a keyboard simply do not give you the control over the cursor that you need to do customized art.

For that reason, this chapter addresses these important devices that make creating computer art more accurate and more enjoyable. This chapter discusses three very different kinds of tools: the mouse, the graphics tablet, and the scanner.

WORKING WITH THE MOUSE

Unless you have been working in a cave with a DOS-based PC since the mid 1980s, you have heard of and probably used a mouse. The *mouse* is a small device used to point to and select items on-screen, reposition the cursor, choose commands from menus, move objects, select text, and draw pictures on-screen. When you move the mouse, the corresponding mouse pointer moves in the same direction. Move the mouse up and to the right on your desktop or mousepad and the mouse pointer moves up and to the right on-screen.

To select an item (such as a menu) with the mouse, do the following:

1. Position the mouse pointer on the item you want to select.
2. Click the mouse button. This "opens" the menu (or the item you selected).

The first mice were available with early Macintosh computers. Because the graphical, point-and-click interface of the Mac was so dependent on the mouse, using the computer without the mouse was next to impossible. The mouse brought a whole new method of using the computer to a new generation of computer users.

The Macintosh had one button instead of the two (or three) on a PC mouse.

PCs were slower to add mouse technology to both their hardware and software systems. Users either love the mouse or hate it. New users typically prefer using the mouse because the point-and-click method seems easier than memorizing cryptic keyboard commands and typing them at an unfriendly DOS prompt. Users who are familiar with the DOS prompt, however, seem to prefer "the old way" because they do not have the change the placement of their hands on the keyboard. Even seasoned DOS veterans, however, find themselves reaching for the mouse (often unconsciously) after working with it a few times.

The introduction of Microsoft Windows legitimized mouse use for PC users. A few programs—and computer manufacturers, as well—had built-in mouse support before Windows arrived on the scene, but the overwhelming acceptance of the mouse was not there before the advent of Windows. PC users now have a point-and-click interface similar to the one that their Mac friends enjoy. Starting programs and opening files—at least in Windows—now is as simple as a click of a mouse button.

One major difference between the Macintosh mouse and the PC mouse is the number of buttons on each one. The Mac mouse only has one button, used in all Mac programs for the same purposes.

PC mice have two or three buttons, the uses of which are as varied as the PC programs themselves. Generally, the left mouse button emulates the press of the Enter key, which means you click the left

mouse button for important command selections. The function of the right mouse button (or on the three-button mouse, the two right buttons) is pretty much up for grabs. Some programs totally disable the use of the second button so it does nothing when you click it. Other programs display attributes or options when you click the right mouse button on a certain item. As more and more applications are written to run under Windows, however, you will see more uniformity among mouse button operations.

WHAT DOES A MOUSE DO?

You know how to use a mouse, but how do the little rodents work? It almost seems like magic. Somehow you can push a rectangular shaped object around on your desk and control things on your computer screen.

The mouse, technically called the mechanical mouse, is commonly referred to as a pointing device, although it also is a drawing device, a painting device, and a text tool. It consists of several small but important parts: the mouse body, the mouse buttons, the mouse tail, the mouse feet, and the mouse ball. Figure 7.1 shows the mouse from top and bottom views.

Figure 7.1: The mouse: right-side up and up-side down.

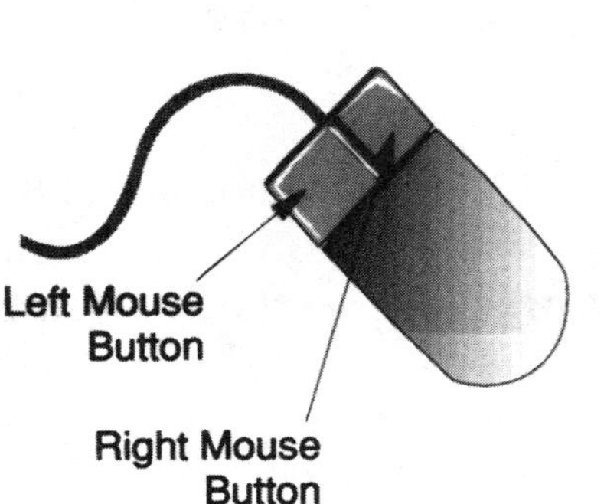

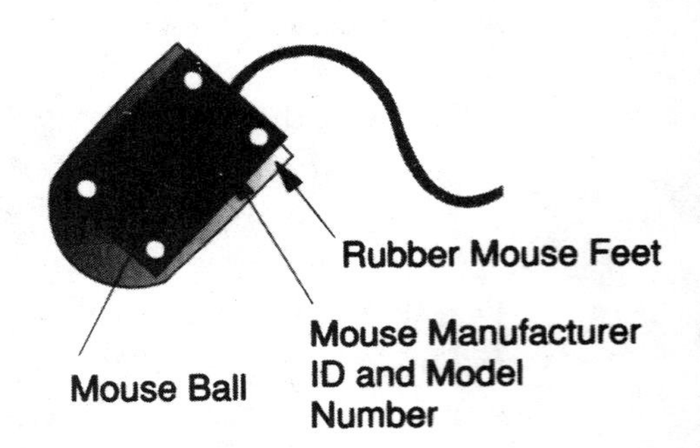

The mouse shown in figure 7.1 is a Microsoft Mouse, manufactured by Microsoft. This two-button mouse is more oblong than it is square, and the rounded shape on top fits nicely into the palm of your hand. On the flip side of the mouse, you see several different objects. The little rubber mouse feet keep the mouse from sliding on your desktop (which could cause skipping on the screen). A label underneath identifies the mouse and the model number (important things to remember if your mouse ever goes belly up). Within the small circular disk, you see only a portion of a black or gray object: that is the mouse ball.

Inside the mouse (you can see these items if you remove the disk), is a large removable mouse ball and several sensors along the edge of the cylinder. When you roll the mouse across the desktop, the mouse ball touches the sensors. The sensors send directional information to the CPU, which in turn sends the information to the screen. If dirt or dust has adhered to the mouse ball or the sensors, your mouse may skip, jump, or refuse to move.

To clean your mouse, do the following:

1. Carefully open the circular disk.
2. Remove the ball from the chamber. Use a cotton swab to clean the ball and the sensors.
3. Blow into the chamber to remove any dust.
4. Reassemble your mouse.

The Coach Says...

Always remember to unplug your mouse before cleaning it.

MEMBERS OF THE MOUSE FAMILY

When you first purchase a mouse, someone will ask you whether you want a bus mouse or a serial mouse. (The temptation to add a bad pun is almost overwhelming.)

A *bus mouse* requires the addition of a board that is plugged into one of the expansion slots in your system. A *serial mouse* uses the serial port in the back of your computer. Little or no performance difference exists between the two mouse types, however, some users prefer the bus mouse because it frees the serial port for other peripherals.

If you use a Macintosh, you do not have to worry about which mouse type to use. Only one mouse type can be used with a Mac, and it is already built into your computer. The mouse is installed, configured, and ready to use from the first time you boot up the system.

Another type of mouse that has different hardware is the *optical mouse*. An optical mouse—as opposed to the mechanical mouse—internally tracks coordinates by reading its position on a special pad. This pad consists of a grid of wires that the mouse sees by shining a beam of light onto them. Then it can read its position and send the coordinates to the CPU.

The high-res mouse is a typical mechanical mouse that has extra sensitive sensors capable of reading movements in extremely small increments. Some high-res mice are capable of responding to movements at a resolution of 400 dots per inch (dpi), which is double the 200 dpi resolution of a regular mouse. A high-res mouse responds to even the smallest movement, so you can move the mouse much less and have it go greater distances. High-res mice are great when working with a minimum of desk space.

The mouse may have been one of the first pointing devices available for personal computers, but it certainly is not the last.

The trackball, another type of pointing device that enables users to control the placement of the cursor, was designed as a potential mouse replacement. Many computers, including Macintosh Powerbooks, include a trackball as part of the computer keyboard. Trackballs are popular for laptop and notebook computers because, unlike the mouse, they do not move. Only the ball inside the trackball housing is moved to reposition the cursor on-screen.

You can use a mouse with a laptop or notebook but it is very difficult. Suppose, for example, that you are working in your car. Where are you going to put the mouse? You need a flat surface. A trackball uses a different positioning scheme—almost like turning the mouse upside-down and moving the mouse ball—to move the pointer on the screen, select objects, and open menus.

Figure 7.2 shows a small trackball that clips onto the side of a laptop computer. This clip-on trackball grabs onto the edge of your computer and attaches to the serial or mouse port in the back of the system through a cable. Two programmable buttons enable you to use the trackball whether you are right- or left-handed (a consideration not addressed for most mouse users).

Many different manufacturers create trackballs and mice. Generally, you can pick up a mouse for anywhere from $29 to $129. Trackballs usually cost from $69 to $129, unless included with a system as standard equipment.

HOW WILL YOU USE THE MOUSE?

Think about how often you pick up a pad of paper and pencil and sketch out ideas, draw directions, design a logo, or just doodle. Using paper and pencil is so easy; you just let your mind wander and your hand follows.

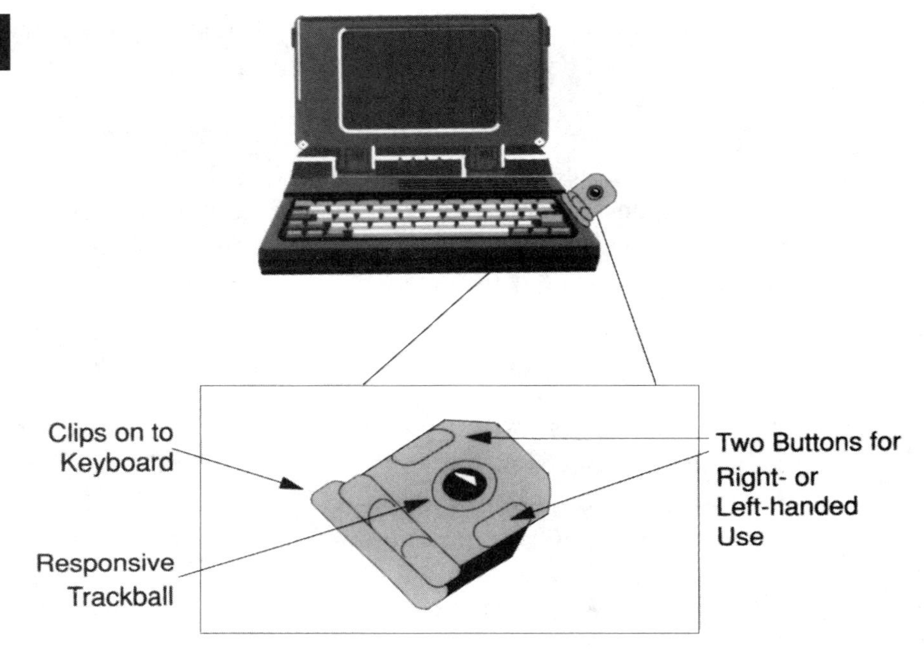

Figure 7.2:

A clip-on trackball.

Computers constrict us, even as they give us more power. Paper and pencil as art tools are as flexible as they come. Paper and pencil, however, have one major disadvantage: you cannot reuse them. After you sketch a drawing, you cannot rotate it, fill it, move a line, or stick it directly into a quarterly report. To turn that drawing into something you can use electronically, you have to digitize it (which is why a scanner comes in handy).

The advantage of using paper and pencil is that you can draw freehand. If you have ever used an Etch-a-Sketch, you know how hard it is to re-create an image when you are limited to using only horizontal and vertical lines (and not very good ones, at that).

If you try to draw graphics using the keyboard, you must work in the Etch-a-Sketch realm, only worse. Sure, you may be able to use the arrow keys to move an object across the screen, but it will take forever. You might be able to get the hang of drawing lines and creating polygons using the keystroke commands, but creating art

that way will never be close to the freehand method as long as you must punch keys.

The mouse provides the flexibility and intuitive power to do just about anything on-screen that you would do with your pencil on paper. Using a mouse, you can do the following:

★ Point to tools

★ Draw circles, squares, and polygons

★ Resize elements

★ Change the color of individual pixels

★ Move, copy, and paste objects

★ Flip art horizontally or vertically

★ Rotate objects

Some users find that even the mouse is a bit too restrictive for true freehand art work or not accurate enough for sophisticated CAD (computer-aided drawing) projects. The next section introduces you to an art tool often used in more artistically demanding situations.

USING A GRAPHICS TABLET

A graphics tablet is an electronic pad on which you can draw images using an electronic pen. The movements of the pen on the pad are then relayed to the screen. The graphics tablet comes with either a *stylus*, which is an electronic pen, or a *puck*, which is a sensitive mouse-like device that reads the location by determining where on the grid it is placed. Most graphics tablets offer either the stylus or the puck (or both for an additional cost).

HOW DOES A GRAPHICS TABLET WORK?

The graphics tablet is a popular graphics input device among users who enjoy the freedom of drawing freehand. Graphics tablets originally were made for high-end graphics and primarily used by those who make a living in graphics work. A recent drop in prices and greater awareness of the benefits, however, has brought graphics tablets within reach of the average user. Figure 7.3 shows a graphics tablet and an optional puck.

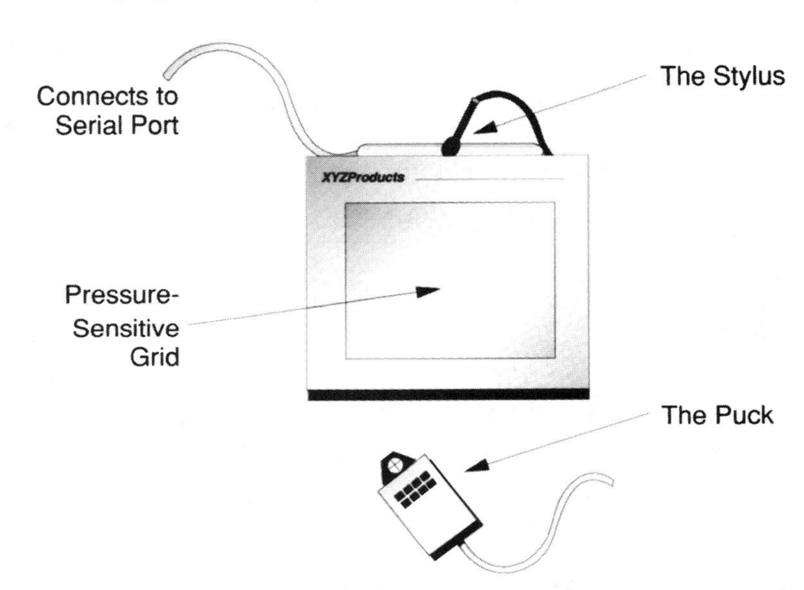

Figure 7.3: A graphics tablet with stylus and puck.

The graphics tablet offers other benefits as well as the convenience of drawing in a more natural way. The graphics tablet actually is an electronically charged grid, and the stylus (or puck) is an extremely sensitive pointing device. The mouse and trackball, at best, provide a relative position on the screen. You will notice, for example, that in some up-close work you may use the mouse to connect two lines. Then, when you zoom the display, you find the lines are not even close to touching. The stylus, however, gives you a fine-tuned precision that the approximate placement of the mouse cannot offer.

AVAILABLE GRAPHICS TABLETS

The range in size and capabilities of graphics tablets is staggering. For high-end CAD applications, you will find large tablets (often up to 12-by-12 or 18-by-12 inches in size), CAD templates (so that you can use the tablet with popular design programs), pucks with 16 programmable buttons, and up to 2000 lines-per-inch resolution. You also will pay several hundred dollars or more for these high-end tablets.

Other mid-range graphics tablets also are available. The AceCat is a new 5 x 5-inch graphics tablet that offers the drawing flexibility you need. Because of its small size, you can use it anywhere—on your lap, on your desk, or leaning back in your favorite recliner. The AceCat, which costs $129, plugs into the serial port in the back of your computer and includes drivers for both DOS and Windows. Another benefit is that the stylus has a button that enables you to change it (functionally speaking) from a pen to a mouse, and your programs will not know the difference.

HOW DOES THE PUCK WORK?

The puck is similar to a mouse but it performs functions in a different way. You might use the puck, for example, to plot points on a schematic or trace over a detailed CAD design. The cross-hair on the end of the puck helps you align your work with pin-point accuracy. Most pucks have multiple buttons that you can customize to perform functions specific to your computer software.

> **The Coach Says...**
>
> Most graphics tablets offer pucks as an option to the stylus (for an additional fee).

USING A SCANNER

You have drawn a really cool logo, but you drew it on your napkin at lunch. You rushed back to the office and tried re-creating it with your draw program, but it just does not look right. Now what?

A scanner is another type of input device that can help you when you already have the art you want to use, but it is not in electronic format. A *scanner* is an input device that digitizes photos, drawings, or text and saves the digitized information in a file that you can use in desktop publishing, graphics, or even word processing applications. Scanners enable you to bring items you create on the fly into your computer art repertoire.

HOW DOES A SCANNER WORK?

The scanner works by shining a beam of light on the image being scanned. The beam moves back and forth across the page, line by line, sending the digitized information through the scanner's cable. The image is then "written" in memory and saved as a file.

You can scan graphics or text. The scanner turns the information into an electronic format that resembles a bit-mapped graphic. Scanned images, however, often have jaggies—easily apparent jagged edges caused by the individual pixels in the file.

When you scan text, it essentially becomes artwork. Therefore you cannot resize the text or change the font and style as you could with text entered in a word processing program. You can, however, use optical character recognition software to change scanned text back into real text so that you can work with. To solve this text problem, use optical character recognition (OCR) software to change the scanned text back into real text.

When you work with graphics, the scanning process works the same way. The image is read into memory, comprised of electronic bits of data. Then, the image is saved as a bit-mapped graphic (usually TIFF format) that you can modify and enhance as necessary.

Some scanners scan at a higher resolution than others and create a better scanned image. No matter which type of scanner you use, however, you will need some kind of program to smooth out the jaggies in your scanned image. Many high-end drawing programs, such as CorelDRAW!, include an autotrace feature that automatically traces the edges of your scanned image turning it into a vector graphic and removing jagged edges. Other stand-alone utilities, such as Adobe Streamline, provide an autotrace feature if your drawing program does not include one.

WHAT TYPES OF SCANNERS ARE AVAILABLE?

You will find a wide variety of scanners available for a wide variety of uses. If you are just trying to find some way to get that new logo into your computer, you do not need a $7,000 scanner complete with all available bells and whistles. A simple hand-held scanner will work for simple scanning tasks. This section introduces you to some of the scanners currently available.

Starting at the low end are hand-held black and white scanners. These scanners, which cost about $120, scan the page as you manually move the device (see fig. 7.4).

The advantages of a hand-held scanner include the following:

★ Cost (a hand-held scanner is inexpensive)

★ Flexibility (you can use it to capture a single small picture)

★ Small size

The disadvantages of a hand-held scanner include the following:

- ★ Wobbly image (you cannot hold a hand scanner still enough to create a clear picture)
- ★ Low resolution (usually only 200 to 400 dots-per-inch)

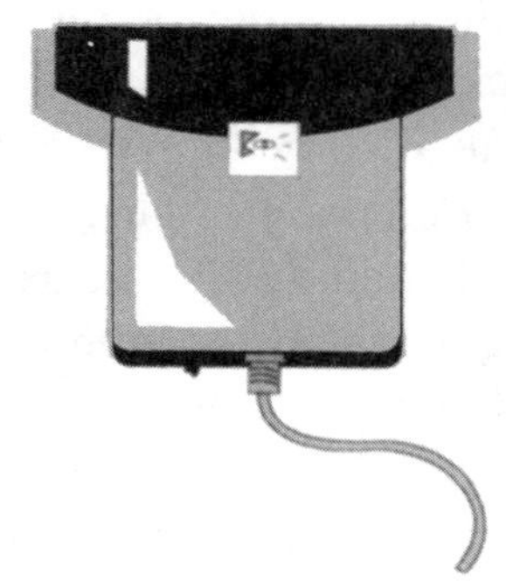

Figure 7.4: A hand-held scanner.

A cousin to the hand-held scanner is the half-page scanner, a large version of the moveable scanner. You move a half-page scanner down the page in the same way you do hand-held scanner. Output and resolution are basically the same, although the image captured with a half-page scanner is wider than the image captured with a hand-held scanner. You also may pay slightly more for a half-page scanner than you would a hand-held scanner.

The next level up on the scanner scale is the flatbed gray scale scanner. A flatbed scanner is different from either a hand-held scanner or a half-page scanner in two ways: the scanner itself does not move (which eliminates wobblies), and the output is displayed in up to 256 shades of gray.

A flatbed scanner is smaller than a printer. In most cases, you use a flatbed scanner like you would a copier: lift the cover, place the page on the glass top, close the cover, and scan the entire page.

The light beam travels down the page, digitizing the image with no loss of clarity because of a moving focal point. Flat-bed gray scale scanners are more costly than their moveable counterparts, costing anywhere from $1,500 to $2,000. Often, you can achieve results from a flatbed gray scale scanner that look better than the original photo or piece of art.

The Coach Says...

One of the most popular gray scale scanners available today is the HP ScanJet, which works with both the Macintosh and the PC.

The highest standard available in scanners today is the color scanner. Color scanners are expensive and cost anywhere from $3,000 to $10,000. Color scanners contain the technology that make it possible for you to scan images with up to 16 million colors (the variety of colors is limited only by the scanning software, not the scanner itself). Scanned color image files eat up a lot of space, so make sure that you have plenty of RAM on your computer. You probably do not need a color scanner unless you work with true color photographs for high-end graphics applications. Although the output is stunning, a color scanner can take quite a chunk out of your computer budget. A gray scale scanner may better fit your needs and your applications needs.

WHAT CAN YOU DO WITH A SCANNER?

When you are first starting out in graphics work, you may be somewhat intimidated by a scanner. It seems a bit too specialized, right? Truthfully, how often would you use that type of technology? Daily? Weekly? Monthly?

You might be surprised. Having a scanner handy (no pun intended) uncovers possibilities you might otherwise miss. You will find yourself looking for opportunities to use scanned images in your work.

The Coach Says...

Copyright infringement is a major problem facing the industry today. Now that scanners are so popular, users are scanning illustrations and photographs that do not belong to them and using them in their own work. If you plan to "lift" a photo or illustration from another source, you must get permission from the publisher or photographer to use it in your work. Otherwise, you may find yourself in copyright trouble.

The following are just a few ways you can use your new scanner:

- Scan "mug shots" of coworkers for the corporate newsletter
- Scan a cartoon drawn by a fellow employee
- Import artwork published in the last corporate report
- Create a library of illustrations used in a recent presentation
- Scan the corporate logo to be included on desktop published stationery, business cards, and envelopes
- Scan a large manual using OCR software to turn it into "real" text (so you don't have to type the entire thing in)
- Scan a character in an unusual font so that you can create your own font based on that object
- Import full-color, lifelike photos into your four-color publications

CHOOSING YOUR TOOLS: A CHECKLIST

This chapter introduced you to a few of the graphics input tools you may want to consider as you launch your graphics career. Think of the way you draw now. What is most comfortable? Are you accustomed to a mouse, or would a graphics tablet and stylus feel more natural? Would a scanner provide access to a library of artwork you might otherwise not have? Consider the tools carefully before choosing any. Table 7.1 contains a few items that might help.

Table 7.1
Graphics Tools Considerations

Tool	*Considerations:*
Mouse	
	Do you currently use a mouse?
	Are you comfortable using the mouse for drawing tasks?
	Would you prefer using a bus mouse or a serial mouse? (PCs only)
	Does the mouse respond quickly enough to small movements? (If not, consider a high-res mouse.)
Trackball	
	Does your computer keyboard already have a trackball?
	Would a trackball be more convenient for your laptop or notebook computer?
	Do you have a limited amount of desk space?

continues

Table 7.1
Continued

Tool	*Considerations:*
	Do you need a right- or left-handed trackball?
	Do you need a full-sized trackball or would a miniature clip-on trackball do?
Graphics Tablet	
	Would you be more comfortable with a paper-and-pen type of drawing?
	Do your applications require more on-screen accuracy than a mouse or trackball can offer?
	Do you have the desk space for a larger graphics tablet, or do you need a smaller size?
	Do your applications require the tracing of elements or large amounts of free-hand drawing?
Stylus	
	Are you more comfortable using a pen or a mouse?
	Do you do a lot of freehand illustration?
	Would you prefer to select menu options, choose objects, or make on-screen choices with a pen?
	Do your applications require pen-point accuracy or can you use approximate placement of a mouse or trackball?

Tool	Considerations:
Puck	
	Do you work with high-end graphics or CAD applications?
	Would your work benefit from the use of CAD templates?
	Do you plot and trace in your graphics work?
	Could you make use of programmable puck buttons?
Scanner	
	Do you need to import art or text from printed media?
	Would your projects benefit from scanned images?
	Do you need to add hand-drawn artwork to your newsletters?
	Could you use a scanner to create a library of art you created manually?
	Would a low-cost hand-scanner meet your needs?
	Do you work primarily with black-and-white photos?
	Will you be incorporating full-color art in your graphics files?

INSTANT REPLAY

In this chapter, you explored the various art tools you could use to create, modify, and import graphics. If you are a Mac or Windows user, you already have a mouse, which may be all the "input" you need as you get up to speed with graphics. On the other hand, if your graphics needs are more specialized, requiring that you do a large amount of freehand work or use photos—half-tone or full-color—in your projects, you may need to consider a graphics tablet and a scanner. The next chapter explores your graphics output options—printers and plotters.

Specifically, this chapter covered the following:

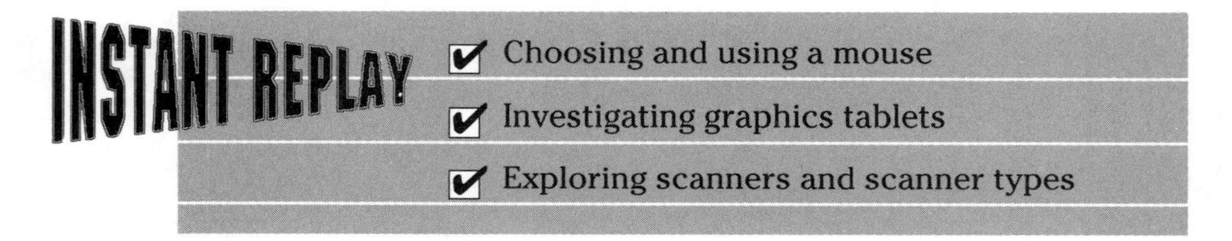

- ✔ Choosing and using a mouse
- ✔ Investigating graphics tablets
- ✔ Exploring scanners and scanner types

UNDERSTANDING PRINTERS AND OTHER OUTPUT OPTIONS

Well, the award-winning graphics you created on your computer are not going to do you much good if they are forever trapped inside that metal box. Sure, you can use them in on-screen presentations, but you need options for output as well. Something you can hold in your hands. Pass around. Autograph.

This chapter explores the various options you have for outputting your favorite graphics files. Specifically, this chapter covers the following:

GAME PLAN

- Discovering dot-matrix printers
- Investigating ink-jet printers
- Thinking about thermal transfer printers
- Looking at laser printers
- Considering color choices
- Understanding printer considerations

PRINTER PRELIMINARIES

If you are investing quite a bit of money and time in the latest graphics software and trying to either find a suitable computer or upgrade the one you have, you do not want to scrimp on a printer. The printed output, after all, is your statement to the world. Even the best piece of art looks shoddy when printed on a low-quality printer with lower-quality paper.

Several years ago, it was financially draining to purchase a printer capable of producing the highest standard of output. If you jumped on the PostScript bandwagon when the printers were first introduced, for example, you probably paid (or are still paying) $4,000 for a printer that today costs about half that much. With the drop in prices and the increase in features and resolution, a good printer is within reach of even the tightest budgets.

As you will see in this chapter, there are several different types of printers available. Each type of printer offers different advantages and limitations. Some printers are capable of high-quality output and some are not. But high quality, in this case, translates to clear, crisp characters, professional-looking art, and, hopefully, a good first impression.

UNDERSTANDING PRINTER TYPES AND CAPABILITIES

The range of printers available in the market today is almost staggering. You can pick up a printer for as little as $100 (of course, the old adage "you get what you pay for" applies), or you can pay up to—and over—$10,000 for a top-of-the-line color laser printer. Chances are, your output needs fall somewhere between the two extremes.

What types of printers are available and which are best for graphics work? This section takes a close look at some of the printers in the market today—dot-matrix, ink-jet, thermal transfer, and laser printers—and helps you make a more educated decision about your output choices.

DOT-MATRIX PRINTERS

One of the most affordable printers on the market today is the dot-matrix printer (see fig. 8.1). Often companies, such as Panasonic and EPSON, offer dot-matrix printers for less than $200, which does not put too much of a cramp in most budgets.

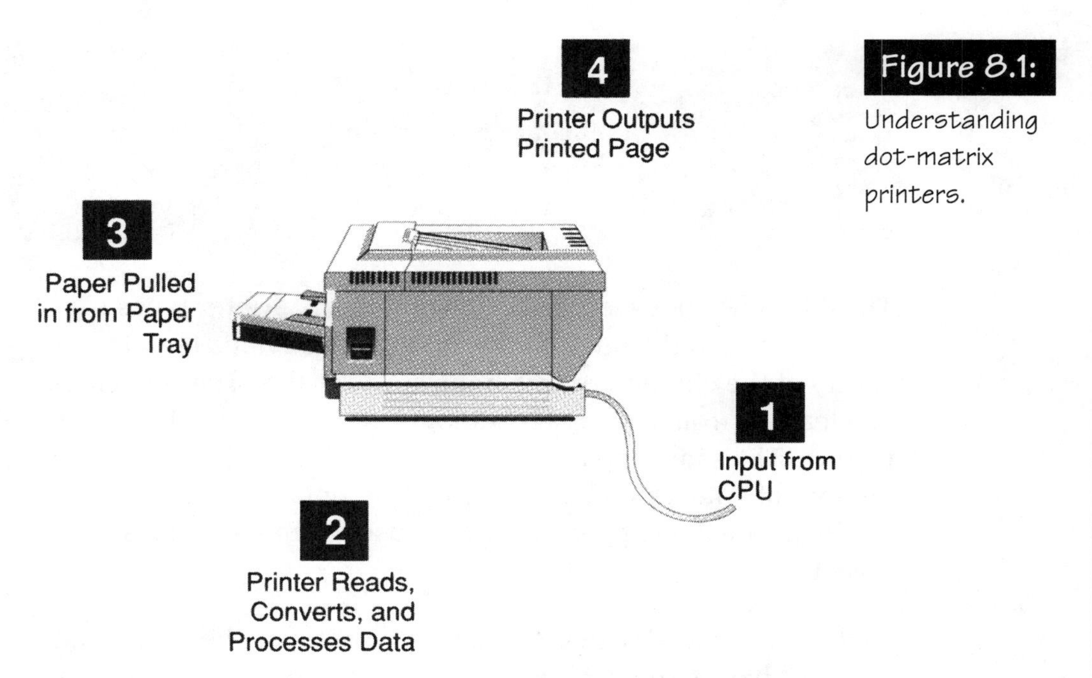

Figure 8.1: Understanding dot-matrix printers.

The upside of working with a dot-matrix printer is that you can get a fast printout at a low cost. The downside is that you cannot achieve high-quality printing from a dot-matrix printer.

The dot-matrix printer prints characters and graphics on the page by pushing a series of pins through a printer ribbon, leaving the print on the page. This means the letter A is not really an A at all but a matrix of dots (hence the name) arranged to look like an A. No matter how you slice it, those dots are dots, and the quality available to you will always be limited by that fact.

Dot-matrix printers are available in two different categories: 9-pin and 24-pin. This terminology refers to the number of pins in the print head that are pushed against the printer ribbon to form the character. With a 9-pin printer, 81 dots are used to print the letter A in a 9-by-9 grid. In the same amount of space, a 24-pin printer uses 576 dots to produce that same A in a grid 24-by-24.

> **The Coach Says...**
>
> Not all characters require the 24-dot width. Some characters may be printed, for example, in a 24-by-9 grid.

The difference between these two dot-matrix printer types (9-pin and 24-pin) and the output they produce is obvious both in the clarity of the characters and in the speed of the printer itself. As you learned from display technology, the more dots, the better the picture. The same applies to dot-matrix printers. The higher the number of dots used to print the picture or character, the more "filled in" the item appears, which causes a smoother-looking object.

Speed is enhanced with a 24-pin printer because the print head does not have to go back across the page and "reprint" dots that were left out in the first pass. Typically, 9-pin printers make up for their thin scattering of dots by taking two or more passes over a line, filling in characters. This does not do a whole lot for printer speed. The 24-pin, on the other hand, can fill in all necessary holes

the first time across and move on to the next line. As you can imagine, the time savings can be dramatic.

Early on, a big selling point of the dot-matrix printer was its graphics capabilities. When graphics technology was in its infancy, virtually no other type of printer enabled you to print charts and other images created in prehistoric paint programs. Dot-matrix printers do print graphics—although for high-end, smooth objects they do not give you the quality you seek.

Dot-matrix printers print graphics in the same way they print characters: dot by dot. This means you can get a pretty good printout of a photo with various color blends on a dot-matrix printer. When you need to print a perfectly round circle with no jagged edges, however, you get a circle comprised of readily apparent dots.

The Coach Says...

Some high-end dot-matrix printers have extensive smoothing features, can print in a variety of modes, and support fonts (type in different typefaces, styles, and sizes). These printers, however, also occupy the high-end of the dot-matrix price scale (which may, if you do some careful shopping, also be the low end of the laser printer scale).

Many dot-matrix printers can now support a wide variety of fonts—typefaces available in a certain size and style. Pause a minute and brush up on some font technology. Arial (a font available with Windows 3.1) 10-point bold text is one example. The type family (Arial) is called the *typeface*. The *size* is measured in points (one point is roughly equivalent to 1/72 of an inch, so a 72-point letter is one-inch high). The *style* is the special text attribute you assign to the letter, such as bold, italic, underline, or normal.

The Coach Says...

For more information about selecting and working with fonts, see *The Fonts Coach*, written by Cheri Robinson, published by New Riders Publishing.

The quest for more and more fonts has been prevalent in the minds of computer users for several years now. Fonts can be used in your text and graphics work to give your reports or presentations any number of different personalities. You can loudly make your statement, quietly express a reflective thought, humorously jab at a co-worker, or carefully represent the professional attitude of your corporation—all by choosing the right typeface family to convey your message.

Dot-matrix printers give us the option of working with fonts in our documents and in our graphics projects. These fonts are called downloadable fonts and are sent to your printer at print time. (In other words, the fonts are not kept permanently in your printer's memory.) Not all dot-matrix printers can support fonts, and not all software programs can work with fonts from companies other than their own. To check the compatibility of your printer with a specific font type, consult your printer manual or contact your dealer.

So if dot-matrix printers can give you fast output for a very small investment, what's the problem? Even though it is possible to print different fonts and create graphics on a dot-matrix printer, you always return to the same stumbling block: everything you see is made from a pattern of dots. Like the paint programs discussed in Chapter 3, no matter how you slice it, dots are dots. When you print anything, some amount of jaggedness exists and you lose some professional quality. If your graphics needs are limited and you are not concerned about a few (or many) jaggies, the speed

and flexibility of the dot-matrix printer may suit your output needs. If, however, you depend on finely printed, smooth characters and graphics, you will be endlessly frustrated by dot-matrix output.

What is the best use for a dot-matrix printer? Many people use dot-matrix printers to print rough drafts; pages used to show placement of items, to pass around for technical review; to check content, grammar, and style. The corrections are made, and the final version is printed on a higher quality printer. Dot-matrix output often is fine for documents—such as memos and inter-departmental reports—that stay inside the company, as well. High quality output, such as that created on a laser printer, is used for materials sent outside, such as quarterly reports to shareholders, public relations pieces, newsletters, and routine business correspondence.

INK-JET PRINTERS

Until recently, ink-jet printers were among the largely overlooked minority of printers that belonged to neither the dot-matrix or laser categories. As you might expect, ink-jet printers create the characters and objects on the page by spraying ink from the print head. Like the dot-matrix printer, the ink-jet composes the items on the page in a pattern of dots. Unlike the dot-matrix, the ink-jet is almost silent because the print head sprays—rather than strikes—the page. Instead of using a printer ribbon, ink-jets work with ink cartridges, which means that you can easily use a variety of colors (a feature limited—or nonexistent—and at the very least, impractical, for dot-matrix printers).

Today's ink-jet printers often boast laser-like quality at a dot-matrix price. Some printers offer a resolution of over 300 dpi (dots per inch), which is the standard resolution of most laser printers. One newer printer, the Star SJ-48, claims 360 dpi, which is 20

percent higher than most laser printers. Additionally, today's ink-jets often offer features such as Windows font support, high-resolution graphics output, and a variety of print modes.

THERMAL TRANSFER PRINTERS

If affordable color output is what concerns you, you already may have investigated thermal transfer printers. This type of printer creates characters and graphics by melting a wax-based ink off the ribbon and transferring it onto the page. Thermal transfer printers generally produce output at a pretty good rate; substantially slower than a dot-matrix, but the quality is worth the trade off.

> **The Coach Says...**
>
> Thermal transfer printers often cost as much as laser printers, but give you the option of adding full-color printing to your work. Many thermal printers can support PostScript and PCL (two page-description languages used by today's laser printers) so that you can get both a color printer and a laser printer if you purchase the right thermal transfer printer.

Although the resolution is high, the thermal printer still prints dots on the page. To create color output, colors are blended by placing dots of ink closely together on the page, giving the illusion of the intended color. To create a purple hue, for example, cyan and magenta dots are patterned in such a way that the image appears purple. Typically, for color output, the printer makes several passes—one pass for cyan, one pass for yellow, and one pass for magenta. This multiple-pass approach for color output takes a bit longer than a simple black-and-white printout, but probably not quite as long as you might think. Most thermal transfer printers can print a full-color chart in about a minute.

A newer, high-end form of the original thermal transfer printer is now being produced. Known as the *dye-sublimation thermal printer*, this printer uses the thermal transfer process but places colors on the page using a different technology. Instead of placing the dots strategically to trick the eye into seeing purple, this printer places one dot of cyan on the page and then places a dot of magenta on top of it, creating a "real" purple. This process produces an image that has truer color and consistency.

The Coach Says...

One such printer, the Tektronix Phaser IISD, features a new image technology, called Photofine, to print darker on transparencies giving the acetate sheets a deeper look that holds the hue for projected color. This printer, available for a retail price of just under $10,000, cuts the costs of most dye-sublimation printers (high-end color output devices) in half.

LASER PRINTERS

The laser printer is no newcomer to business printing (see fig. 8.2). Having been around for years, lasers now are an affordable option for the highest possible print output. Unlike the dot-matrix printer, the laser printer is completely silent and the quality available is not inescapably subject to the jaggies. You do not have to settle for less than your ideal with a laser printer, unless, of course, your heart says "Yes" but your checkbook says "No."

Laser printers have grown up in two very different neighborhoods. One group, PCL printers, is largely governed by the Hewlett-Packard family of printers (including all the manufacturers that are producing HP-compatible printers). PCL (printer control language) printers use the PCL page description language—which initially

consisted only of the simplest set of print instructions—to explain to the printer the way the text and graphics should be placed on the page.

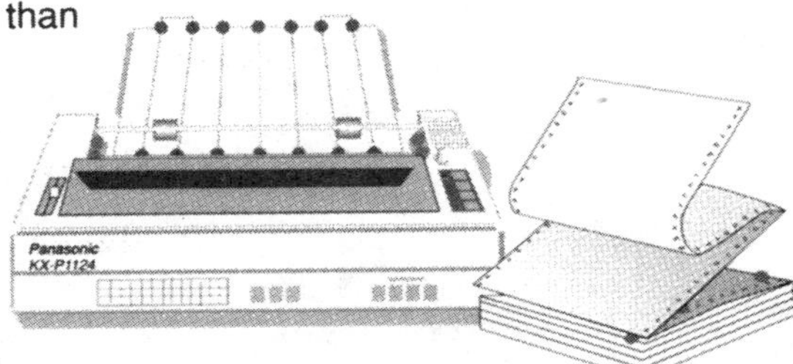

Figure 8.2: Printing with a laser printer.

> **The Coach Says...**
>
> What about color? In the last section, you learned that thermal transfer printers are popular for color output. Today, color laser printers are available, but the price is still high. Because of the way the image is placed on the page (see "How Does a Laser Printer Work?" later in this section), color features require more of the standard laser printer than black-and-white printing allows. Expect to pay from $7,500 to $10,000 for a quality color laser printer.

Early PCL printers provided better output than dot-matrix printers but were limited in the types of text and graphics they could produce. To use different fonts (which were not quite as big a deal five years ago as they are today), you had to purchase font cartridges—little plug-in Nintendo-like things you physically inserted

in a slot on your printer. These font cartridges contained the description of the font and the memory to support it. When your printer received a file that included a font different from those it was capable of producing internally, it automatically looked to the font cartridge for instructions on how to reproduce the desired font.

Long after PCL printers began making a big splash, PostScript printers appeared. PostScript, which is actually a page description language created by Adobe, offered users scalable fonts; the laser printer they purchased had many fonts the printer could replicate automatically, and each of those fonts could be used in any size or style. PostScript uses mathematical calculations to create text and graphics (which you may remember from the discussion of EPS graphics). When you want to enlarge a 10-point Times Roman A, for example, to a 72-point character, all you have to do is change the size. The printer refigures the character to the size you want without jaggies, distortion, or additional font cartridges. The first PostScript printers were expensive, often carrying a $4,000 price tag (or more). For the money, you were guaranteed 35 different fonts (nine different typefaces), and smooth, high-quality text and graphics.

Although PostScript printers were expensive, their success mushroomed. After the technology was available, people lusted for large font libraries and the clearest possible print. The PCL printer, while still the affordable alternative to its well-endowed cousin, suffered from the popularity of the PostScript printer and eventually, with the current revision of the page description language, the PCL5 was developed, which for the first time offered scalable fonts and compatibility with PostScript graphics.

Current technology is seeking ever higher resolutions. Stuck for many years at 300 dpi, both PostScript and PCL have been looking for ways to increase the number of dots per inch. One new printer, the LaserJet 4M (from Hewlett-Packard) is a PCL printer that

includes both PostScript and AppleTalk support. Another major difference of the LaserJet 4 is the quality of output: up to 600 dpi, at no significant loss of speed, producing dramatically increased quality. Many users studying characters and graphics produced at 600 dpi and images outputted on a typesetter could see no visible difference. For under $3,000, you now can purchase a printer that works with PCs and Macs, uses both PCL and PostScript, and gives you a higher quality output than any other laser printer currently available.

The Coach Says...

A cousin to the laser printer, the desktop typesetter, is a high-quality, super-high-resolution output device. The desktop typesetter, so named because it produces output up to (and sometimes over) 1,000 dpi and can sit on your desktop like an ordinary laser printer, is capable of producing text and graphics at a resolution that rivals true typeset materials. Desktop typesetters are still an expensive option to high-quality text, but some manufacturers, such as LaserMaster, offer upgrade boards that can turn your existing laser printer into a desktop typesetter.

HOW DO LASER PRINTERS WORK?

Laser printers look mysterious from the outside and the fact that they make virtually no noise (except as the paper is being drawn through) leaves us wondering what actually happens inside that rectangular device. How do laser printers work?

Figure 8.3 shows the process a laser printer uses to turn the electronic data sent from the computer into a printed page. When

you open the File menu and choose Print (or whatever process is necessary for your particular program), the computer sends the file to the printer. The file goes to the image processor, which contains the PCL or PostScript page description language, and is converted into a form the printer understands. If the file contains instructions for a font not supported internally by the printer, the printer looks to the font cartridge (or to the printer's RAM, if the printer does not support cartridges) to find the font descriptions.

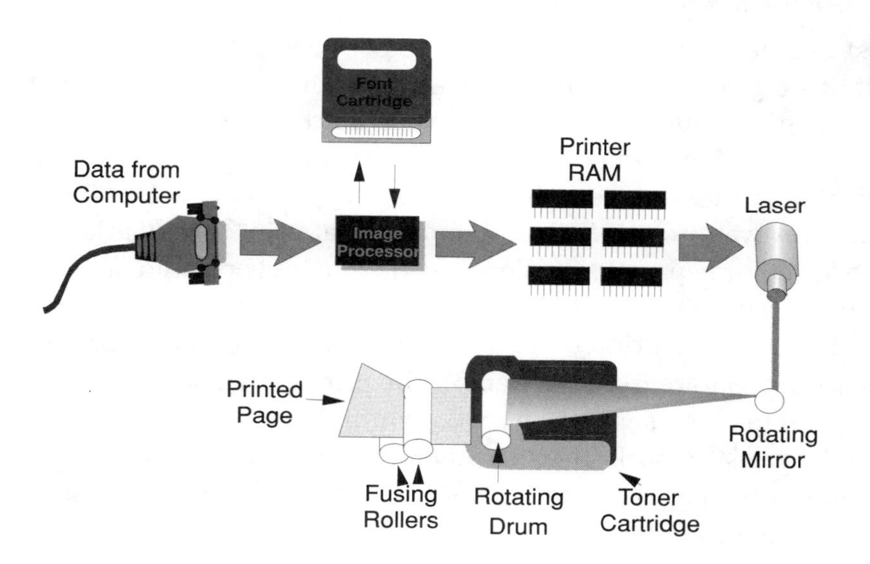

Figure 8.3: The process of printing on a laser printer.

When one page is stored in the printer's RAM, the data is sent, bit by bit, to the printer's laser. The data turns on and off the laser quickly, sending a modulated beam to the rotating mirror. The mirror reflects the beam—a line at a time—into the toner cartridge, onto a cylinder called the *drum* coated with a light-sensitive substance that holds the charge from the light. The drum rotates past a cartridge that stores electronically charged *toner*—a substance that is drawn to the portion of the drum that has been charged by the laser.

The paper, which enters the picture at this point, also has its own electric charge that draws the toner from the drum to the page. The page, which now has the necessary text and images on it, passes through the fusing rollers, which use both heat and pressure to set the toner onto the page. Then, voila! The page is outputted, ready to be used.

UNDERSTANDING COLOR CHOICES

Most people do not have access to a color printer (unless they are part of a big corporation that budgets in such things), and to print pages professionally done in color, they need to create color separations. Many high-end graphics programs (and desktop publishing programs, as well) give users the ability to select the items they want to print in color and then, at print time, mark the page for color separations. When the document is printed, a separate page is printed for each color assigned. If you select the page header to be printed in blue, for example, that item is printed on a page separate from the items to be printed in black. Then, when you take the separations to a printing service, the printer uses the register mark (the small symbol in the upper and lower margins of the page) to align the pages so that the different colors align on the printed page.

The Coach Says...

If your graphics or desktop publishing program enables you to print color separations, chances are it also lets you select a color model. A color model, like the Pantone Matching System, is a standard color system used by professional printers. This helps you ensure that you are creating graphics in colors that can be reproduced professionally. Check your software manual (and talk to your printer) to find out which color model is best for you.

LASER PRINTER CONSIDERATIONS

Just a few years ago, laser printers were used by only the business elite—people who just could not make it without the highest possible quality output. Today, most businesses—big and small—have laser printers in some form; and lasers may be shared between computer workstations. Keep in mind that laser printers are out there at an affordable—almost attractive—price.

When you prepare to purchase a laser printer, ask yourself the following questions:

★ Is the printer a PCL or PostScript printer?

★ Will you use the printer with PCs or Macs?

★ If you use the printer with a Mac, is AppleTalk built-in or do you have to purchase it separately?

★ How many pages per minute (shown on the PR materials as ppm rate) does the printer produce? Most laser printers can output four to six pages per minute when printing text, two to three pages of graphics.

★ How much internal memory does the printer have? (Most PostScript printers need at least 2M of memory to store a PostScript document and a couple of fonts. If you create sophisticated graphics, you will need more than 2M of memory.)

★ What kind of output quality can the printer produce? Is 300 dpi enough, or would your word processing and graphics applications benefit from 600 dpi or even 1000 dpi?

★ If you are looking for a high-resolution (600 dpi) printer, make sure that special memory considerations do not keep you from printing at that resolution. Check with the manufacturer for memory requirements before buying.

★ Do you need to print in special paper sizes or types? Will you be outputting acetate sheets for transparencies? If so, make sure the printer supports alternative paper styles before you purchase. The printer manufacturer (and the sales literature) should include all this information.

The Coach Says...

Want more? Many high-end laser printers, like NEC's Silentwriter Model 95, is not only a laser printer complete with PCL5, PostScript, and AppleTalk support—it is also a fax, and claims "600 dpi-equivalent" quality, to boot. If that is not enough, $4,999 will bring Doc-It to your office: a "document processor" by Okidata that acts like a PCL printer, a fax, a scanner, and a copier—it does everything except water the plants.

OTHER OUTPUT OPTIONS

Now you have investigated the different types of printers available for many business uses. But what if printing is not that important to you? Perhaps you are designing large sheets of plans for an upcoming business park, banners for an executive conference, or patterns for a new line of clothing you plan to introduce. You may want to consider a plotter, a large output device that places text and graphics on the oversized page (paper is usually on a roll) by using colored pens controlled directly from the computer itself. This provides high accuracy in output, something necessary for CAD applications and other projects where technical accuracy and placement is a high priority. Most users, unless they are working in the CAD realm, do not need plotters for routine business work.

On the flip side, you may not need to produce printed output at all—requiring only on-screen presentations that you can save to

disk and distribute to your major clients. (Some presentation graphics programs—such as Lotus Freelance Graphics for Windows and Micrografx Charisma—can create a slideshow your viewers can run on their own machines whether or not they have the same program you do.)

Another option might be sending the finished files—via modem—to a slide service which can produce high-quality, full-color slides for your presentations at a nominal cost. Many presentations graphics programs include support and direct linking to popular slide services such as Autographix, Genigraphics, MagiCorp, or Slidemasters.

WHAT TYPE OF OUTPUT DO YOU NEED? A CHECKLIST

In this chapter, you explored the different types of printers popular for traditional business and graphics work. Each of the printer types—dot-matrix, ink-jet, thermal transfer, and laser printers—offers a different kind of technology and different trade-offs of quality and price. Table 8.1 shows the differences among these printers and provides a few questions for you to consider as you evaluate your existing printer or consider purchasing a new one.

Table 8.1
Printing Considerations

Printer	*Considerations:*
Dot-matrix	
	Do you need to print rough drafts of graphics?

continues

Table 8.1
Continued

Printer	***Considerations:***
	Will you be working with a paint or draw program?
	Will "jaggies" bother you?
	Do you need a fast printer? (Some dot-matrix printers can output text at up to 850 characters per second.)
	Will the output you produce be circulated only in the office or will it be sent to clients?
	Is cost a limiting factor?
	Do you need color printouts?
Ink-jet	
	Do you need an output device that is quieter than a dot-matrix printer?
	Would color benefit your applications?
	Do you want laser-like resolution (300 or over) for a dot-matrix-like cost?
	Are fonts a major consideration (some ink-jet printers support Windows scalable fonts)?
Thermal transfer	
	Is color a major issue?
	Do you need a quieter printer than a dot-matrix printer?
	Would your applications benefit from PCL and PostScript support?

Printer	Considerations:
	Is the cost-per-page are big consideration in your decision?
	Is the traditional method of wax-based transfer good enough for your applications, or do you need dye-sublimation technology?
Laser	
	Are you using a PC or Mac?
	Do you need compatibility with different types of printers?
	Would you prefer PCL or PostScript technology?
	How much can you afford to spend?
	Do you need any additional bells and whistles, such as fax, scanning, or copying support?
	Do you need scalable fonts?
	Do you work with paint or draw graphics?
	Does your printer have the memory to support sophisticated graphics files?
	Do you need color output?
	What is your price range? (You can now purchase laser printers for under $1,000.)
Desktop typesetters	
	Do you need 1,000 dpi resolution?

continues

Table 8.1
Continued

Printer	*Considerations:*
	Do you have room to add an expansion board inside your computer?
	Is the typesetter you are considering compatible with your graphics program?
	Will purchasing the typesetter save you money over traditional typesetting costs?
	Can you upgrade the printer you now have to reduce initial cost and make better use of your system?

INSTANT REPLAY

In this chapter, you explored the various output options available as you think about getting your graphics into print (or onto film). You learned that there are several different printer types, each better for some applications than others. In the next chapter, you start Part Three by considering graphics design issues that help you create effective on-target graphics.

Specifically, this chapter covered the following:

INSTANT REPLAY

- ✔ Discovering dot-matrix printers
- ✔ Investigating ink-jet printers
- ✔ Thinking about thermal transfer printers
- ✔ Looking a laser printers
- ✔ Considering color choices
- ✔ Understanding printer considerations

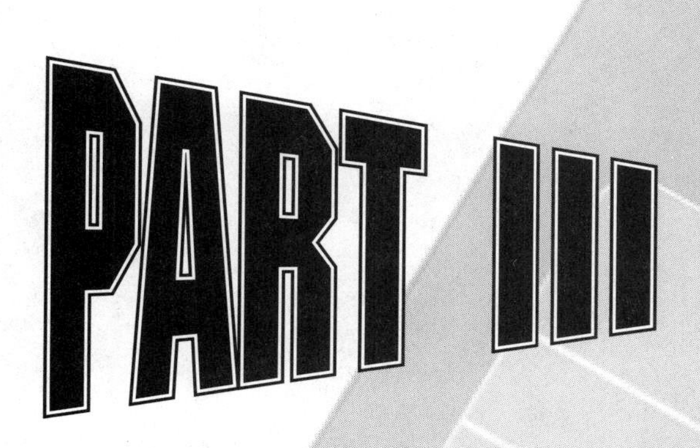

PART III

WORKING WITH GRAPHICS

GRAPHICS DO'S AND DON'TS

This chapter opens up Part Three by providing some basic background information on creating effective graphics. Not everyone can be a graphics artist. Most of us aren't even close, and yet that excuse doesn't buy us any Brownie points when its our turn to put on the departmental presentation. The audience doesn't want a resume of our past artistic accomplishments: They want glamour; they want glitz. They want us to wow them with our captivating artwork.

This chapter covers the following:

GAME PLAN

- Starting out in graphics
- Reaching your audience
- Fine-tuning graphics personalities
- Thinking about space requirements
- Using your resources

A GRAPHICS RULEBOOK

No doubt, if someone bottled artistic talent, we'd all be buying some. Most of us, who use our computers for a wide range of capabilities including word processing, spreadsheeting, and other data management tasks, don't have a lot of time or creative energy to spend on practicing and improving what limited art talents we have. Picassos, perhaps, are born and not made, but with the right tools and a few common-sense guidelines to help us with the art we create, we have a better chance of creating effective graphics.

As soon as you sit down in front of a graphics program for the first time, you feel a heavy burden resting on your shoulders. What makes good graphics good?

The best cure for a runaway case of the what-ifs is action. Don't think about what your boss wants or what your coworker created yesterday. Consider your audience, consider your tools, and brainstorm a little. Think about the goal of your work. Are you illustrating a magazine article about scanners or a children's book about elephants? The answer will make a big difference in the overall feel of the finished piece.

With all the software and hardware tools available to today's wanna-be artist, we can leave some of our artistic insecurities behind. Tools exist in our programs to help us make that perfect circle, that sweeping curve, or that drop-shadowed rectangle. We can import photographs and then touch them up. We can even use other peoples' art—clip art—in our own projects. Any number of resources exist to help us create the image we see in our minds (assuming, of course, that we see it in our minds before we try to create it on the screen).

The following do's and don'ts will help you get started with some common-sense graphics tenants:

Do keep a notebook of art pieces you like. We learn much of what we eventually do by imitation. We see an image we like and then ask ourselves why—and the next time we create something, we try a little of the same technique. Everyone does it—from movie directors to writers to artists. Imitation is the sincerest form of flattery, but remember that too much imitation isn't flattery anymore—it's grounds for a lawsuit. Remember to study the technique (did they use an airbrush tool? a different color palette? a unique pattern?) and apply it to your own work—don't just lift the fruit of someone else's labor and use it in your own piece.

Do carefully consider the goal of your work. Before you start, think about what you're trying to accomplish with your art. Are you creating a menu for a local restaurant? Your graphics will be much different than the graphics used in a quarterly report to company shareholders. Are you trying to inform or entertain? Enlighten or persuade? Keep a clear focus on the work's goal as you create the piece: that keep you from getting carried away and creating a piece of art that is inappropriate for your intended audience.

Do think about the intended audience. The audience, of course, is the group of people who will see your work. Are you designing an anti-drug presentation for high-school teens, or are you illustrating the flow of data through Micro Channel Architecture for a technical manual? In either case, you'll be using a different language, a different tone, and different tools. Remember to design a piece that will appeal to and communicate with your intended audience.

Do consider any additional materials that will go along with your art. If you are doing the artwork for a book, think about the overall tone of the book before beginning your artwork. The two go hand-in-hand, and lighthearted graphics with really heavy text is going to confuse the reader. Key off of any materials that will accompany your work, whether those materials include press releases, quarterly reports, or bulleted lists for presentations.

Do be consistent with the look of the piece. It's been proven that we are repetitive animals—we like to see similar shapes and themes used in materials because those similarities help us recognize patterns in communication. When you are designing the art-side of a publication, think about a central theme and then stick to it. If you use rectangles to highlight text items on Page 2, for example, don't switch to ovals on Page 4. The consistency will help readers understand—and enjoy—the materials you create.

Do clean up photos whenever possible. In many cases, when you scan photos (or have them scanned at a service), the photos aren't usable in their initial form. You may see a passable image; you might see bad blends and rough edges. Fight the temptation to say "Oh, it's good enough," and place it in your piece. Use a paint program (preferably something that works well with photo touch-ups, like PC Paintbrush V), to fine-tune the color blends and do away with rough edges. You'll be amazed at the difference a few minutes' editing can make.

Don't steal other peoples' work. This may sound like common sense, but with today's technology, the temptation may be overwhelming. Multimedia presentations, for example, only use hundreds of photos, video clips, and custom-drawn art pieces to create a presentation.

Multimedia producers find themselves in the not-too-pleasant position of either having to design all their own work or request permission and pay for the use of other people's work. Scanning capabilities and CD-ROM storage technology, which provides us with thousands of images instantly available, make using work without permission easy to do. Better to be safe—and legit—and ask the original artist for permission (in writing) before you use work that doesn't belong to you.

The Coach Says...

With multimedia blooming the way it is, new businesses are springing up that serve as "clearinghouses" for permissions of video and graphic clips. These services research libraries of pieces multimedia producers might want to use, and have the permissions and costs of individual pieces available for questioning producers.

Don't close your eyes to possible improvements. Whenever you work with one particular file for any length of time, you can get blind to the flaws in the piece. After you finish working on a graphics project, put it away for an hour or so and then look it over carefully. If you see two lines that don't meet exactly where they should, fix them. If one of the colors you used doesn't look right in print, change it. One of the keys to creating good art is the extent to which you're willing to perfect it. Leaving even minor flaws that may go unnoticed by viewers will compromise your own feelings about the piece.

Don't underestimate the value of space. White space is as important a design element as text or graphics on a page or presentation slide. White space gives the

reader's eye a rest and leads attention to the key areas on a page. Don't cram the page or slide with lots of text or graphics that are too big; take care to create a balanced effect that gives the reader room to breathe.

Don't forget that type can be art, too. If the piece you're creating involves text, whether that text is in the form of paragraphs, figure labels, or bulleted text, think carefully about the font and style you choose. If your piece warrants it, use a font with some personality that does along with your work. Depending on the program you are using, you may also be able to create special text effects like rotating, curving, filling, or inverting text.

Don't delete your art pieces without saving them to disk. After struggling to create a piece of art with just the right "something," it would be terrible to use it once and lose it forever. For example, suppose that you created some cool freehand graphics for a presentation. After you give the presentation (congratulations—it was a big success), you delete the file from your hard disk. After all, you won't use that presentation again. But what about the art? You could use that again in documents, as a logo, on press releases, or on any number of other materials. Save the art out to disk and keep it—no matter how simple or complex. This helps you build your own library from which you can later pick and choose.

GRAPHICS GUIDELINES

Suppose that your boss walks in late on Friday afternoon and asks you to prepare a presentation for Monday morning's manager's meeting. You're in charge of research and development on a new line of products, so she figures you're just the person to do it. The problem? You've never done anything like this before. She puts a

new presentation graphics program on your desk, picks up her briefcase, and leaves for the night. You sit there, for hours, in a quiet office on a Friday night, trying to wing your way through your first presentation. This section provides you with guidelines for creating that on-the-fly artwork. Your artwork should be on target if you stick with the following guidelines while you're creating it:

★ Think about your audience.

★ Plan the right tone for your presentation.

★ Work within the amount of space available.

★ Use your art resources.

The sections that follow explore these considerations in more detail.

THINK ABOUT YOUR AUDIENCE

Who will be seeing what you do? In this case, managers. In other cases, it may be the general public, elementary school kids, or corporate shareholders. Are these artistically savvy people, or will they be wowed with minor graphics? Is the piece an illustration for a magazine or backup material for a speech?

Perhaps more than any other factor, the audience for your art will control its content and tone. If your presentation is for scientists, you'll use one type of language and style. If you're creating artwork for a first-grade reading book, the art will be totally different. Consider carefully who the people in your audience are. Think about their comprehension levels, art awareness, and attention skills. Consider how best you can reach them—with humorous drawings, technical sketches, or CAD designs.

> **The Coach Says...**
>
> If you are including a wide range of graphics in your project, the audience may also control the type of graphics you create. If you're doing a presentation to motivate real estate salespeople, for example, showing a range of colorful charts explaining new sales trends and illustrating successful sales techniques will pump them up more than pictures of houses. If you're doing illustrations for a trendy magazine, pictures reflecting new fashion trends might speak to the audience more than an abstract piece of art would.

PLAN THE TONE

The tone of your art is its personality. Does your project call for humor, lightheartedness, or seriousness? Will you be illustrating a dry, technical manual or a humorous book? Does the work call for a modern style (like you might find in a computer magazine) or an older look (for a flier advertising antique furniture)?

Think about the way the material will be presented. How much time will the viewer have to see what you've done? If your work will be used in a presentation, your art may need to be from the "quick-look" school; viewers may have only a few seconds to see and understand your work. If your graphics will be used in a report or book, on the other hand, the reader controls when the page is turned and can therefore look as long as necessary at the art you create. That doesn't mean you should make book or magazine art more complex or harder to understand; rather, you can count on the reader having more time to get your point than the presentation viewer might have. This "timing" issue will contribute to the tone you select. You might need something serious but simple. Or lighthearted and fast. Or more involved, with figure labels and

arrows and other elements that leads a reader's eye through a particular thought process.

In most businesses, the corporate logo is an important identity feature. If you're creating something for your company, the logo may control the tone to some degree. If your company logo is "artsy," your artwork can be, too. If your company logo is more serious, you may be taking more of a chance if you take a whimsical approach to your art project (at least without the okay of superiors).

WORK WITHIN SPACE REQUIREMENTS

The space you have for your artwork is an important consideration. If you've been asked to do an illustration for a newsletter, and you know that on the finished page you'll have less than a 3-by-5-inch spot, you know that the item you create can't be too complex. Remember to allow white space for margins around your art to call the reader's attention to the piece.

If you're working on a CAD design, on the other hand, you may output your plans on a plotter and have all kinds of room. In this case, the plan itself, and not the accompanying materials, may be the focal point of your whole meeting. In this case, space isn't as much of an issue, at least as it relates to corresponding materials. Even with a schematic, or plan, you need to make sure the item is placed well on the page with plenty of white space to enable viewers to follow your design more clearly.

If you're using a drawing program to create your art, you can easily resize the item you create by using a simple command and the mouse. So, you may be thinking, the available space for the illustration doesn't really concern you. Not true. If you create a complex piece of art—one that looks good by itself on an 8 1/2-by-11 inch piece of paper—and then resize it to fit a 3-by-5-inch space,

the image will look cluttered and be confusing to viewers. For small spaces, keep it simple. When you have a larger space (and more viewing time), go for more elaborate illustration.

USE YOUR RESOURCES

This is a big one. You can dream about multimedia presentations, with video clips, animation, and stereo sound, but if you're working with a Mac Classic or a 286 PC, it's just not going to happen. We don't all have access to an unlimited corporate budget that allows for things like color scanners, mega RAM, and gargantuan hard disks. Realism is a part of the graphic artist's life. Think carefully about the resources you have available before you set out to create something you won't be able to finish.

As the idea for your art is taking shape, think about where you can tap into resources that already exist. Can you use one of the graphics fonts on a coworker's computer? Does someone in your department have clip art? Is there a file, somewhere in a company database, that contains some of the elements you want to use in your own art? If so, gather these resources together before you begin.

Also consider the resources available to you in terms of hardware and software. If you don't have access to a scanner, you can dream about importing photos, but it's not going to happen unless you pay an outside agency to scan the photos for you. (Which is a great potential resource and often used by people who have infrequent scanning needs.)

> **The Coach Says...**
>
> You may want to use a draw program instead of the paint program you currently use, but unless you purchase one (or borrow one from a friend), you're going to be limited to paint graphics.

You don't have to re-invent the wheel every time you sit down to do a new piece of art. Think carefully about your resources and use them to the fullest. That way, at least when it comes to graphics work, you can work smarter rather than harder.

WHAT MAKES FINE ART FINE?

No doubt, you have seen pieces of art that have left you with that "huh?" kind of feeling, and you have seen art that really did a good job of communicating a certain message. What makes one a dud and the other a success? In many cases, the success or dud-quality of a piece of art has more to do with its concept than the actual artistic ability of the artist. A Picasso-like painting might look cool for the cover of a book about motor sports, but unless you tie the art in somewhere—make it apparent to the reader that it has a reason for being there—you're going to get a "huh?" response (and worse, you may not sell many books).

> **The Coach Says...**
>
> The continuity of your work lets the reader (or viewer) know that your art has a reason for being there. Key off important concepts, phrases, or designs used in accompanying text to add continuity to your work.

When you're up to your eyeballs in on-screen composition, keeping sight of one thing will help you ensure a better graphic: continuity. If your picture reinforces the text, it provides continuity with the on-going discussion. If the art plays off your company logo, there's visual continuity.

Continuity helps your readers or viewers understand your message. There are three types of continuity that will improve any piece of art you're working on: Conceptual continuity, tone continuity, and visual continuity.

Conceptual continuity keeps the concept similar throughout the piece. What's your concept? Are you entertaining a convention of businesspeople or will you be teaching a new sales technique? If you're teaching, teach all the way through. Don't add a page to entertain in the middle; it will distract your audience. If you're creating graphics—such as icons—to help readers find special tips in a how-to book, remember to repeat a certain theme—functionality—through all the art pieces.

Tone continuity ensures that the tone you use in your art provides the same feeling throughout. Switching from schematics to cartoons may be a bit of a shock. Using an impressionistic look on the page after an 18th century etching is going to bring back that dreaded "huh?" quality. If the tone of your work is lighthearted, stay lighthearted. If you need to inform, use a consistent tone throughout.

If you are illustrating an article comparing two new software products, you might include a chart comparing features, a photo of the software's CEO (perhaps to go along with a quote), and a screen shot or two of the programs' main menus. The tone is factual but friendly. The tone is consistent, showing informational pieces through all the graphics. Adding a cartoon, or importing a technical schematic would make the tone too light or too serious.

Visual continuity is a much easier to achieve. Visual continuity holds the piece together by repeating similar design elements on different pages or in different pieces of art. Often a certain "motif" is selected to add visual continuity to a piece (such as a rectangular design used for all pages of a booklet).

INSTANT REPLAY

This chapter discussed various things to do—and not do—as you start to create your own graphics. Remember that these are just guidelines and they won't apply to every piece of art you do. Perhaps the best advice for any person dipping a toe into the cold waters of artistic endeavor is to let yourself go and have fun. Brainstorm, and let the creativity come out. You might not design the perfect logo, or the best illustration, or a serious-enough design, but your experience won't be wasted. You'll be getting to know your graphics programs and your own abilities.

This chapter covered the following:

INSTANT REPLAY

- ✔ Starting out in graphics
- ✔ Reaching your audience
- ✔ Fine-tuning graphics personalities
- ✔ Thinking about space requirements
- ✔ Using your resources

A GRAPHICS PRIMER

Okay, enough theory. Get started working with some of these graphics programs. No matter what type of program you use—paint or draw—certain similarities exist. Each program provides you with a set of tools you can use to paint or draw shapes on-screen. Every program includes menus and menu options that enable you to modify and manipulate the graphics you make. This chapter introduces you to the tools and commands available in paint and draw programs.

This chapter concentrates on describing the commands and tools common to paint and draw programs. Specifically, you explore the following:

GAME PLAN

- Understanding paint tools
- The paint toolkit
- Paint features
- Understanding draw tools
- Draw features

AN INTRODUCTION TO GRAPHICS TOOLS

Any painter needs a palette, a good set of brushes, and plenty of clean canvas. A designer needs a variety of angles and rulers, good sharp pencils, and blank grid paper. When you work with electronic art, the tools are different, but similar. You still find tool sets, and color palettes, and controls that help you measure and fine-tune angles. This section introduces you to the electronic on-screen tools you find when you work with either a paint or draw program. The two programs bring you two different sets of tools because each type has its own unique approach to the process of creating graphics.

PAINTING TOOLS

As you read in Chapter 3, a paint program places graphics on the screen by painting individual pixels, or dots. This type of program creates what's known as a *bit-mapped graphic*, so named because the image is actually stored as a map of bits in memory. Paint programs are popular for working with scanned photos, for creating realistic images from custom color blending, and for drawing freehand.

The downside of the paint program is the limited quality of final output; because the image is comprised of dots, bit-mapped graphics sometimes suffer from the *jaggies*, or jagged edges along which the individual pixels are easily seen. Some users get around this by starting their project in a paint program and then importing the paint file into a draw program. Many draw programs have "smoothing" or autotrace features that can cure even the roughest case of the jaggies.

The sections that follow explain the set of tools and commands that is a part of paint programs. If you are a Windows user, you

already have a paint program: Windows Paintbrush. This program is used to illustrate the examples in the following sections. Figure 10.1 shows three of the primary tool sections used when you paint with Paintbrush: the toolkit, the line width settings, and the color palette.

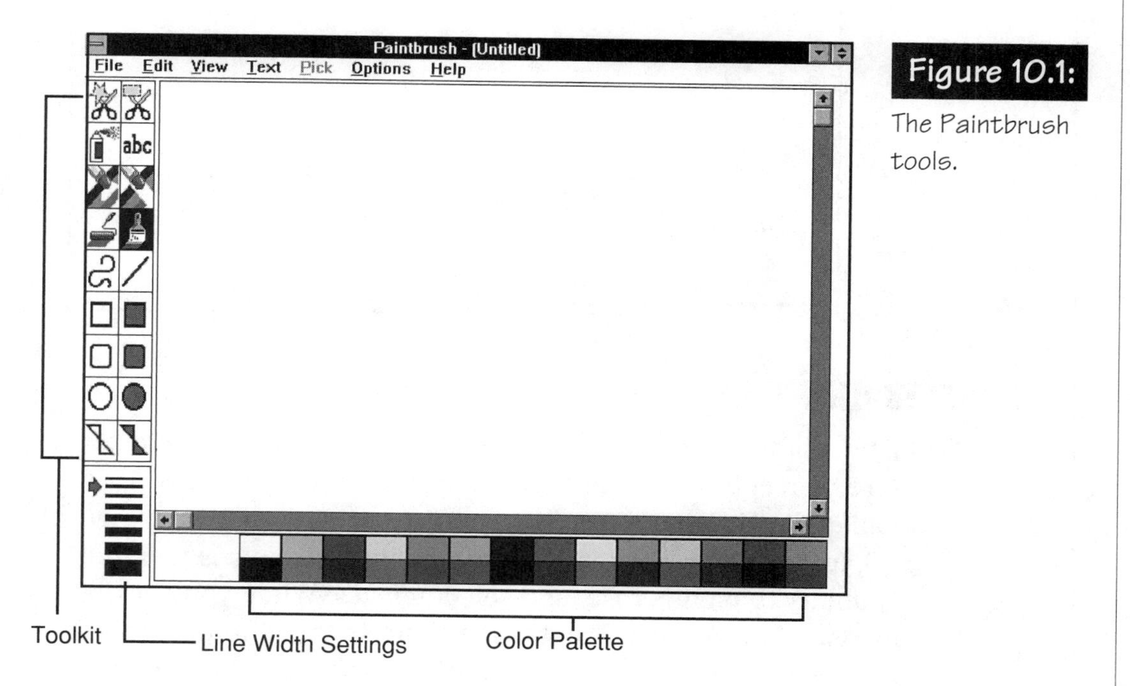

Figure 10.1: The Paintbrush tools.

The sections that follow explore each of these items in more detail. Remember that your program may show slightly different tools from the one shown here. In addition, some line width and color palette settings are shown as commands in the pull-down menus rather than in an on-screen palette. Figure 10.2, for example, shows the initial screen of Painter for the Mac.

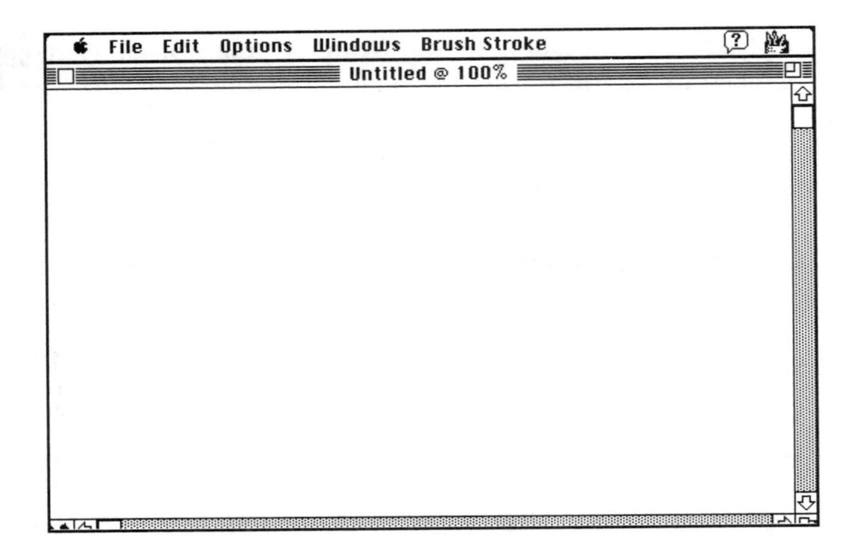

Figure 10.2:

A new work screen in Painter.

THE TOOLKIT

Instead of the traditional set of paintbrushes you might use on more conventional media, paint programs provide "tools" that emulate real-world items. Consider the tools row shown in figure 10.3, for example. A set of 18 tools in Paintbrush gives you the capability to paint, erase, and select images. When you click on any one of these tools, Paintbrush changes the function of the cursor so that it "becomes" the tool. For example, when you click on the paintbrush tool, the cursor acts like a paintbrush.

At the top of the row, you see two tools showing scissors. These are both selection tools you will use to highlight items you want to copy, move, erase, or otherwise modify. You use the tool on the right to draw a flashing selection rectangle around the item you want; you use the tool on the left to draw a freehand line around the item, so that only the image you want is selected. The primary difference between these two selection tools is that one captures a rectangular area (white space in the corners and all) and one captures only the image in the border you draw. (On the Mac, this is known as the Lasso tool.)

The Painter (Mac) toolkit includes different tools, as shown in figure 10.4. You see several tools for painting, similar to Windows Paintbrush, but you also have magnification and arrangement tools right in the toolkit.

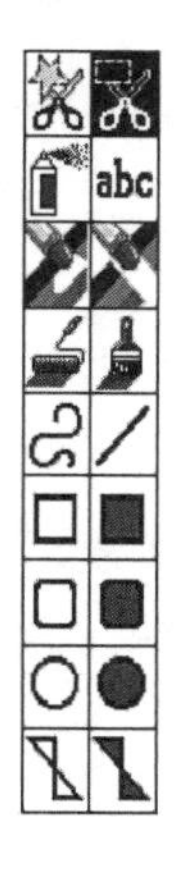

Figure 10.3:

The Paintbrush toolkit.

Figure 10.4:

The Mac Painter toolkit.

The first tool in the next line of figure 10.3 is the spray paint tool. When you use the spray paint tool, a spattering of paint is "sprayed" on the page whenever you press the mouse button. Like paint from a spray can, you can control the thickness or heaviness of the paint by spraying a more concentrated amount of color in one area.

Beside the spray paint tool, you see the text tool. This tool enables you to position the cursor in the work area, click the mouse button, and type text in your painting. You might use text, for example, to highlight certain items, to add a title, or simply as part of a painting. You can control the font, style, and size of text by using the commands in the Text menu, as shown in figure 10.5. You can

make text bold, italic, underlined, outlined, or shadowed; you can also choose a different font and size by selecting the Font command.

Figure 10.5:

Controlling text settings.

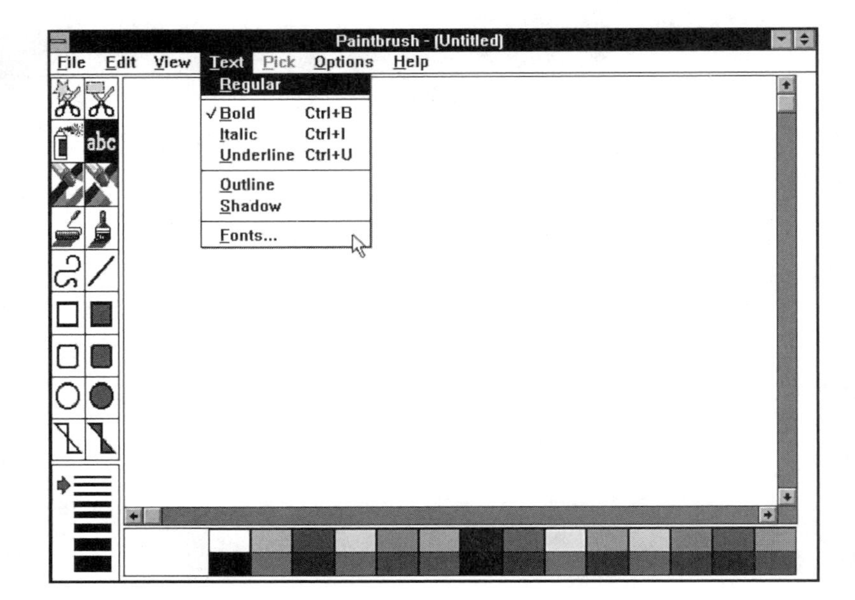

The Coach Says...

If you want to change the text settings for text in your painting, click on the text tool and use the commands in the Text menu to change settings *before* you enter the text. You cannot change the font, style, or size of text after you enter it. Because you're working with a paint program (and therefore everything entered on the screen is actually a pattern of dots). After you type the letters, they become dots on-screen, just as everything else.

Beneath the spray paint and text tools in figure 10.3, you see two kinds of eraser tools. The eraser tool on the left erases only the top layer of your painting. For example, if you place a circle on top

of a rectangle, this tool erases only portions of the top item, the circle. The eraser tool on the right erases all layers down to the blank page.

The next two tools in figure 10.3 are the paint roller and the paintbrush. The roller paints the area you specify with the color selected in the color palette. If no enclosed area is selected, the paint roller paints the entire screen. (In some paint programs, a paint can is used as the tool icon to perform this function.) The paintbrush enables you to "hand paint" selected portions of the screen. You can easily change the color painted by the paintbrush by clicking on the color you want from the color palette.

The Coach Says...

It is easy to fill a screen area accidentally with paint. The roller may slip or you may click in an area that isn't completely enclosed and the paint "runs" out into other areas of the screen. If this happens, don't panic: just open the Edit menu and choose the Undo command. Paintbrush will then cancel the last operation you performed (in this case, using the paint roller). Most paint programs have some kind of Undo command, which typically is found in the Edit menu.

The next two tools are line tools: one produces a curved line, and the other draws straight lines. Their uses are obvious. Be careful when using the straight line tool; you can easily move a fraction of a space and leave a "crimp" in your line. Most line tools have some way around this annoyance; your program may enable you to press and hold down the Shift key, for example, to constrain the tool to drawing a straight line. Remember, if you goof and leave a crimp, you can use the Undo command or magnify the view and straighten the line pixel by pixel.

Below the line tools in figure 10.3 are the rectangle tools. The one on the left is an open rectangle; the one on the right is a filled rectangle. When you draw an open rectangle, Paintbrush uses the currently selected line width setting to control the width of the borders (this is true for the curved line and line tools, as well). In addition, the color of the square's border is determined by the color selected in the color palette. When you select the filled rectangle tool, the color selected is used to fill the entire rectangle.

The next tools are the rounded rectangle tools, which work the same as their square-cornered counterparts. The open circle and filled circle tools and the open polygon and filled polygon tools enable you to draw their assigned shapes with your preferred line width and color settings.

THE LINE WIDTH SETTINGS

The small line width box, located in the lower left corner of the Paintbrush screen, controls the width of the lines used for the curved line tool, the line tool, the open rectangle, the open rounded rectangle, open circle, and open polygon tools. Figure 10.6 shows the line width settings box.

Figure 10.6: The line width settings box.

The arrow shows which line width is currently selected. The second line width from the top is the one chosen by default when you start Paintbrush. To change the line width selected, you simply position the mouse pointer on the width you want and click the mouse button. The next time you use one of the tools affected by this setting, the new width is used.

Not all paint programs put the line width settings right on the screen where you can reach them easily. Some paint programs

incorporate the settings in menus; to change the settings, you first must open the menu and choose the Line Width command. Some programs, such as Fractal Design's Painter, do not include line tools at all; instead, you have three different options that control the thickness, style, and behavior of the brush.

THE COLOR PALETTE

The paint palette, also called the *color palette*, is usually positioned along the bottom of the screen in most paint programs. This palette displays the various colors you can use as you are painting the screen. (The number of colors displayed in a color palette varies widely with the capabilities of the paint program. Paintbrush V, for example, displays many more colors than Windows Paintbrush.) The currently selected color is displayed at the left end of the palette (see fig. 10.7).

Figure 10.7: The color palette.

When you want to select a new color, simply move the mouse pointer to the one you want and click the mouse button. The color you select becomes the current color displayed to the left of the color palette.

> **The Coach Says...**
>
> If you choose a different color for a specific tool—to draw a yellow filled rectangle, for example—click on the color and then draw the shape. You cannot change the color of an already drawn item by clicking on a new color. In that case, you must use the paint roller—carefully—or the paintbrush to change the color of the new item.

Other features included with color palettes include patterns and color shading features.

SPECIALIZED PAINT FEATURES

Now that you have explored the various tools available to you on-screen, you may wonder what features exist behind the scenes, in the menus at the top of the work area. Paintbrush displays seven menus:

- File
- Edit
- View
- Text
- Pick
- Options
- Help

The Coach Says...

Remember that not all paint programs will have these same menus. These menus are the ones available in Windows Paintbrush. Other paint programs have similar commands and share features with the program used here, but many have their own unique menus. Painter, for example, includes a Brush Stroke menu not available in Paintbrush.

Like all Windows applications, the File menu contains commands you use to open, save, close, and print graphics files. The Edit menu, shown in figure 10.8, provides commands for undoing, cutting, copying, and pasting images.

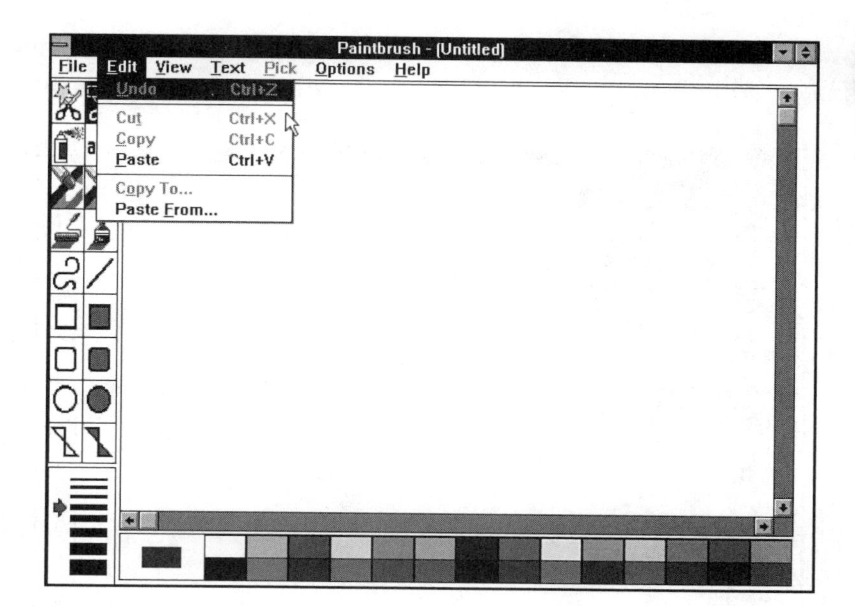

Figure 10.8: Commands in the Edit menu.

> **The Coach Says...**
>
> Before you can use most of the commands on the Edit menu (the Undo and Paste commands are the exceptions), you first must select the item you want to cut or copy by using one of the scissors tools at the top of the tool row.

The View menu contains important commands not found in a draw program. With a paint program, you need a way to zoom in on the individual pixels in the image. That way, you can change the color of pixels or erase stray pixels. The View menu, shown in figure 10.9, contains these commands.

The Zoom In, Zoom Out, and View Picture commands enable you to change the way you look at the picture. Zoom In magnifies the image to display the pixels that make up the painting. Figure 10.10

shows how the screen looks after Zoom In is selected. (A rectangle has been added so that an image appears in the zoomed view.)

Figure 10.9:

Commands in the View menu.

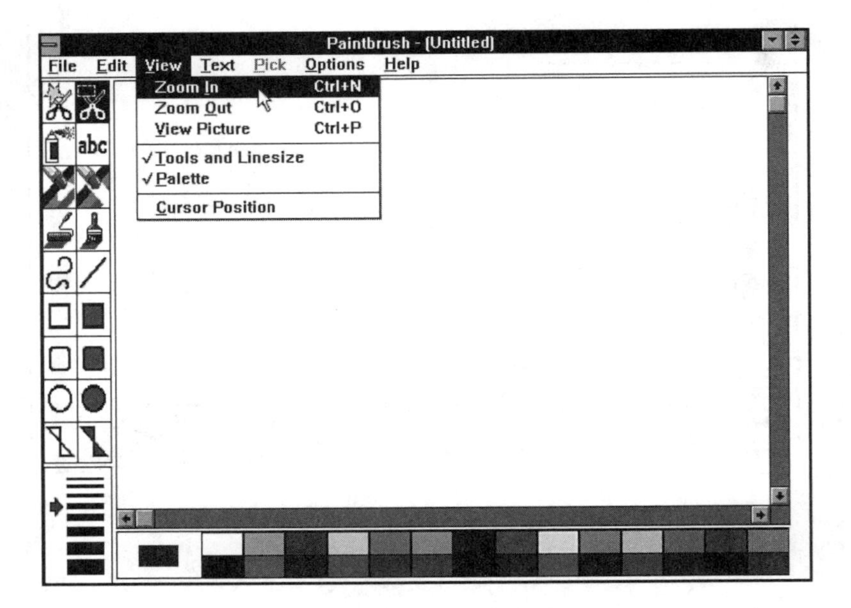

Notice that a small window in the upper left corner of the work area shows the image in normal view. You can make changes in magnified view by clicking on the color you want and using the mouse pointer to change the color of individual pixels. When you are ready to return to normal view, open the View menu and choose Zoom Out.

The other commands on the View menu—Tools and Linesize, Palette, and Cursor Position—control whether the toolkit, line width box, color palette, and cursor position box are displayed in the work area. (The cursor position box, which is not displayed by default, is a small box that appears in the upper right corner of the screen and shows the coordinates of the cursor position.) To disable the display of any of these items, click on the item. The checkmark tells you that the item is currently displayed.

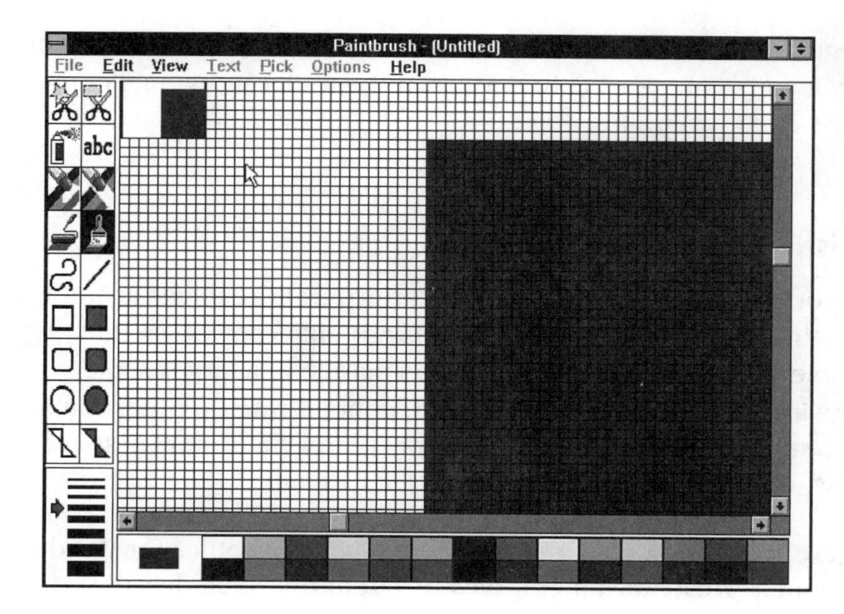

Figure 10.10:

The magnified view.

The **T**ext menu controls the style, typeface, and size used for text created with the text tool.

The **P**ick menu enables you to change the placement of a selected item. (You first must select an image you want to work with using one of the selection tools.) The first two options flip the selected image horizontally or vertically. The third option, **I**nverse, creates a "negative" version of the image, turning the dark area light and the light area dark. The **S**hrink + Grow command enables you to make the image larger or smaller. **T**ilt, a command available only with Windows Paintbrush, enables you to tilt a shape you've created by clicking the mouse button and dragging the shape in the direction you want the angle.

Finally, the **O**ptions menu enables you to control the way you work with your paint program. You can change the height, width, and measurements of an item; change brush shapes; customize color selection; and work with the overall picture format. The **H**elp

menu, at the far side of the menu bar, provides you with a set of commands you can use to find out more about individual commands and program features.

DRAWING TOOLS

As you can see, everything in a paint program revolves around painting. You have paintbrush tools and different views that enable you to see what you paint on-screen in a larger scale. Drawing tools, as you might expect, concentrate on precision and placement of various items. Draw programs have similar shape tools, but no spray paint or paint roller items.

Figure 10.11 shows a screen from Freelance Graphics for Windows, a popular presentation graphics program that includes all the drawing tools you could ever want. Freelance Graphics offers many more features than just drawing capabilities, which results in a very busy screen with many potential tools.

The drawing tools are located in the bottom portion of the tools row. In the sections that follow, you explore the toolkit, the line options, the color palette, and other specialized draw features.

THE TOOLKIT

Although in Freelance Graphics you see tools stretching across the top of the work area and along the left edge of the screen, the actual drawing tools are found in the bottom half of the tools row. Figure 10.12 shows the tools palette and points out the drawing tools.

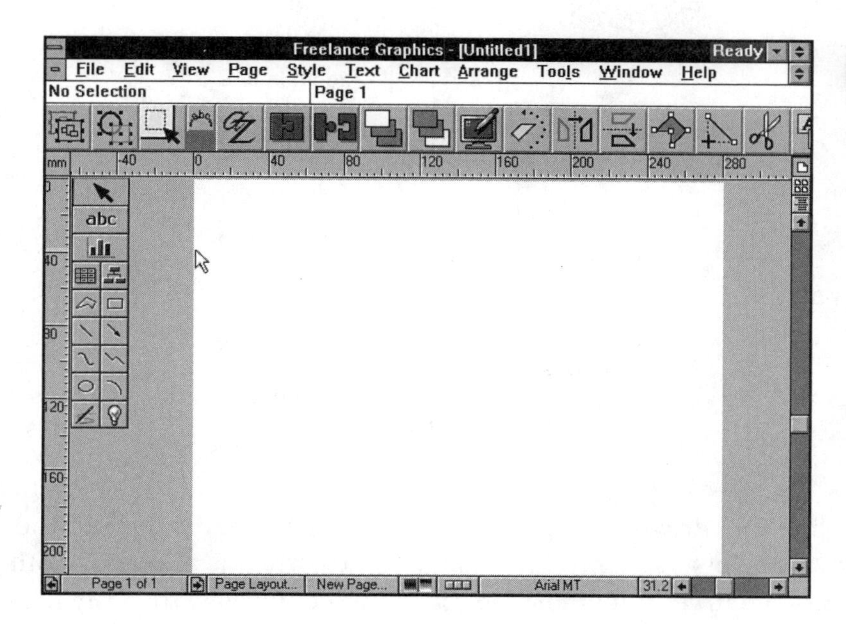

Figure 10.11: The Freelance Graphics drawing area.

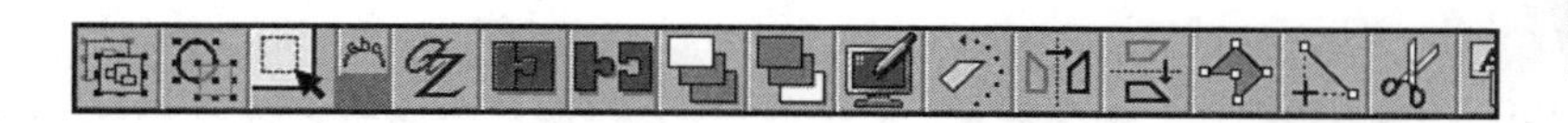

Figure 10.12: The drawing tools.

Again, it is almost impossible to show you every type of drawing tool included in a draw program. The tools in your draw program may be very different. Consider, for example, the tools used in Adobe Illustrator for the Mac (see fig. 10.13).

The first drawing tool in Freelance Graphics is the polygon tool. This tool enables you to create an enclosed polygon by drawing a series of connected lines. (A polygon is considered any closed, multisided object.) The rectangle tool, as you might expect, enables you to create rectangular shapes.

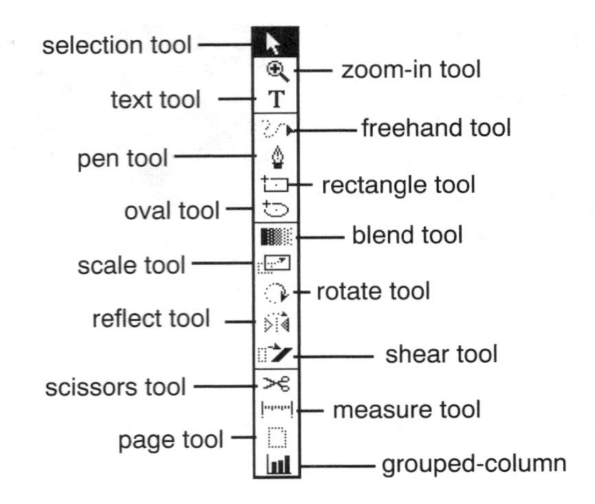

Figure 10.13: The Adobe Illustrator (Mac) toolkit.

The line tool draws straight lines, up, down, or vertically; and the arrow tool lets you draw lines and add arrowheads at one or both ends. The curve tool helps you make perfect curves; the polyline tool lets you create a series of connected line segments. The oval tool draws circles or oblong ovals; the arc tool allows you to draw a straight line and then move the center point to the place at which you want the arc to reach. Finally, the freehand tool lets you use the cursor like a pencil, drawing images on-screen in freehand fashion.

CHOOSING LINE OPTIONS

As you learned earlier in this chapter, when you create a paint image—whether that image is text, a shape, or a spattering of color—it is really just a pattern of dots. When you want to work with any of those images, you have to manipulate the dots. Draw programs, on the other hand, see all the items you create as objects. When you create a line, that line appears as an object you can select, move, rotate, and resize. When you click on the line, it appears with handles so that you can easily work with it. Much different from dots on a page, draw graphics are easy to change in almost every way. Because of the added capabilities, they also can be more complicated.

You change the line width settings in a draw program by double-clicking on the object itself or by choosing a defaults or attributes command. With Freelance Graphics, the **D**efault Attributes command in the **S**tyle menu displays a dialog box from which you can choose the line width, color, and style used for all objects you create (see fig. 10.14). To change any of the settings, click on the down-arrow symbol to the right of the option. A drop-down box appears showing you the various settings you can choose.

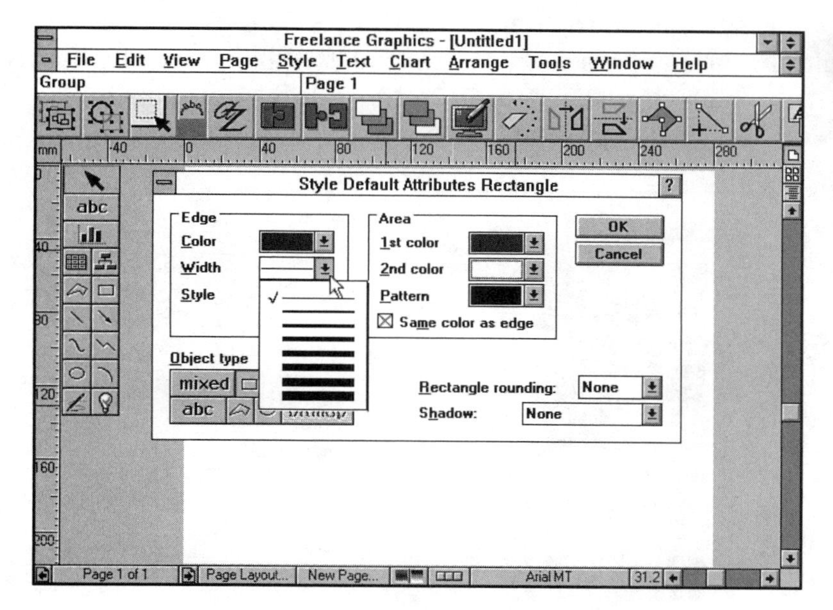

Figure 10.14:
Selecting line width.

CHOOSING COLORS

Selecting colors is also an object-specific action in a draw program. Unlike a paint program, the color palette is not displayed on-screen but is available when you double-click on an enclosed shape or choose one of the palette commands from the **S**tyle menu.

The Coach Says...

In a draw program, an object must be enclosed before you can fill it with color. In a paint program, you can spray paint on the screen without creating an enclosed shape.

Figure 10.15 shows the color palette displayed after the Color option is selected in the Default Attributes dialog box. This particular program offers a specialized palette taken from the library palette, which contains 256 colors. Most draw programs offer several color palettes from which you can choose.

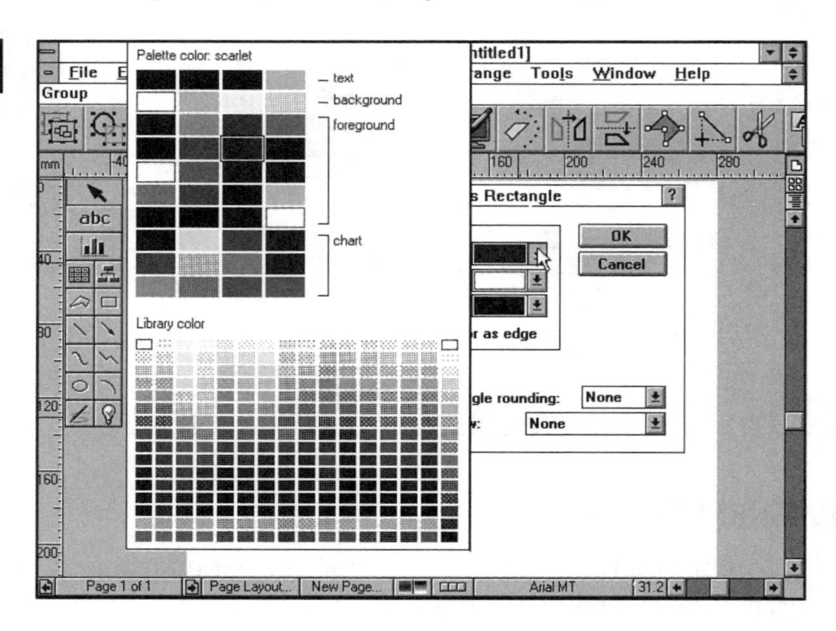

Figure 10.15: The color palette in a draw program.

Draw programs such as Freelance often enable you to choose a second color for color blends. To use this feature, you choose a first color and a second color, then select a pattern to control the way in which one color flows into another.

SPECIALIZED DRAWING TOOLS

As you get used to a drawing program, you may feel both limited and overwhelmed. Gone, you may think, is the freewheeling kind of art of splashing paint wherever you want it and cleaning up the mess later. Drawing programs seem to represent more of a think-before-you-draw kind of attitude.

This is only an initial reaction, however. After you play around with your drawing program a little, you discover how easy it is to change lines into shapes, colors into patterns, and large images into small images.

Grouping Objects. One specialized feature a drawing program offers is the capability to combine many small objects to create a larger object (and vice versa). For example, consider the image of a hand scanner shown in figure 10.16. When you use the pointer tool and click on the object, handles appear around the exterior, showing that it is one object.

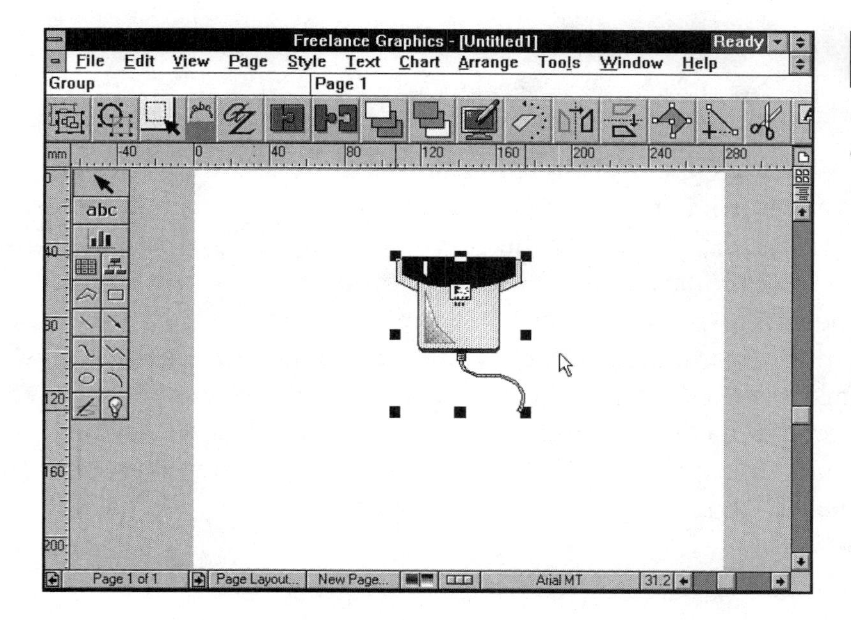

Figure 10.16: A combined object.

After using a "break-apart" command (called Ungroup), you can see that this is not one object at all but the combination of many different objects—lines and shapes—that have been placed this way to create the image (see fig. 10.17). After all the items are in place, the objects are grouped together.

Figure 10.17:

The individual elements of the object.

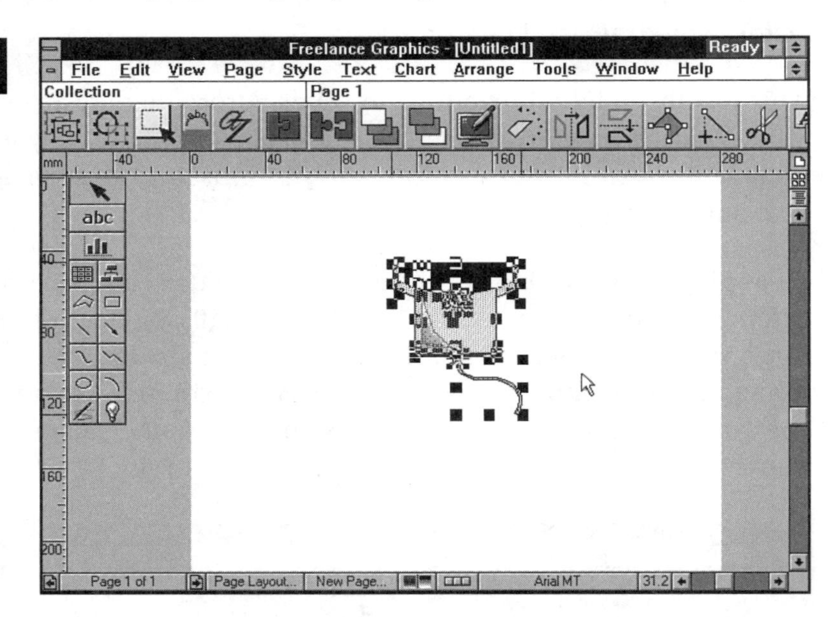

Converting Objects. Draw programs also make it easy to change an object from one type to another. Suppose, for example, that you create an image by using the curved line and the polyline tools. You want to fill the object with a color and pattern but a problem appears: the program sees what you've created as lines and not shapes. Color and patterns can be applied only to enclosed shapes. A Convert command allows you to select the lines you've created and convert them into a polygon, which is an enclosed shape. You can then add color and patterns as necessary. Later, if you want to modify a line, you can convert the polygon back into lines.

Layering Objects. As you learned in Chapter 3, working with a draw program is often like layering paper cutouts to create a desired effect. What if you want only a portion of a shape to show (such as a shadow extending beneath an object)? Your draw program provides a command (or perhaps several commands) that enable you to control the layering of objects. Freelance Graphics uses a Priority command to bring up layering options: Top, Bottom, Send Forward One, and Fall Back One. Other draw programs use different commands, but they perform the same function.

Editing Objects. Not all draw programs are sophisticated enough to allow you to change individual points on the line or shape after you've created it. Freelance Graphics offers a points mode that you can use to add and move points on a specific object, which changes the shape of the image. Figure 10.18 shows a close-up of the image in points mode. You can click on any of the little open handles and drag that portion of the image to a new position, thus changing the shape or alignment of the item.

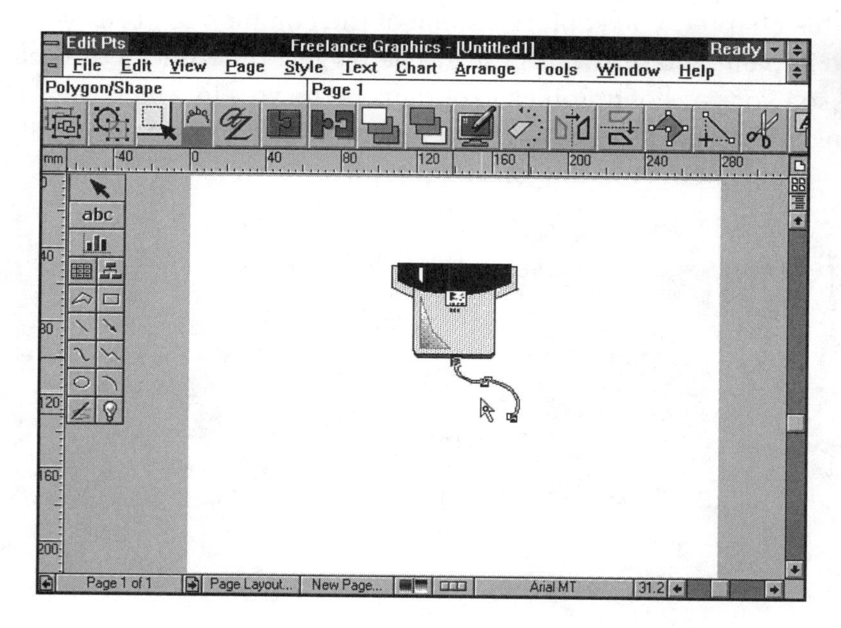

Figure 10.18:
Editing an object in points mode.

Rotating and Aligning Objects. Some paint programs give you the ability to rotate or flip objects; many do not. All draw programs can rotate objects (usually to the exact degree you specify), flip items, and arrange or align objects on a page. Most draw programs also enable you to control the spacing between objects.

Controlling On-Screen Accuracy. Draw programs feature on-screen rulers to help you position the articles you create exactly where you want them. Further, drawing programs often have Grid and Snap To Grid commands that display a dotted grid on-screen and cause the image you're working with to align along the gridlines. This helps you make sure that items are drawn to a specific measurement and placement on the screen. Additionally, you can choose from a variety of measurement standards, including picas, points, millimeters, centimeters, or inches.

INSTANT REPLAY

In this chapter, you explored some of the common features you'll find in paint and draw programs. The biggest difference between these two types of graphics programs is the way in which the image is stored: as a pattern of pixels or as an object. Specifically, this chapter covered the following topics:

INSTANT REPLAY

- ✔ Understanding paint tools
- ✔ The paint toolkit
- ✔ Paint features
- ✔ Understanding draw tools
- ✔ Draw features

CREATING AND EDITING GRAPHICS

Now that you know the differences paint and draw programs have to offer, you're probably anxious to start using one or the other. The best method of learning, in this case, is to grab a mouse and get busy. You'll learn more from trial and error by creating a drawing than you will from descriptions.

This chapter takes the tutorial approach to creating a few simple graphics. Specifically, this chapter explores the following topics:

GAME PLAN

- ☐ Using a paint program
- ☐ Using a draw program
- ☐ Editing paint graphics
- ☐ Editing with the shareware programs on the bonus disk
- ☐ Editing draw graphics

CREATING GRAPHICS

In this first portion of the chapter, you learn some of the basic techniques, tools, and commands you can use to create graphics in both paint and draw programs. Remember that the programs used to illustrate examples were chosen because they are easy to use and have many tools in common with other programs—individual tools, commands, and menus may look different on your paint and draw programs.

USING A PAINT PROGRAM

This chapter shows you how to draw a set of billiard balls. The first step in using any paint program is starting it. If you haven't already done so, install the program by following the instructions in your program manual. Then start the program according to program directions. If you're following along with Windows Paintbrush, open the Accessories group window by double-clicking on it and start Paintbrush by double-clicking on the program's icon. Then the process of working with your paint program—creating a simple piece of art—involves basically these steps:

1. Begin a new file
2. Select a tool
3. Select a line width
4. Select a color
5. Draw your image
6. Enhance the image
7. Add text
8. Save the file

Beginning a File. As soon as you start the paint program, a blank screen area is displayed. You have two options: you can begin creating a new art file, or you can open an art file you've already created. If you want to begin a new art file, you don't have to do anything except begin painting. If you want to open an existing file, open the **F**ile menu and choose the **O**pen command. A dialog box appears, allowing you to select the file you want to open (see fig. 11.1). In Paintbrush, the available files in the current directory are listed in the box beneath the File **N**ame list box. The extensions in the File **N**ame list box (in this case, *.bmp and *.dib) show the file types displayed.

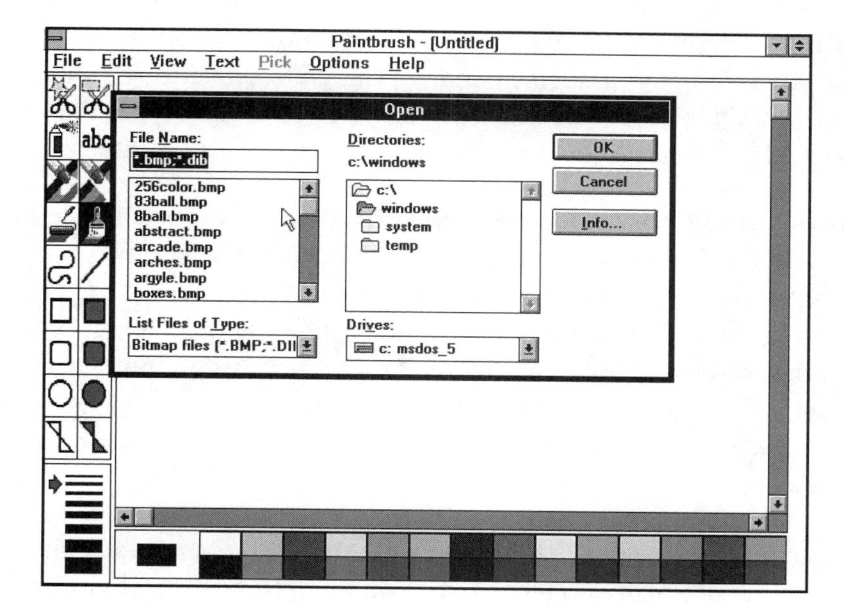

Figure 11.1: The Open dialog box.

The Coach Says...

If you don't see the file you want but you know it's there somewhere, check to make sure you're looking in the right drive and directory. To change the drive, click on the down-arrow at the end of the Dri**v**es box. To change the directory, click on the icon beside the name of the directory you want.

Selecting the Tool. First, choose the tool you need by clicking on it. (For this example, click the filled circle tool.) As soon as you click on it, the tool appears darkened. The cursor changes from an arrow to a cross-hair.

Choosing Line Width. Take a quick look at the line width selected for the item. Are you happy with it? For this example, use either the second line thickness (the default thickness chosen when you start Paintbrush) or select the thinner line. Things are okay the way they are, for now.

Selecting Color. You do not have too many color choices if you're creating an eight-ball. Black is the default color, and black is the color you need. If you need to change the color (for future reference), just click on the color you want. The chosen color is displayed as the larger rectangle to the left of the color palette.

Drawing the Item. Now position the cross-hair pointer where you want to draw the circle. Imagine you are putting the cursor at the top left corner of the item. Press and hold the mouse button and drag the mouse down and to the right, diagonally from where you started. A circle outline is drawn on the screen as you move the mouse. When the circle is the size and shape you want, release the mouse button. The paint program fills in the shape with the color you selected, as shown in figure 11.2.

Enhancing the Image. That leaves a pretty flat-looking black circle on the screen. Hardly an eight-ball. You need to add another circle and a few other effects. Make sure the filled circle tool is selected (it is); check the line width (it's okay); and choose your color (click on light blue). Now move the cross-hair cursor up to a point close to the left edge of the first circle. Press and hold the mouse button while dragging the mouse down and to the right. When the

circle is the size you want, release the mouse button. The circle looks more like an olive than an eight-ball, but it's taking shape.

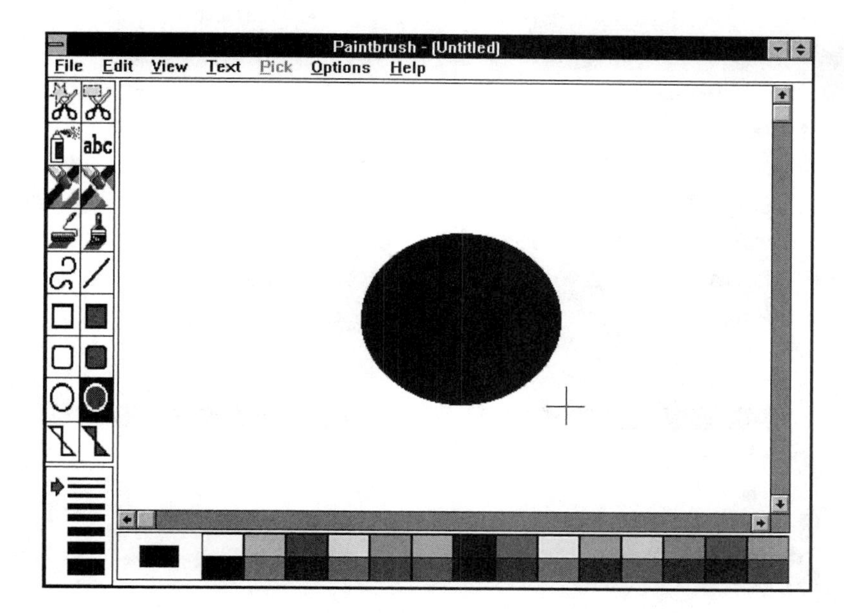

Figure 11.2: Drawing a filled circle.

Adding Text. Next, you need to add the 8 to the eight-ball. First, click on the text tool. The pointer changes to an I-beam cursor. Click on the image and type 8. (Remember that once text is placed on the picture, it blends in, pixel-wise, with the rest of the image. To change text, you need to erase it with the eraser tool and retype it or edit it, pixel by pixel.)

The Coach Says...

Remember that because text is a graphic element just like anything else, you need to set the color, font, and size of text *before* you enter it. After you select the text tool, click on the color you want to use (in this case, black) and make text settings by choosing Font from the Text menu.

Adding Highlights. The highlights on the top right side of the eight-ball are simply a few splotches of paint sprayed along the ball's edge. To use the spray paint tool, click on it (it's right beside the text tool). Move the pointer to the color palette and click on white. Now, move the cursor to the point inside the upper right edge of the pool ball. Click the mouse button once quickly and move the mouse. You can see a small splotch of white dots have been added to the top right edge of the ball. Carefully position the mouse cursor beside the set of dots you just added and click the mouse button again—another dot splotch. Add as many sets of dots as necessary to get the desired effect. Figure 11.3 shows the finished eight-ball.

Figure 11.3:

The finished eight-ball.

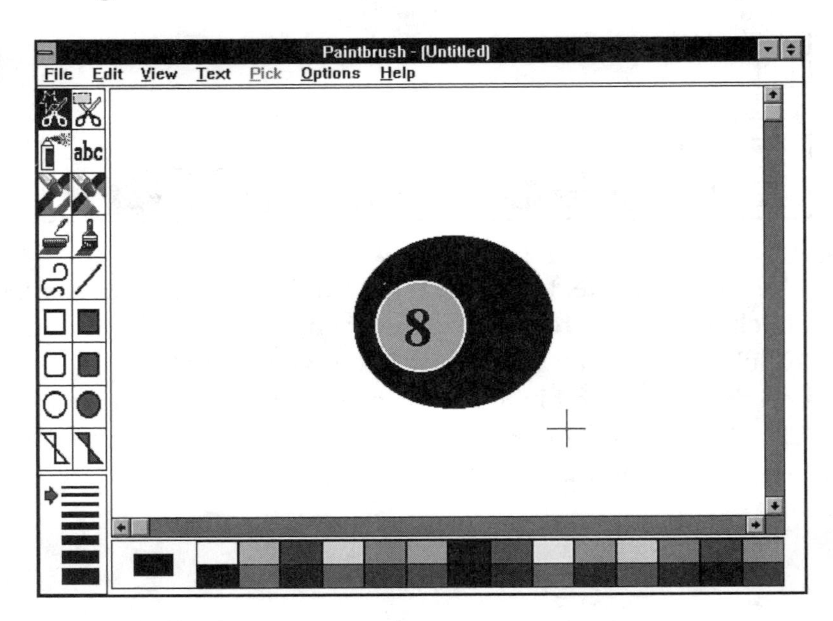

Saving the File. Now that you've created the graphic, you need to remember to save it to disk. Any time you spend more than a few minutes modifying or creating art, be sure to take a second and save what you've done. To save the file, open the **F**ile menu and choose the **S**ave command. (Every program has this command

somewhere in the File menu.) Type a name for the file and click on OK.

The Coach Says...

Some programs give you the option of saving files in a variety of formats: PCX, TIF, GIF, PNT, EPS, etc. You'll find the commands you need to change the file type somewhere in the File menu or in one of the Save or Save As dialog boxes.

USING A DRAW PROGRAM

Draw programs are a different kind of animal. Instead of finger-painting, you're working in an adult's world of object creation and manipulation. Still, it doesn't have to be more difficult than creating and moving objects around on the screen. The process for working with a draw program includes the following steps:

1. Beginning a new file
2. Choose the tool
3. Draw the object
4. Changing object color
5. Drawing additional shapes
6. Moving objects

Beginning a New File. In many cases, as soon as you start a program (such as Adobe Illustrator), a new blank screen is displayed. Some programs, such as Aldus Freehand, require you to open the File menu and choose New.

The Coach Says...

In the example in this section of the chapter, you create a picture of a 5 1/4-inch disk using Lotus Freelance Graphics. Remember that the examples shown here were chosen because the tools are easy to explain and to use; the tools in your draw program may look and act differently from the ones shown here.

Selecting the Tool. To draw a square, click on the square tool. The tool appears to be "pressed," indicating that it has been selected. Move the pointer—which changes to a cross-hair cursor—to the point on-screen where you want the upper left corner of the floppy disk to begin.

Drawing the Object. Press and hold the mouse button while dragging the mouse down and to the right. When the square is the size you want, release the mouse button. The square appears on-screen, white in the middle, with handles around the perimeter (see fig. 11.4).

Changing Object Color. Now make the rectangle black. This is a simple process; with Freelance, just double-click on the item you've just created. (It's not this easy with all draw programs. With some, you may need to look for a Fill or Color command.) Click on the Color option and, when the color palette appears, select the color you want by clicking on it (for the disk, choose black).

Drawing Additional Shapes. The process of drawing in a draw program requires that you think in shapes. The disk, for example, is a rectangle with two circles (one gray and one white) in the center. Other shapes include the white rectangle and ovals used to block out the notches on the disk. As you create the image, click

on the tool you need, draw the image, and change the item's color as necessary.

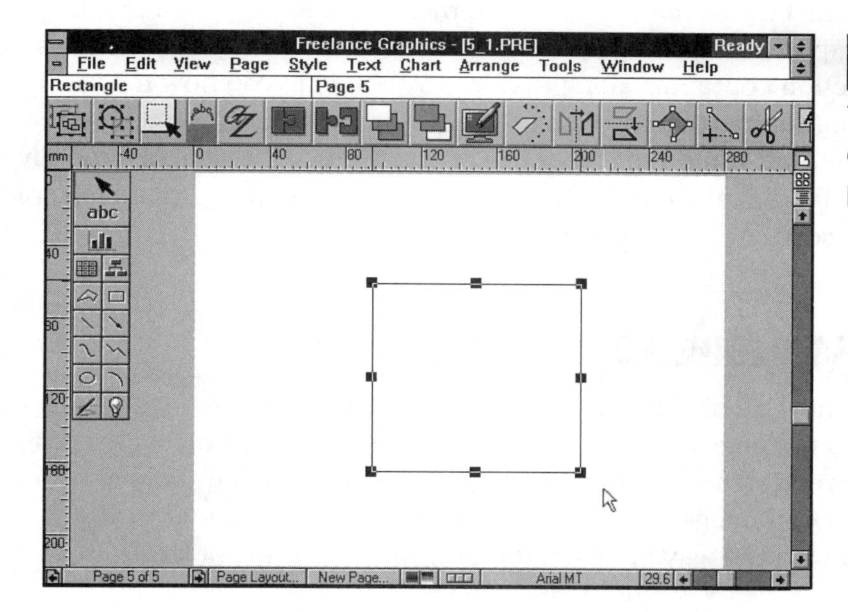

Figure 11.4: The rectangle created in a draw program.

Saving the File. When you're ready to save the file, you'll find the process to be a simple one. Again, look in the File menu for the Save command. When you choose this command, the Save As dialog box appears. Enter the file name you need and choose the appropriate drive and directory for the file. When you're finished, click on OK or press Enter.

The Coach Says...

Remember to save all the images you create on a disk you can put away for later use. You may be able to use bits and pieces of files you've already created. That saves you the trouble of re-creating something you've already done.

EDITING GRAPHICS

In the last section, you learned the difference between creating a simple art object in a paint program and in draw program. This section continues along that line by showing you how the two program types approach editing tasks. Editing, in this sense, is anything you do to the (more or less) finished object. If you move a shape, that's editing. Changing the size is editing. Changing color or position also is editing.

UNDERSTANDING EDITING DIFFERENCES

By now, you've heard it over and over again: bitmaps are maps of bits (or pixels); vector images are collections of objects that can be resized and changed with no loss of quality. The way in which you edit images in each of these program types has everything to do with the way in which the program sees the object.

If you use a paint program, the image you create on-screen is simply a pattern of dots. You can perform all kinds of operations with those dots, including changing their color, erasing them, or moving them to different parts of the page. You can select paint images and flip them, rearrange them, and perhaps even tilt them (with Paintbrush, at least). No matter what operation you perform with the dots, they remain dots. When you're editing a paint graphic, you'll probably spend much of your time working in pixel mode (that is, in magnified view) so that you can change the color of individual pixels. You might also spend some time with the Copy and Paste commands, but, if you're like most people, you'll primarily be working on a pixel-by-pixel basis.

A draw program supplies a different approach to editing. Because each item you create in a draw program is an object unto itself (a line, a circle, and a curve represent three different objects), you select the object with which you want to work and then change

that object in any manner necessary. Now it's not a matter of dots; you can move, resize, rotate, copy, paste, twist, flip, layer, or change the color of objects you select. It's hard to say which editing tasks will get the most attention from one edit to the next; the wide range of editing possibilities in a draw program make all kinds of things possible. Whether you want to do something simple such as move a square from one side of the screen to another or something more complex like add and then edit an individual point on an object, the draw program gives you the potential to edit your object in any way necessary.

The Coach Says...

Other types of programs contain editing features, as well. Three such programs, Paint Shop Pro for Windows, Graphic Workshop (for DOS), and the Mac's GIFConverter are included on the Graphics disk enclosed with this book. These programs enable you to do a considerable amount of editing; in fact, with the wide range of support for different file types and variety of editing features, they may offer more extensive editing capabilities than your paint or draw program can give you. Later in this chapter, you'll find out more about the editing capabilties of each of these programs.

EDITING PAINT OBJECTS

This section shows you how to perform some basic editing tasks on the painted eight-ball created in the last section (see fig. 11.5). Editing operations include the following:

1. Selecting the object
2. Copying the object

3. Pasting the item
4. Changing color
5. Editing pixels

Figure 11.5:

The eight-ball in its current form.

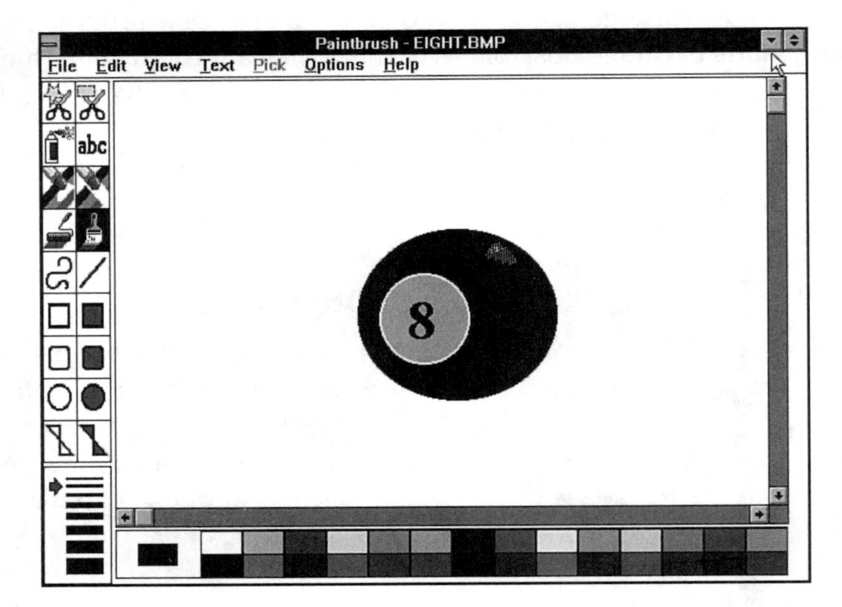

When you are finished with this paint graphic, another pool ball—the three-ball—will be on the right side of the existing eight-ball. You can create this second image easily by copying the one that's already there and making a few modifications.

Selecting the Item. Because you are planning to make a copy of the image shown in the figure, select the item you want to copy. This lets the paint program know which portion of the screen is to be involved in the copy procedure. To select an item, click on the selection tool and drag a rectangle around the object you want to select.

The Coach Says...

If you capture too much white space or decide you don't really want to capture the item after all, you can remove the highlight box by clicking the cursor outside the box.

Copying Paint Objects. The next step involves making a copy of the selected item. To copy the image, open the Edit menu and choose the Copy command. (If you prefer to do it from the keyboard, you can press Ctrl-C.) Although nothing new appears onscreen, the paint program has made a copy of the selected item and placed the copy on the clipboard.

The Coach Says...

The clipboard is an unseen, reserved area of RAM that stores images and text you cut or copy. Although the clipboard used in this example is called the Windows Clipboard (because, of course, it's part of Windows), DOS and Mac programs also use clipboards to store graphics and text in copy and cut operations.

Pasting Paint Objects. Now you need some way to get the copy off the clipboard and onto the page. That's where Paste comes in. Open the Edit menu a second time and choose the Paste command (or press Ctrl-V, from the keyboard). The image is placed in the upper left corner of the work area.

Changing Color. Before you move the item into place, however, make some changes right where it is. First, change the color—from black to red. Click on the paint tool you want to use; then select the color from the color palette; and finally, click within the area you want to fill with color.

The Coach Says...

Why not move the copied image first and then change the color? One simple reason: because the original ball is black and the copied ball is black, when the two overlap there will be no boundary for the red paint "poured" into the image. The red will fill both balls, and then you have to figure out how to turn only the first one black again. It's easier to make the modifications in a "safe" part of the page—one that does not affect the finished portion of the screen—and then move the modified image to its proper place.

Changing the View. The next editing step is to change the 8 into a 3. This involves a two-fold process: changing the view and changing some pixels. When you want to magnify the view and display the individual pixels in the piece, open the View menu and select the Zoom In command (or press Ctrl-N, in Paintbrush).

The Coach Says...

All paint programs have some method of magnifying the view. The commands in your program may not be called Zoom In; you might have Magnify, Enlarge, or 200% View. Look for these commands in a View menu. Mac programs often have a magnifying glass tool that you can use to zoom on the area of the screen you want to see more closely.

Pixel-Level Editing. Now that you can see the individual pixels, it's time to edit them. First, click on the paintbrush tool (which is right beside the paint roller in Paintbrush). Move the pointer down to the color palette and click on the light blue. The color selection box changes to reflect your choice. Now move the pointer up to

the 8 and click on individual pixels to turn them from black to blue. Notice that the zoom area in the top left corner of the screen reflects the changes you make. Figure 11.6 shows the edit in process.

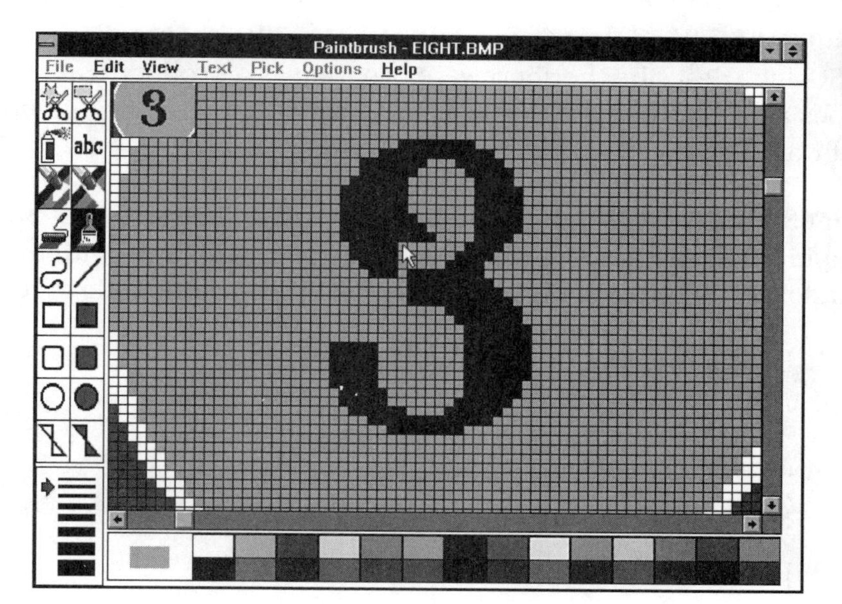

Figure 11.6: Changing the 8 into a 3.

> **The Coach Says...**
>
> If you make a mistake and paint a few pixels blue that should be black, simply click on the black and fix the pixels.

By using a combination of these techniques, you can modify any image you create in a paint program. In addition, you can use other products—including the three shareware programs available on *The Graphics Coach* bonus disk—to do other types of editing operations. The sections that follow explore editing with these three programs.

EDITING WITH PAINT SHOP PRO

On your Graphics disk included with this book, you'll find another kind of graphics tool that provides not paint tools and palettes but a specialized type of editing and conversion utility called Paint Shop Pro for Windows. The manufacturers of Paint Shop Pro, JASC, Inc., describe the shareware program as a product that "does all those things that you wish a painting program would do, but doesn't."

Paint Shop Pro for Windows enables you to take files in all sorts of graphics file formats and view, edit, and print them from within Windows. The program supports the following graphics file types:

BMP	DIB
GIF	IMG
JAS	MAC
MSP	PIC
PCX	RAS
RLE	TGA
TIFF	WPG

Paint Shop Pro for Windows can display your image in a variety of views, allowing you to zoom in up to 10 times the normal display. Editing capabilities include flipping and rotating, resizing, cropping, and color adjusting. (You won't find pixel-level editing in Paint Shop Pro, however.)

STARTING PAINT SHOP PRO

To start Paint Shop Pro for Windows, begin at the Windows Program Manager. (If you haven't yet installed Paint Shop Pro, do so now. Consult Appendix B for instructions on installing the program.)

Double-click on the Paint Shop Pro group window icon. The window opens, revealing the program icon. Double-click on it. After a moment, the Paint Shop Pro screen appears, as shown in figure 11.7. All you see is the window title and the menu bar stretched across the top of the screen.

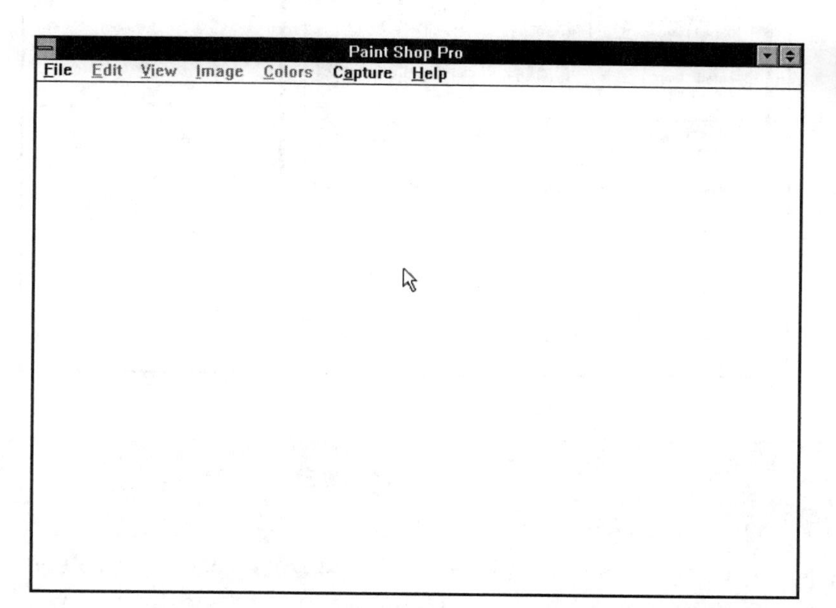

Figure 11.7: The blank Paint Shop Pro for Windows screen.

LOADING AN IMAGE

What's the program waiting for? Only you. The first step in using Paint Shop Pro is loading an image. To do this, open the **F**ile menu and choose the **O**pen command. (You can press Ctrl-O to bypass the menu selections.) When the File Open dialog box appears, click on the format of the file you want to see; then choose the file from the Fi**l**es list on the left side of the dialog box (see fig. 11.8).

Figure 11.8:

The File Open dialog box in Paint Shop Pro.

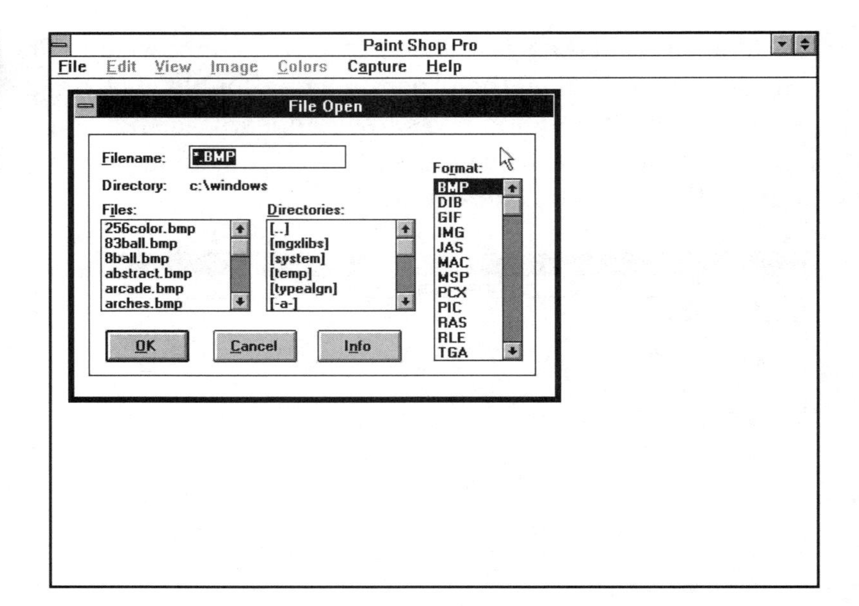

The Coach Says...

If you don't see the file you want in the displayed list, look through the **D**irectories list to see whether you've stored the file in another directory. By default, Paint Shop Pro looks in the Windows subdirectory for files you've created.

After you enter the settings you want (select the EIGHT.BMP file edited earlier in this chapter), click on OK or press Enter. The file is then loaded into Paint Shop Pro. If you're opening a large file, you'll see a status box that tells you how much of the file has been loaded. (If the file is small, you may miss the status box if you blink.)

EXPLORING THE EDITING OPTIONS

Paint Shop Pro for Windows is meant to be an add-on utility for whatever paint program you normally use. This means you won't be able to change individual pixels on the screen, but you will be able to perform editing tasks not usually available in a traditional paint program.

Paint Shop Pro includes seven different menus: **F**ile, **E**dit, **V**iew, **I**mage, **C**olors, C**a**pture, and **H**elp. Each of these menus contains a set of commands that enable you to work with the image in different ways. Table 11.1 provides you with an overview of the options available in the Paint Shop menus.

Table 11.1
Paint Shop Pro Menus

Menu	*Description*
File	Contains commands for opening, closing, saving, and printing files. Also allows you to set preferences for screen capture and file compression features
Edit	Includes an **U**ndo command that reverses the most recent operation, **C**opy and **P**aste commands, and a command for emptying the clipboard
View	Allows you to select a variety of views, from full screen to zoom up to ten times the normal display
Image	Manipulate the image by flipping, rotating, resizing, cropping, and applying filters to the item

continues

Table 11.1
Continued

Menu	*Description*
Colors	Helps you adjust various color controls including the RGB mix, the brightness and contrast, the grey scales used, and fine-tune the gamma level for display. Additionally, this menu contains commands for counting colors, reversing the image (to create a negative), and decreasing and increasing the color depth (by changing the number of bits per pixel used to store color).
Capture	Starts the screen capture utility and enables you to specify which area of the screen you want to capture (Area, Full Screen, Client Area, or Window)
Help	Provides you with several commands for using Paint Shop Pro's extensive help feature. You can choose the help you need from a displayed Index, display a list of keyboard commands, or following the instructions in Using Help.

SAVING YOUR CHANGES

After you've made your changes using Paint Shop Pro for Windows, be sure to save the file by opening the File menu and choosing the Save As command. You'll see, from the wide variety of file formats in the Format window, that you can choose many different output options for the file (see fig. 11.9).

Click on the format you want for the saved file, and type a name (up to eight characters before the extension) in the Filename box. (Change directories if necessary.) When you're finished entering the file name, click on OK or press Enter; Paint Shop Pro for Windows then saves the file.

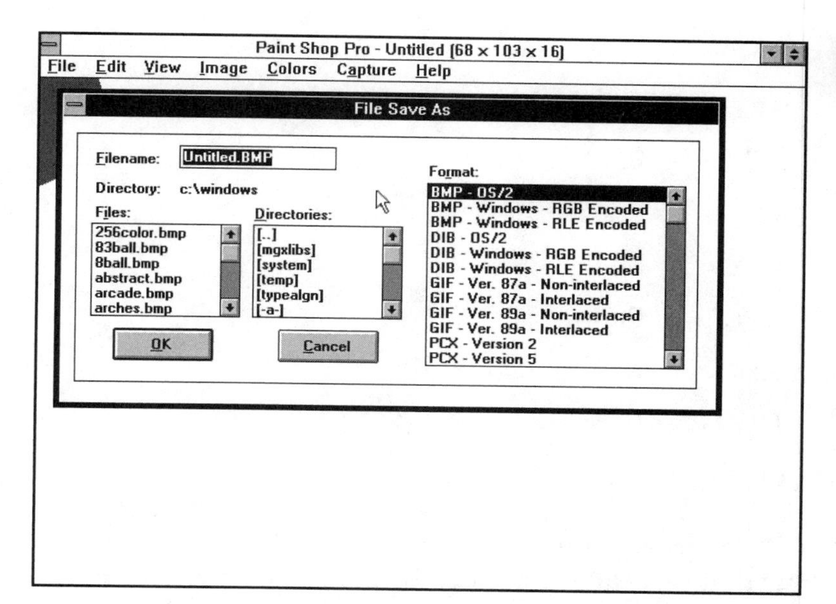

Figure 11.9: Saving the modified file.

EXITING PAINT SHOP PRO

When you're finished working with the graphics files in Paint Shop Pro for Windows (and you've already saved your files), open the File menu and choose Exit. If you've forgotten to save your changes, a dialog box appears prompting you to do so. After you click Yes (or No, if you want to abandon what you've done), you are returned to the open Paint Shop Pro group window. To close the window, double-click on the close box in the upper left corner of the window.

EDITING WITH GRAPHIC WORKSHOP

Graphic Workshop is a DOS-based image conversion and editing utility. Produced by Alchemy Mindworks, Inc., Graphic Workshop enables you to work with the following graphic file types:

- MAC
- IMG
- GIF
- IFF
- TGA
- WPG
- TIFF
- TXT
- CUT
- GEM
- PCX
- BMP
- LBM
- MSP
- PIC
- EXE
- EPS

Graphic Workshop comes with several files in the GIF and IMG formats that you can experiment with as you try out the program. In addition to the file conversion utility (covered fully in Chapter 14), the Graphic Workshop includes several editing features, including scaling, cropping, reversing, dithering, rotating, and flipping images.

A big bonus Graphic Workshop offers is the addition of a special effects feature. When you press F9 to display the Special effects popup menu, you are given the options of reducing color, changing to grey scale, sharpening, softening, smudging, spacing, or deepening the color of pixels.

> **The Coach Says...**
>
> The process of modifying an area of pixels—such as sharpening, softening, or modifying spacing—is known as an *area process*. These operations change the way a certain area of your graphic looks (such as when you sharpen the outline of an element).

STARTING GRAPHIC WORKSHOP

To start Graphic Workshop, first copy the program to your hard disk in a directory named GWS. (For specific installation instructions, see Appendix B.) Then, when the DOS prompt is displayed (it may be C:\ or D:\ on your computer), type the following line and press Enter:

CD GWS

This makes the Graphic Workshop directory the current directory. Now you can start the program by typing the following and then pressing Enter:

GWS

After a moment, the Graphic Workshop screen appears, as shown in figure 11.10.

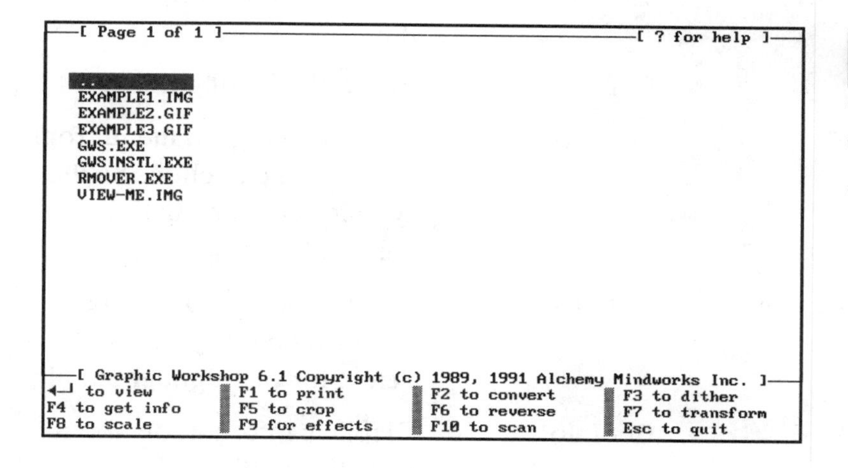

Figure 11.10: The Graphic Workshop opening screen.

LOADING AN IMAGE

Graphic Workshop comes with several images you can experiment with. You'll find four different files: two ending with IMG and two ending with GIF. To load an image, simply highlight the one you want by pressing the arrow keys and press Enter. The program

displays a status box that shows the file's progress as it is unloaded.

INVESTIGATING EDITING POSSIBILITIES

As you can see in figure 11.10, the layout of GWS is much different from that of Paint Shop Pro for Windows. Graphic Workshop uses function keys—not the mouse—for command selections. At the bottom of the screen, you see the menu showing the different available options. Table 11.2 provides a description of these various commands.

Table 11.2
Graphic Workshop Commands

Key	*Command*	*Description*
Enter	View	Loads the currently selected file
F1	Print	Prints the highlighted file
F2	Convert	Displays a popup menu from which you can choose a file type for converting the selected file
F3	Dither	Displays a popup menu of dithering types you can select for the highlighted file
F4	Get Info	Displays information about the chosen file
F5	Crop	Allows you to trim the displayed image

Key	Command	Description
F6	Reverse	Inverts the display (for example, a black background and white text becomes a white background with black text)
F7	Transform	Lets you rotate or flip the image
F8	Scale	Displays a popup box in which you can enter the new scale for the modified image
F9	Effects	Displays a popup box of special effects
F10	Scan	Allows you to scan an image (if you've already hooked up a scanner and installed the scanner driver).
Esc	Quit	Leaves Graphic Workshop

As you can see, Graphic Workshop contains many different kinds of image editing commands that enable you to stretch the capabilities of your standard paint program. When you choose one of the commands by pressing the appropriate function key, a popup box appears, displaying further options about the command you have chosen. For example, figure 11.11 shows the popup box that appears when you press F2.

After you modify a file in GWS, the program saves the original and the copy for you; there's no save command to issue. When you're ready to exit the program, simply press Esc.

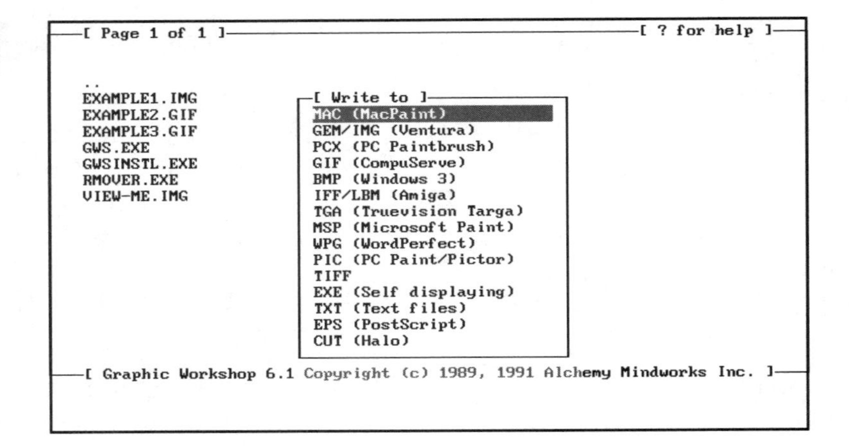

Figure 11.11: The conversion popup box in Graphic Workshop.

EDITING WITH GIFCONVERTER

The final image-editing program is the GIFConverter, a Macintosh shareware utility offered by developer Kevin Mitchell. GIFConverter (pronounced jif, like the peanut butter) is a multifaceted image editing and conversion utility that you can use to view, edit, convert, and print graphics in different formats. GIFConverter can work with files in most popular formats; rotate, crop, and flip graphics; control color depth and greyscaling; and control image resolution.

GIFConverter supports files in the following formats:

GIF	RLE
paint	scanned image
PICT	RIFF
TIFF	PostScript EPSF
PostScript EPSF (text only)	

STARTING GIFCONVERTER

To start GIFConverter, open the Apple menu and choose GIFConverter 2.2.10 by clicking on it. The GIFConverer symbol appears in the upper right corner of the screen, and the menus in the menu bar change to show the GIFConverter menus.

LOADING AN IMAGE

When you want to load an image, open the File menu and choose the Open command. When the dialog box appears, choose the folder or desktop where the file you want to use is stored. Then click on the Open button. After a moment, the image you select is displayed in the GIFConverter work area.

EXPLORING EDITING FEATURES

GIFConverter contains many different types of editing features. In addition to the file conversion tasks (explored fully in Chapter 14), GIFConverter allows you to move, stretch, scale, rotate, crop, and print graphics images. Table 11.3 describes the various menus displayed in GIFConverter.

Table 11.3.
GIFConverter Menu Functions.

Menu	*Description*
File	Begin a new file, open existing files, set up the page, prepare for printing, print a file, save a file, or revert to an older file version
Edit	Includes commands for undoing the last operation and for cutting, copying, pasting, clearing, and selecting images

continues

Table 11.3
Continued

Menu	*Description*
Display	Enables you to control the color depth of individual pixels, fine-tune color balance, choose grayscaling, or hide on-screen items
Image	Scale, rotate, crop, enhance, set resolution, change the selected color palette, and reduce the number of colors used in the display
Special	Enables you to change the background colors, set dithering, and specify other options
Tools	Lets you choose the tools you'll use to work with images
Windows	Enables you to display various on-screen items or select other active files

SAVING THE IMAGE

After you've worked with the image, remember to save it by opening the File menu and choosing Save As. When the Save dialog box appears, select the folder in which you want to save the file. If you want to choose a file type different from the one displayed in the File Type box, click the mouse button in the box to display a list of supported file types. When you've entered the filename, click on OK or press Return.

EXITING GIFCONVERTER

When you're ready to exit GIFConverter, open the File menu and choose the Quit command. You are then returned to the desktop (or to a different active application).

EDITING DRAW OBJECTS

The process of editing an object you create in a draw program is different in that the various items you create in a draw graphic are individual objects themselves. This section shows you some of the basic principles involved in editing draw objects. Specifically, you'll review the following tasks:

1. Selecting an object.
2. Resizing the object.
3. Grouping and ungrouping objects.
4. Arranging objects.
5. Deleting objects.
6. Working with object points.
7. Tracing bitmaps.

Selecting Objects. When you want to select an object that is part of a draw graphic, you simply position the mouse and click on the item. Handles appear around the edges of the object. With some draw programs, such as Micrografx Designer, you first must click on the selection tool before you can select the item. With other programs, the selection tool is chosen for you automatically.

Resizing Objects. Resizing the object is a simple task. Just move the pointer to one of the object handles. When you do so, the arrow changes to a double-headed arrow. You then can press and hold the mouse button while dragging the object in the direction you want. If you want to make an object wider, drag one of the side handles. If you want to increase the overall size of the image, drag one of the corner handles outward. Figure 11.12 illustrates your options for resizing an object.

Grouping and Ungrouping Objects. Often, when you're finished working with a draw graphic, you will want to group them together to make working with the items easier. After you combine them all in one group, you've got only one item to resize: the entire object.There also will be times when you need to break apart—or ungroup—the object you've combined. Suppose, for example, that the fact that the center hole of the disk is slightly off-center. You try to ignore it, but cannot. You can't fix it by simply clicking on it and moving it, because when you do, the entire object is selected. Before you can move that individual item, you must ungroup the object.

Figure 11.12:

Resizing an object.

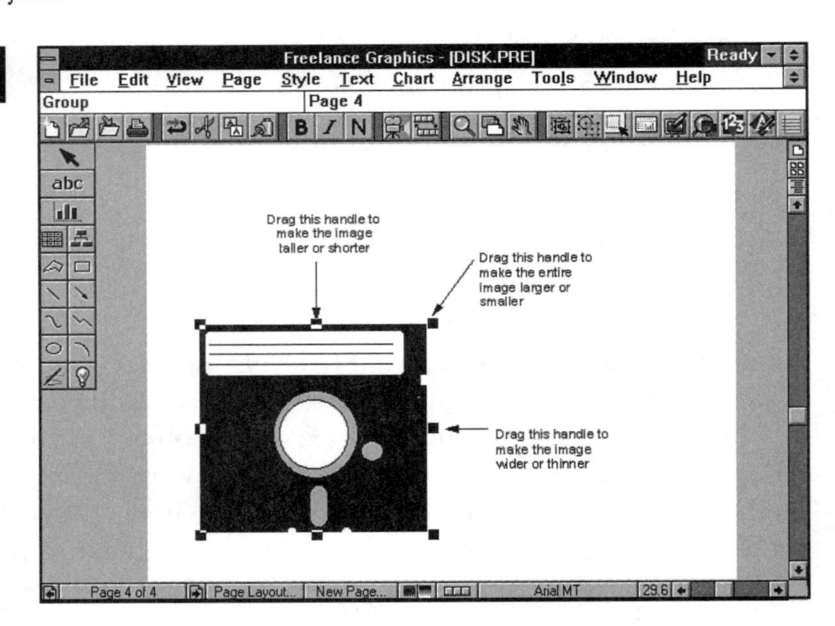

The Coach Says...

In other draw programs, the commands for lumping and separating a bunch of objects are different from Group and Ungroup. Micrografx Designer, for example, uses the Combine and Break Apart commands for the same function.

Layering Objects. When you're working with multiple objects on a page—whether that means you have used several items to create one, as in the disk example, or you have several overlapping elements for a larger graphic—you need some way to change the placement of items that overlap. For example, in the picture shown in figure 11.13, the layered effect is important. In this picture, the bottom layer is a yellow enclosed curve; the second layer is a black enclosed curve, and the stars occupy the top layer, scattered in an overlapping pattern on top of both the black and yellow curves. You can change the layer on which an item is placed by clicking on the item you want and choosing a command such as Move back or Move forward. This changes the position of the item in relation to other items in the object.

Figure 11.13: A logo with several layers.

Arranging Objects. Draw programs make it easy for you to arrange the items you create on-screen. After you select the object, you can flip it horizontally or vertically or rotate it according to an increment you specify. Figure 11.14 illustrates various flipping and rotating tricks.

Figure 11.14:

Flipping and rotating graphics.

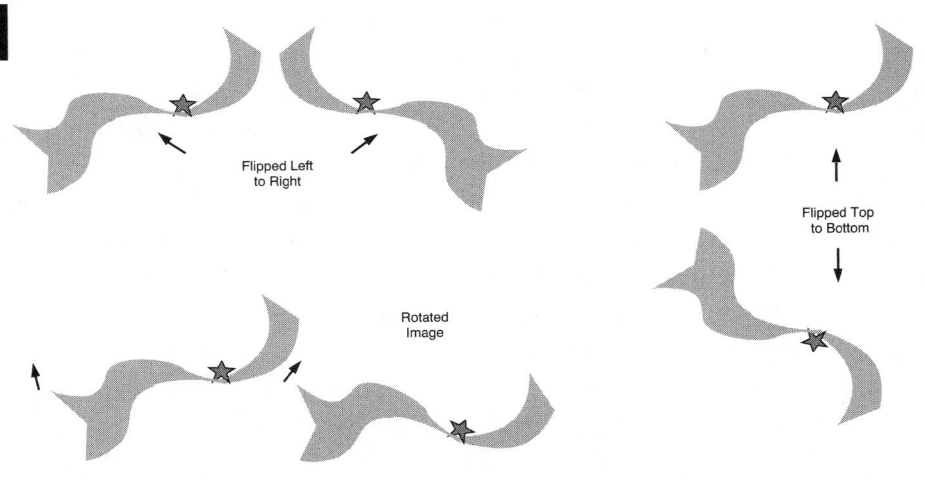

Deleting Objects. Of course, you need some tool for getting rid of graphics (or portions of graphics) that just do not work anymore. All programs have at least one way you can delete objects; some programs have more than one. In the **E**dit menu of most programs, you'll find a C**u**t command; this command removes the selected item from the page and places it on the Clipboard. Other programs have a **D**elete command, which removes the item from the page without retaining a copy.

The Coach Says...

If there's even a remote chance that you might want an image again later, use C**u**t instead of Delete. Remember, however, that the clipboard stores only one image at a time and any subsequent items you copy or cut will replace the item already there.

Editing Fine Points. One of the early criticisms of high-end drawing programs was working with portions of shapes—such as the side of a polygon—was pretty much impossible. After you created a shape, you had no recourse for working with a small piece of it.

In the revised editions of draw programs that have surfaced in the last few years, a built-in feature has been added that enables you to select and edit individual points on a shape or line. This gives you finer control of the drawing and makes editing virtually unlimited. For example, when you want to view and perhaps edit the individual points on the star used in the preceding example, you can select Points Mode (or Reshape Points), usually available in Arrange or Change menus. The points of the star—not just the end points but the points along all linear segments—are made visible, as shown in figure 11.15. Now you can click on the point you want and move it to edit the image as necessary.

Figure 11.15:

Working in points mode.

Autotracing Bitmaps. One major benefit some drawing packages offer is the capability to import and smooth out bitmap graphics you create in a paint program. This gives you the flexibility to paint freehand or bring in scanned photos into a paint program and then save the file, open it in your draw program, and smooth out the rough edges. Not all drawing programs have this capability, but Micrografx Designer and Adobe Illustrator both do.

In the smoothing, or autotrace, procedure, the program transforms the image you import into forms it recognizes: shapes, curves, line segments, etc. Autotrace, in effect, converts a bitmap to a vector image. If you're working with a large number of bitmapped graphics or scanned images, look for this feature before you buy.

If your draw program has no autotrace feature, you can purchase a stand-alone autotrace program to use on your bitmapped files. One such program is the popular Adobe Streamline, an easy-to-use tracing utility that transforms the jagged bitmaps into smooth vectors.

INSTANT REPLAY

In this chapter, you explored a variety of graphics procedures available in both paint and draw programs. As you know, the names of the commands vary from program to program, but all paint and draw packages—unless otherwise noted—have the features listed here. Explore your own graphics software for these basic features and find out where they are. Specifically, you investigated the following topics:

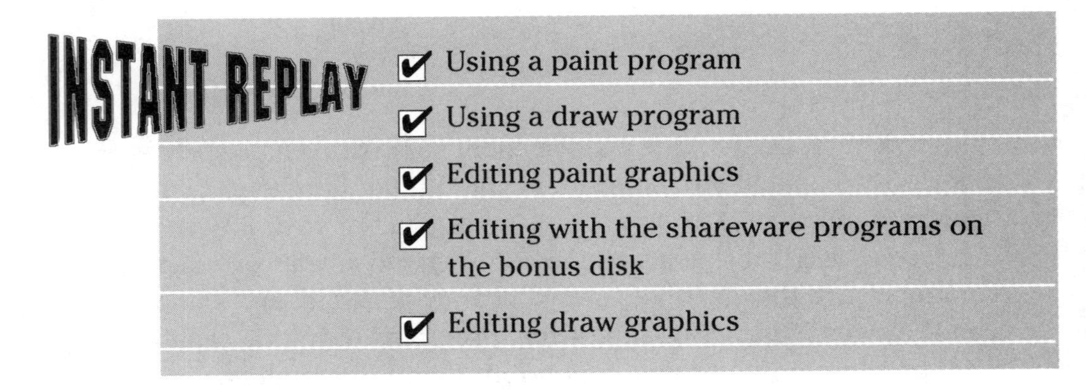

PRINTING GRAPHICS FILES

Now that you've worked with your graphics a bit, you would probably like to see how it "really" looks. This chapter explains some of the different print procedures you will run into as you use the various programs discussed in this book.

Specifically, this chapter introduces the following topics:

GAME PLAN

- Setting up your printer
- Starting the print routine
- Setting print options
- Printing with the programs on the bonus disk

The Coach Says...

All three of the graphics programs included on *The Graphics Coach* bonus disk—Paint Shop Pro for Windows, Graphic Workshop, and GIFConverter—have built-in print utilities. This means that after you modify an image using one of these utilities, you can print the image right away to see the effects of your work.

SETTING UP YOUR PRINTER

It's always a good idea to begin at the beginning. You have a printer, right? It's connected through a cable to the back of your computer. Make sure the cables are tight and the printer is on-line and ready.

Another problem that can hang printers up is a paper deficiency or a bad paper draw. Check to make sure that your printer has enough paper and that, if you're using continuous feed paper, that it is not restricted in any way. (Sometimes the pages get trapped among the cables in the back of the printer.)

If you're using Windows, you may want to take an extra moment and make sure that Windows recognizes the printer type you are using. You can find this out by opening the Main group window, double-clicking on the Control Panel, and choosing the Printers icon, as shown in figure 12.1.

Windows displays the Printers dialog box, in which you can look for your installed printer (see fig. 12.2). If you don't see the one you want to use, you can add a printer driver (you'll need your original or backup copies of your Windows disks to add a driver) by clicking on the Add button and choosing your printer type from the displayed list of printers. When you click on the Install button,

Windows will tell you which disk to insert so that the appropriate printer files can be loaded.

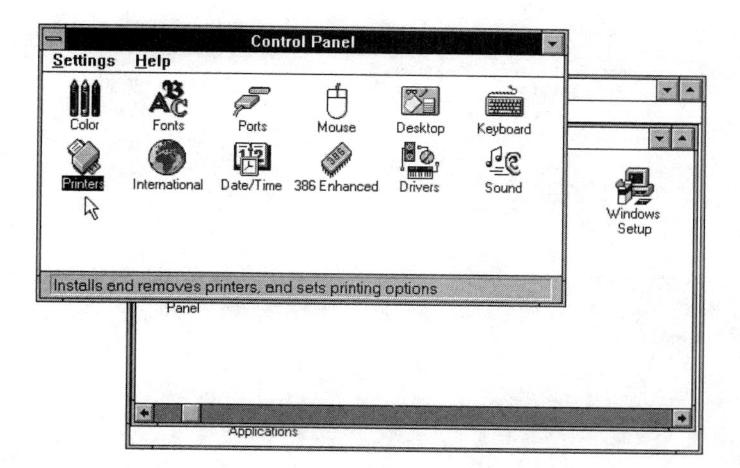

Figure 12.1: Making sure Windows supports your printer.

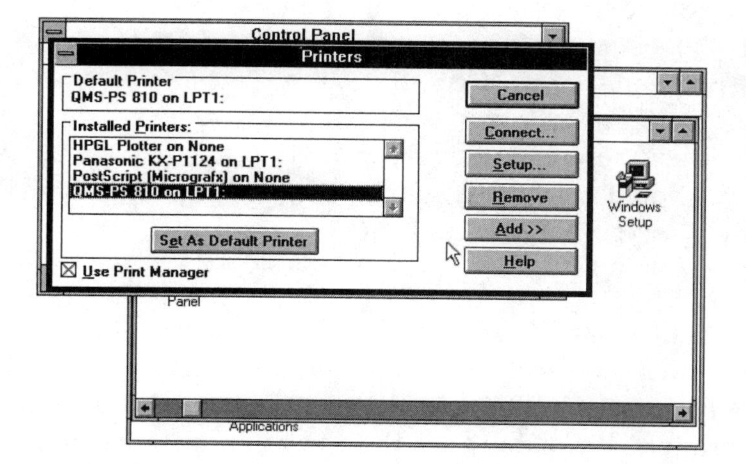

Figure 12.2: Displaying a list of installed printers.

If you're working with a DOS paint or draw program, look for a Printer Setup command in the File or Print menus to make sure your printer is ready to run. With the Mac, open the File menu from within the paint or draw program and select Print Setup to check out the printer to which the Mac thinks its sending the file. You also can determine some of the expectations your software

has by looking at the settings in Page Setup, as shown in figure 12.3.

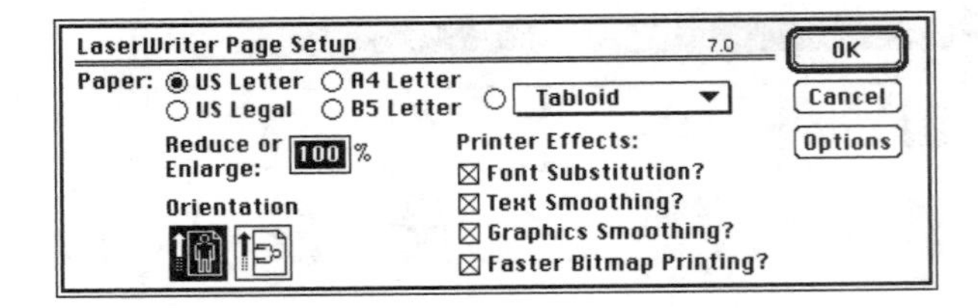

Figure 12.3: Checking page setup options with a Mac draw program.

The Coach Says...

Although the list of programs that support a sweeping range of printers is rapidly growing, you may be using a program that is more limited in its printer selections. If the list of printers your program supports is relatively short, and if you can't find your printer on the list, consult your printer manual for information on emulation modes. Most printers can "act like" another type of printer, which comes in handy when you're trying to make sure your files are going to print. Your printer's manual should tell you everything you need to know about what other types of printers yours can emulate.

If you're using Paint Shop Pro for Windows, you can start the program, open the File menu, and choose the Printer Setup command. A Printer Setup dialog box appears, showing you the installed printers. If you don't see the one you want, click on Setup to specify further options (doing so ties you into Windows' print setups). You can take care of adding printer drivers from the Windows Control Panel. The driver will show up in Paint Shop Pro, as well.

Before you begin working with the print options on the Mac, be sure to select the printer you want to use by using the Chooser on the Apple menu. You then need to use the Control Panel to connect the printer—software-wise—to your Mac.

STARTING THE PRINT ROUTINE

In its simplest form, most print routines are, at their essence, the same. You open or select a file, choose a print command, fill in necessary print options—like number of copies, paper size, and range of pages—then click on OK or press Enter. The file then prints. Sound simple? Keep your fingers crossed.

In the best cases, printing is easy. Those of us who have grown up in the PC neighborhood have learned from experience to be a bit surprised when everything works like a charm the first time. It does happen, though; especially when you're working with a dependable, Windows-based program or a high-end program with good printer support.

When you begin printing with a Windows-based program, such as Windows Paintbrush, the print routine is pretty straightforward. A Print dialog box appears, something like the one shown in figure 12.4. (The next section explains more about selecting print options.)

Life with the Mac is pretty predictable. Because everything designed for the Mac has the same look and feel, standard printer drivers are available for software programs (and developers) which makes the support for printers more consistent. You know, for example, that you'll find the Print command in the File menu (while in some PC programs, Print is in a menu of its own). You can expect to see a somewhat familiar Print dialog box no matter what Mac application you are using. Figure 12.5 shows the Print dialog box displayed when using Adobe Illustrator.

Figure 12.4:

The Print dialog box in Windows Paintbrush.

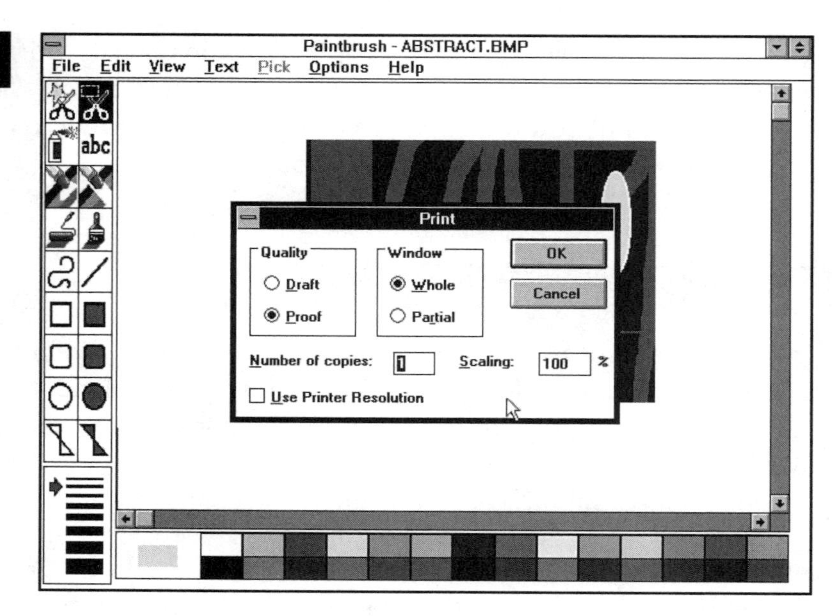

Figure 12.5:

The Print dialog box in Adobe Illustrator.

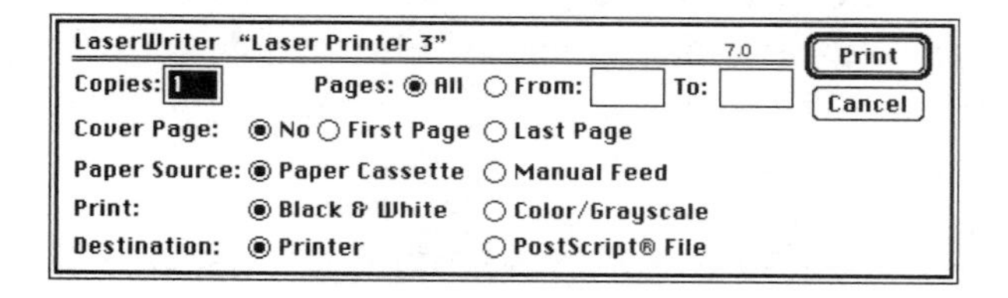

No matter what type of graphics program you are working with, you have certain settings to decide about when you prepare to print a file. These "somethings" are called print options, and they are the subject of the next section.

SPECIFYING PRINT OPTIONS

Some programs have print options and some programs—such as Paint Shop Pro for Windows—do not. When you choose the **P**rint command from the **F**ile menu, Paint Shop Pro starts sending the file right to the printer, with no "What paper do you want to use?" or "How many copies would you like?"

Other programs, however, display a Print dialog box that enables you to specify some important settings for your printout. Those settings include how many copies you want, what type of quality you expect (higher quality takes longer to print), whether the paper comes from a paper tray or manual feed, and the range of pages you want to print. The following sections further explain these options you might find in your own paint, draw, and image-editing programs.

CHOOSING PRINT QUALITY

One of the options your Print dialog box may ask you involves the quality of the printout you want. You may wonder, after you've taken all this time to create stunning graphics, why you would settle for quality less than the best. One reason exists: time.

When you're printing complicated graphics, printing can take several minutes or longer. When you opt to print at a lesser quality—settling for a quick print—you still can check the placement of items, look at the patterns used, and see whether all your lines meet. You won't get the superior printout of fonts and special color blends, but you will get an idea of how the finished piece will look.

If you're using Windows, the selection of print quality will probably appear in the Print dialog box as a checkbox you can either enable or disable. Windows Paintbrush offers you the options of Draft or Proof and provides a Use Printer resolution checkbox to give you the choice of relying on the highest possible quality your printer can offer.

The Macintosh, on the other hand, includes the print quality considerations in the Page Setup dialog box. Here you have a choice of whether you want to allow font substitution (if your printer doesn't have the fonts you've included in your graphics file, do you want the Mac to substitute fonts automatically?). Other

options that affect print quality include text and graphics smoothing (meaning the rough edges are automatically smoothed during printing) and faster bit-map printing, which prints paint images at an accelerated rate. If you want to print at the fastest possible rate, disable the first three options but leave Faster Bitmap Printing enabled, as shown in figure 12.6.

Figure 12.6:

Getting a quick Mac print.

LaserWriter Page Setup 7.0
OK
Paper: US Letter A4 Letter US Legal B5 Letter Tabloid
Cancel
Reduce or Enlarge: 100 %
Printer Effects:
Options
Font Substitution?
Text Smoothing?
Orientation
Graphics Smoothing?
Faster Bitmap Printing?

> **The Coach Says...**
>
> The black-and-white or color option affects the speed at which files print. Color printing generally takes much longer than black-and-white printing because of the number of passes required by the printer. If you want a quick print for a rough draft of your graphic, print it in black and white and save a bit of time.

CHOOSING NUMBER OF COPIES

Another important feature includes the number of copies you want to print. With most programs, printing 20 copies of an image—perhaps for a presentation handout—is no more difficult than printing one.

You'll find the Number of copies option is fairly consistent among all programs: usually, it is stored in the Print menu. The highest number of copies you can print is usually some astronomical

figure—such as 99, or even 999. To enter a new value in the Number of copies box (the default is 1), type the number of copies you want.

CHOOSING PRINT RANGES

Most print routines also give you the choice of printing a range of pages—say, from page 3 to page 5—without printing pages you don't need. When you enter a print range, type the first page you want to print in the From: box and type the last page you want to print in the To: box.

The Coach Says...

Windows Paintbrush enables you to choose a portion of an image for printing. For example, suppose that you have several elements grouped in one file. Rather than printing the entire file, you want only to print a single item. When you choose the Partial option, Windows redisplays the image so that you can use the selection tool to enclose the area you want to print. That portion of the screen is then sent to the printer.

SCALING OPTIONS

The task of choosing the scaling percentage of your image is another common print option. Not all programs offer scaling, although any program that prides itself in its editing capabilities offers a customized scaling option.

> **The Coach Says...**
> Scaling controls the size at which you print the image. Suppose, for example, that you have created an image that fills the screen. When you print, you'd prefer if the image were smaller. You can reduce the size of the image at print time, without changing the size in the file, by choosing a 50 percent scale. If you wanted the image actual size, you'd choose 100 percent; and for double-size, you'd choose 200 percent.

The Macintosh also has a scaling option, but it's called something else: Reduce or Enlarge. You have the same options available (and you can enter your own percentages), and the option is found in the Page Setup dialog box (command available in the File menu).

CHOOSING PAPER SOURCE

Another specialized type of print option not all print routines possess is the capability to choose the paper source. If you're using a dot-matrix printer, your printer comes from one place: the sheet feeder or continuous paper feed on your printer. If you use a standard laser printer, chances are you rely heavily on a paper tray or perhaps feed special pages manually.

Some high-end printers have replaceable paper trays that can store paper in different sizes. If you have a printer capable of printing pages of different sizes, the paper source option is important for you. (Print routines that do not have this option will simply pull paper from the default paper source.)

Most high-end programs are equipped to handle the following paper sizes:

Paper Type	*Size*
US Letter	8 1/2-by-11
US Legal	8 1/2-by-14
A4 Letter	8 1/2-by-11 2/3
B5 Letter	7-by-10

The last two options, A4 and B5 Letter, are both standard European paper sizes.

The Macintosh includes the Paper settings on the Page Setup dialog box. Other programs, such as Aldus Freehand, include the option on the Print dialog box. The Mac also has a drop-down box that offers other alternative paper and envelope sizes, such as Tabloid, A3 Tabloid, Envelope—Center Fed, Envelope—Edge Fed, and LaserWriter II B5.

CHOOSING ORIENTATION

Again, not all programs will give you the option of printing in different orientations. Most desktop publishing programs, presentation graphics packages, and draw programs give you the option of printing in either landscape or portrait orientation.

The term orientation refers to the way in which the image is printed on the page. Portrait orientation is the traditional 8 1/2-by-11 format in which most business memos, reports, and routine letters are printed. Landscape orientation prints the image in 11-by-8 1/2 format, with the page turned longways. This type of orientation is popular for creating charts, transparencies, and presentation graphics. Additionally, flowcharts and organizational charts are usually better represented in landscape orientation.

Figure 12.7 shows the difference between landscape and portrait orientation.

Figure 12.7:

Landscape and portrait orientation.

The Coach Says...

For best results in creating and printing your graphics, consider the orientation issue before you begin creating the file. This may affect the way you place the items on the page. Additionally, some graphics programs change the look of the page when you choose landscape; the work area represents the shape of the printable page space.

CHOOSING PRINTER OR FILE

One of the final choices you'll make when specifying print options is whether you do, in fact, want to print to the printer. By printing to a file (in many applications), you can create a file that can be printed on any standard system, whether that system has access to the same program. For example, when you print a Micrografx Designer image to a file rather than to the printer, the information is sent through the normal channels as though it is going to the printer; but instead, it is stored in a file. That file can be taken to another computer and printed with a simple DOS command.

This capability comes in handy when you create an image on your system but need to print on another. You can print the image to a file and print it on the other system with a minimum of trouble.

PRINTING WITH PAINT SHOP PRO FOR WINDOWS

Now that you have been through all the available print options, look more closely at the programs you have at your disposal. The first of these is Paint Shop Pro for Windows.

Most of the print options for Paint Shop Pro are set in Windows. In fact, the print process in Paint Shop Pro involves only this:

Open the File menu and choosing Print.

Figure 12.8 shows the process of selecing the command. The image in the Paint Shop Pro area is then sent to the printer. No fuss, no bother.

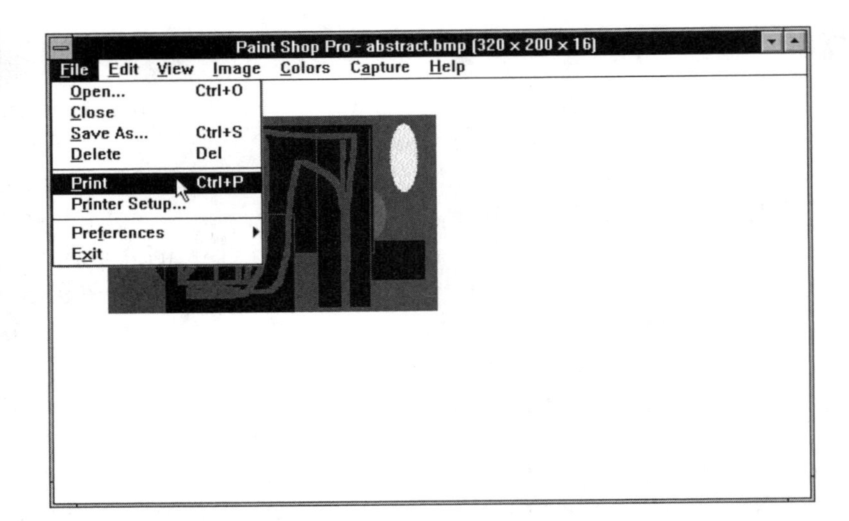

Figure 12.8:

Starting the print process.

PRINTING WITH GRAPHIC WORKSHOP

Printing with the Graphic Workshop is another simple endeavor. Although it seems improbable, it actually involves less than Paint Shop Pro. First display the image you want to print on-screen and then press F2.

A popup box appears so that you can choose the printer you're using (see fig. 12.9). Highlight the printer you want and press Enter. A small status box appears on-screen, showing you how much of the file has been sent to the printer. (You can press Esc to cancel the print).

PRINTING WITH GIFCONVERTER

You've already seen the important dialog boxes that will concern you as you work with GIFConverter. Because Mac applications are look-alikes, the Page Setup and Print dialog boxes contain the same options, whether you're using Adobe Illustrator, Aldus Freehand, or GIFConverter.

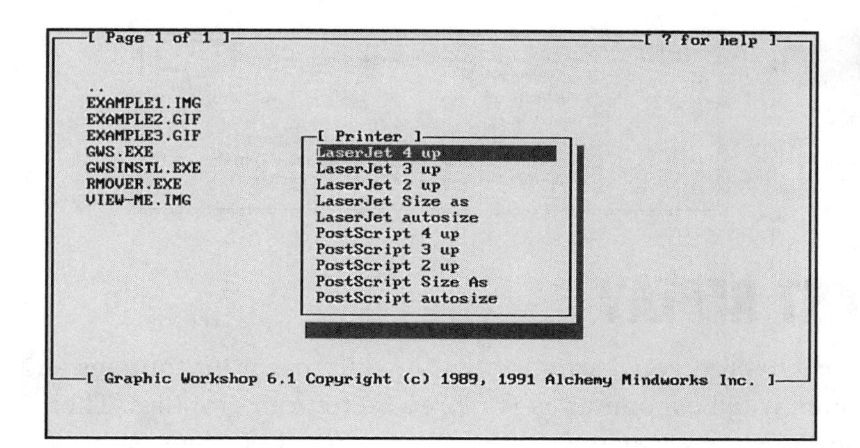

Figure 12.9: Choosing the printer for Graphic Workshop.

When you're ready to print, simply open the File menu and choose the Print command. The Print dialog box appears, and you can change and necessary settings; then click OK. The file is sent to the printer.

The Coach Says...

If you want a quick printout with GIFConverter, open the File menu and choose Print One. This prints a quick draft-quality printout of the image currently displayed in the GIFConverter work area.

Other options you might want to consider as you're printing your GIFConverter images are the LaserWriter Options available from within the Page Setup menu in all Mac applications. The options on this screen enable you to flip the image, invert it (so dark is light and light is dark), align the bitmap, and control the number of downloadable fonts allowed during printing (see fig. 12.10).

Figure 12.10: Additional Mac print options.

INSTANT REPLAY

In this chapter, you learned about the different print routines and options you'll encounter as you prepare to print graphics. There is some consistency among software and computer types, at least when it comes to printing capabilities. Here is what was covered:

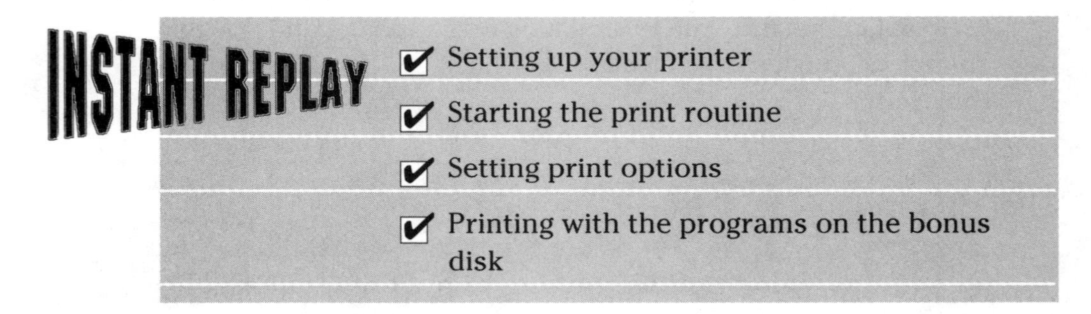

- ✔ Setting up your printer
- ✔ Starting the print routine
- ✔ Setting print options
- ✔ Printing with the programs on the bonus disk

CONVERTING AND MANAGING GRAPHICS FILES

In previous chapters you learned the basic differences among graphics types, you explored the hardware concerns that affect creating graphics, and you had hands-on experience with creating, editing, and printing graphics.

This chapter explores the following procedures:

GAME PLAN

- Converting files with Paint Shop Pro
- Converting files with Graphic Workshop
- Converting individual files and file batches
- Converting files with GIFConverter
- Compressing graphics files

After you start to get comfortable creating your own images or using clip art, you develop an appetite for more visuals. If you're adventurous, you've already tapped into CompuServe and downloaded a few GIF files; if you're creative, you've designed some art of your own.

Graphics files don't always work the way you want them to. They don't always plug right in to applications. Some require conversion, which sounds like a scary word but isn't, thanks to the graphics file conversion utilities included on your *Graphics* disk. Whether you work with a DOS-based PC, a Windows PC, or a Macintosh, you already have a program that converts your graphics files for you.

Another consideration is the size of the graphics files. Not all graphics files are huge—their size depends on their content and the type of graphics program (and format) you've selected. Encapsulated Postscript files, for example, are the Sumo wrestlers of the bunch; PCX files weigh in at a pixie fraction of their cousins.

UNDERSTANDING FILE CONVERSION

The process of changing one type of graphics file into another isn't as mystical as it may sound. In fact, only two types of graphics files exist, although there are dozens of offshoots of one type or another. Two types of graphics programs create two different types of graphics files: bit map and vector images. Bit-mapped graphics are created in a paint program; vector, or object-oriented, graphics are produced in a draw program. Each type of graphic has its own way of producing the image on-screen and in print.

Each of these graphics files types (bit map and vector) have different formats in which the files are saved. Bitmap formats are fairly similar (how many ways can you present a dot) but vector formats tend to be more complex. Different draw programs have different kinds of tools (which use unique calculations to draw the images on screen). If you use a polyline tool in one draw program and then import the vector image into another draw program that does not have a polyline tool, the calculations used to re-create the image produce something close to the original but not exactly the same.

TYPES OF FILE CONVERSIONS

Chances are, when you convert a graphics file, you convert it in one of the following ways:

Bit map to bit map. In this process, you change a bit-mapped graphic from one format to another. Suppose, for example, that you download a few graphics files from CompuServe. You want to use the file in a project you're preparing (don't forget to get the necessary permissions), but your current paint program does not support GIF files. You can use an image editor with a file conversion utility built-in; something like Paint Shop Pro for Windows, GWS, or GIFConverter. This changes the bit map from the version your program can't read (GIF) into one that it can (PCX). (For more information about accessing and downloading files from an on-line service, see *The Modem Coach*, published by New Riders Publishing.)

> **The Coach Says...**
>
> Another reason you might convert bit maps to bit maps involves file size. TIFF files, for example, can be extremely large, often taking up to three times the space a similar PCX file would require. For that reason, many users change their bit-mapped files to PCX to save computer storage space.

Bit map to object-oriented. This type of conversion turns a bit-mapped graphic into an object-oriented graphic. Usually, this is done in a high-end drawing program. Programs such as Micrografx Designer and Adobe Illustrator have autotrace utilities that automatically trace around the edges of a bit map, turning the pattern of dots into a line-art object-oriented image. Adobe also offers a standalone tracing utility, called Streamline, for PC users who don't have the autotrace capability built into their software. CorelDRAW offers a sister utility, CorelTRACE, that also turns bit maps into vectors.

Object-oriented to bit map. The process of changing an object-oriented image into a bit map is also possible. Most drawing programs do not have this capability built-in, and for the results with the least hassle, you'll probably wind up getting a screen capture of the image and then using the screen capture as the bit map. The screen shot of the image may not be as clear as an original bit map, but dots are dots. After you import the screen capture into a paint program and clean up any messiness, you won't know the difference.

Object-oriented to object-oriented. This type of conversion can be tricky because of the unique characteristics of many popular draw programs. Some use unique blending tools; others rely heavily on

shapes and designer line tools. When you move a graphic from one vector type to another, you may have trouble with the inconsistency you find among the way the images are created. Few conversion utilities are capable of converting vector images to other vector formats, although HiJaak for Windows supports conversions between many different vector formats. Your best bet for converting a Micrografx Designer image, for example to a Freelance Graphics image, is to try to import the image into the program. Most high-end drawing programs are flexible enough to support a variety of formats, although they may not show the formats on the screen.

The Coach Says...

If you're working with Windows applications—for example, you're bringing a bit map from Paintbrush into a Windows draw program—you can get around worrying about file inconsistencies by simply copying the image to the clipboard. Then open the receiving application and paste the picture in. In 99 out of 100 cases, Windows places the image without any grumbling. If you're restricted by memory or color capabilities, you may see some popup box alerting you to substitutions or possible memory hang-ups.

A REVIEW OF FILE TYPES

As you learned in Chapter 4, several different formats exist for bit map and object-oriented images. Table 13.1 reviews the formats for bit-mapped images; Table 13.2 shows the formats for object-oriented images.

Table 13.1:
Common Bit-map Formats

Format	*Stands for*
BMP	Windows bit map
DIB	Device-independent bit maps
GIF	Graphics interchange format
IMG	Image
JPG	Joint Photographic Experts Group
MSP	Microsoft Paintbrush
PCX	PC Paintbrush
PNT	MacPaint—early version
MAC	MacPaint—current version
TGA	Targa
TIF	Tagged image file
WMF	Windows metafile
WPG	WordPerfect graphic

The three programs on the graphics disk—Paint Shop Pro for WIndows, Graphic Workshop, and GIFConverter—can be used on your Windows PC, DOS PC, or Mac to convert just about any bit-mapped graphic format you'll encounter. For a program that converts vector formats to other vector formats, however, first check the capabilities of your draw program and then, try a third-party product such as HiJaak for Windows.

Table 13.2:
Common Object-oriented Formats

Format	Stands for
WMF	Windows metafile
DRW	Micrografx Designer
CDR	CorelDRAW
CGM	Computer graphics metafile
EPS	Encapsulated PostScript
HPGL	Hewlett-Packard Graphics Language
DXF	Data Exchange Format
GEM	GEM metafile
PIC	Picture format
PCT	Macintosh PICT file vector format

CONVERTING FILES

In some cases, you'll want to convert files on a file-by-file basis. This is fine for those times when you need to use one piece of artwork in a program that won't support it; then you can use Paint Shop Pro or one of the other programs to change that single file.

Graphic Workshop has a feature for larger-scale conversions. This batch-conversion possibility enables you to select a number of files that can all be converted at once. You don't have to load and enter a new name for each file; just select the file type you want to convert, make a few selections, and go get a cup of coffee while the program does the work. The following sections explore file conversion with each of the three shareware products on *The Graphics Coach* bonus disk.

USING PAINT SHOP PRO FOR WINDOWS

First start the program by opening the Paint Shop Pro group window and double-clicking on the Paint Shop icon. The Paint Shop Pro window appears. Open the **F**ile menu and choose the **O**pen command. The File Open dialog box appears, as shown in figure 13.1.

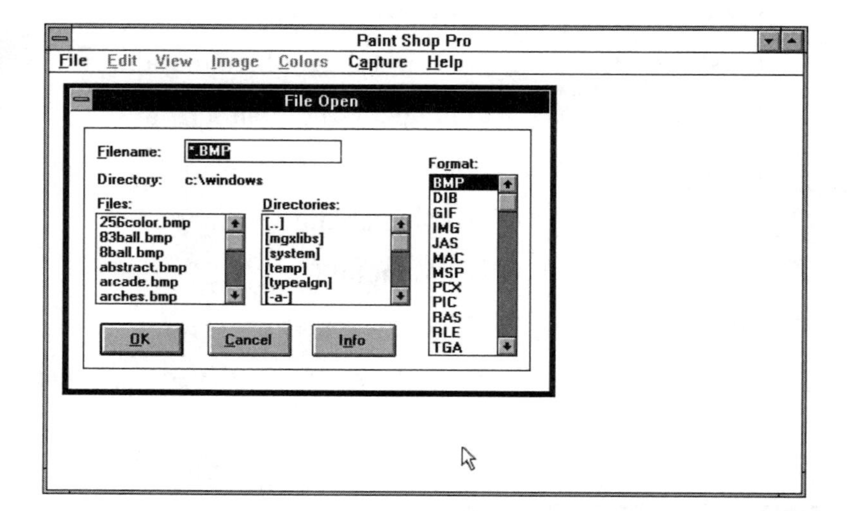

Figure 13.1: Opening a file to convert.

Click on the format of the file by choosing the extension from the Fo**r**mat box on the far right side of the dialog box. Scroll through the list of files in the F**i**les box (change directories if necessary). When you see the file you want, click on the file name; then click on OK. The file is then loaded into Paint Shop Pro.

You can then edit the file if necessary (refer to Chapter 11 for more information on editing with Paint Shop Pro). When you're ready to save the file in a different format, open the **F**ile menu and choose Save **A**s. The File Save As dialog box appears, as shown in figure 13.2.

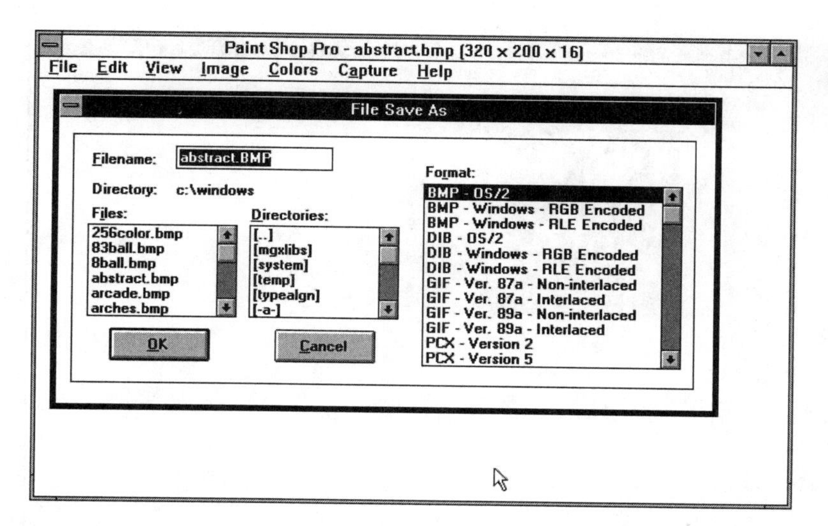

Figure 13.2:
Saving in a different file format.

As you can see, many, many different formats are displayed in the Format window. Scroll through the list and click on the format you want. (If you're unsure which format you need, you may want to save the file in two or three different formats so you increase your chances that one of the formats will work.) When you click on the file format, Paint Shop Pro automatically changes the name of the file displayed in the **F**ilename box. Finally, click on OK.

Paint Shop Pro converts the file and displays a status box, showing you the progress of the conversion. When the file has been converted, the program displays the graphic in the Paint Shop Pro work area. The new file name is displayed in the title bar at the top of the screen (see fig. 13.3).

USING GRAPHIC WORKSHOP

The Graphic Workshop is a DOS-based conversion and editing utility that enables you to convert virtually any bit map to any other bit map. Simple to use and easy on your computer's memory, the Graphic Workshop instantly converts single files and—almost as quickly—converts large groups of files.

Figure 13.3:

The converted image.

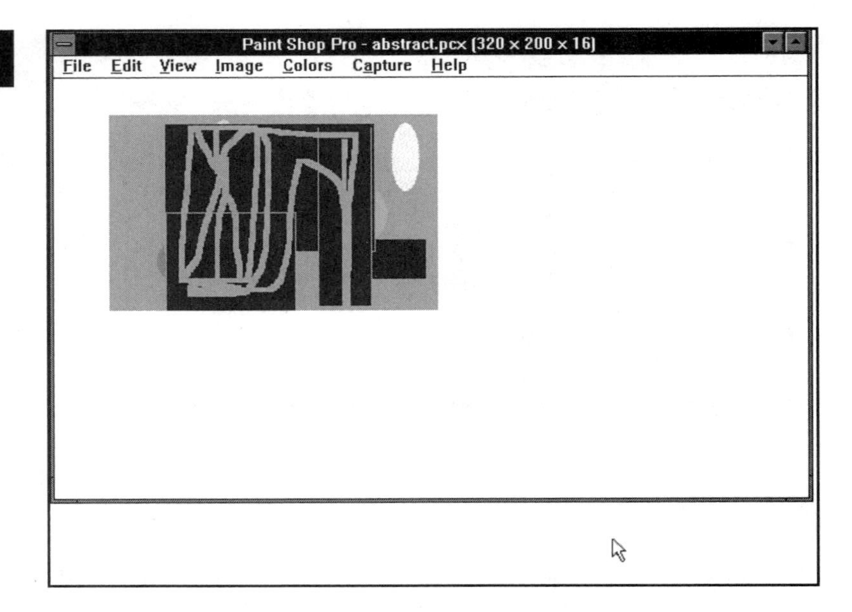

To start the Graphic Workshop, you first start at the DOS prompt (C:\ or D:\). Then change to the Graphic Workshop directory by typing **CD GWS** and pressing Enter. To start the workshop, type **GWS** and press Enter. The Graphic Workshop screen appears (see fig. 13.4).

The Coach Says...

If the files you want to convert are not displayed in the files list on the Graphic Workshop screen, highlight the directory symbol (..) and press Enter. Change to the necessary directory to display the files you want to convert.

The files in the current directory are shown in the main portion of the screen. If you're converting a single file, use the arrow keys to highlight the file you want to convert. If you're converting a group of files, move the highlight to the file you want and press T to tag

the file. Then move to the next file you want and press T again. The tagged files are marked with a small symbol to the left of the file name (see fig. 13.5).

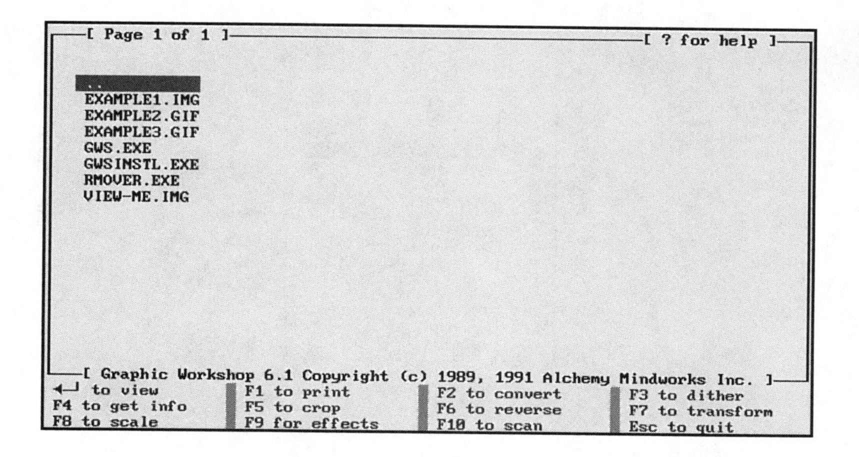

Figure 13.4: The Graphic Workshop screen.

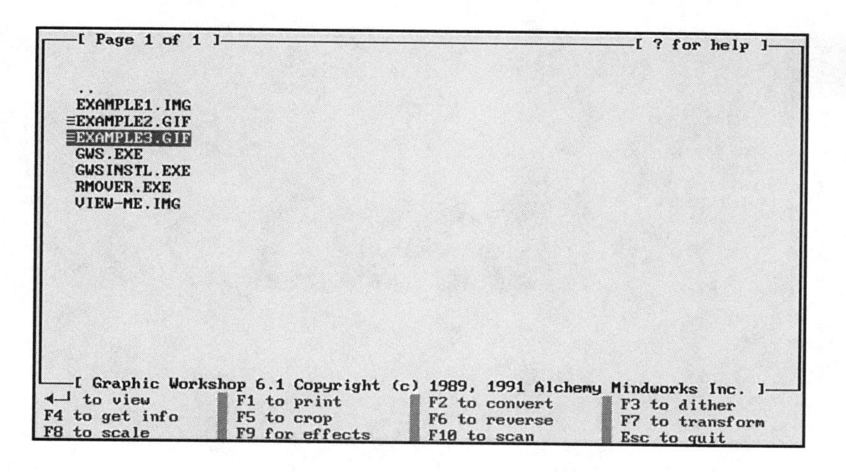

Figure 13.5: The tagged graphics files.

To start the file conversion process, simply press F2. A popup window appears, enabling you to choose the format to which you want to convert the selected files (see fig. 13.6).

After you choose the file conversion format, Graphic Workshop begins the translation process. A status box appears on the

screen, showing you the progress of the conversion (see fig. 13.7). When the files are converted, they are added (with their new extensions) to the displayed file list.

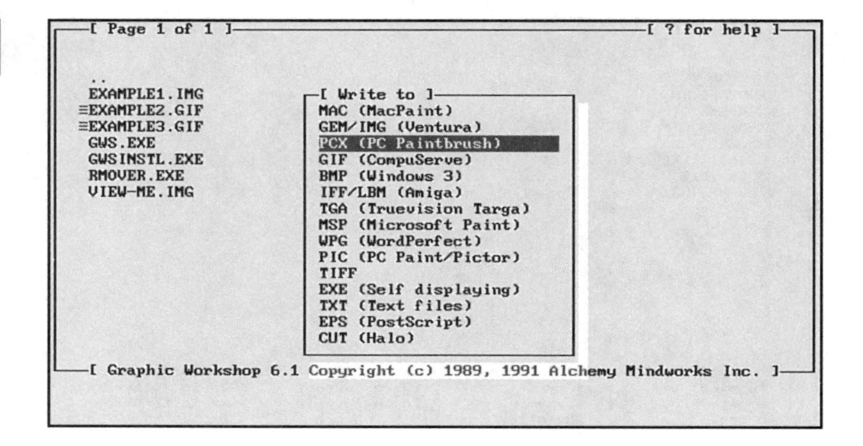

Figure 13.6: The file conversion formats.

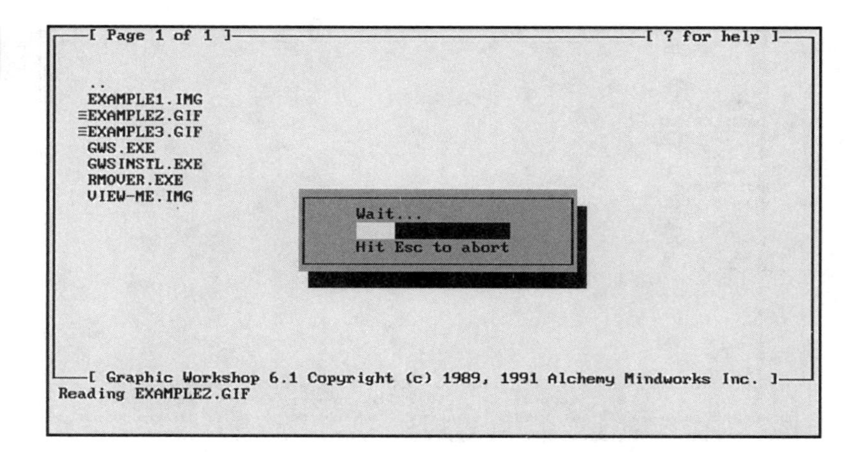

Figure 13.7: The file conversion status box.

USING GIFCONVERTER

The final shareware file conversion and image editing utility included on the Graphics disk is GIFConverter. This Macintosh utility fits into the Apple menu so that you can easily access the program without interrupting your other tasks.

To start GIFConverter, open the Apple menu and select GIFConverter 2.2.10. The menus change to show that the utility has been loaded and the GIFConverter symbol appears in the upper right corner of the screen (see fig. 13.8).

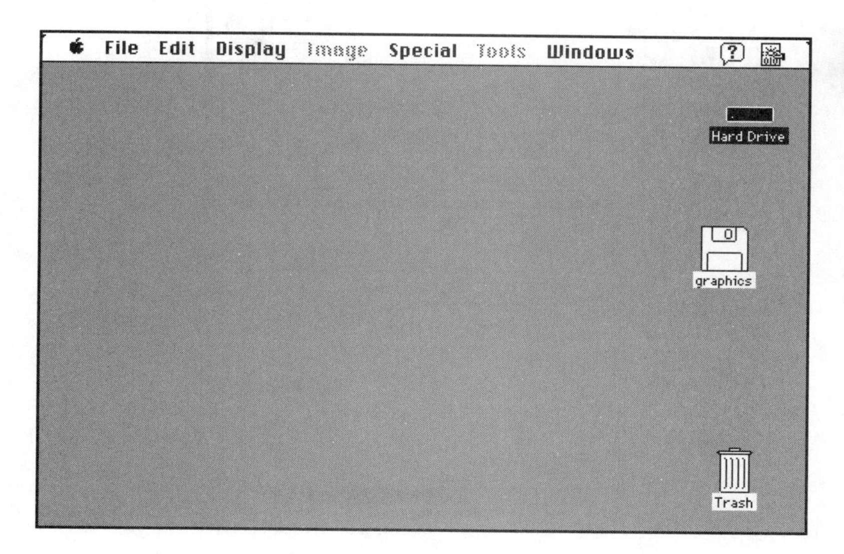

Figure 13.8:

The loaded GIFConverter program.

To load a file to be converted, pull down the File menu and choose Open. A dialog box appears, allowing you to choose the folder and file you want to view. Click on the folder you want; then highlight the name of the file you want to see, as shown in figure 13.9.

After you click on OK, GIFConverter opens the file in the work area. You can then make any necessary editing changes (see Chapter 11 for more about editing) and prepare to save the file in the format you want.

When you're ready to save the file, open the File menu and choose Save As. A popup box appears, allowing you to choose the format in which you want to save the file. First, however, click on the folder in which you want the newly saved file to be placed. Then click on the File Type: line to display a list of possible file types (see fig. 13.10).

Figure 13.9:

Selecting a file to convert.

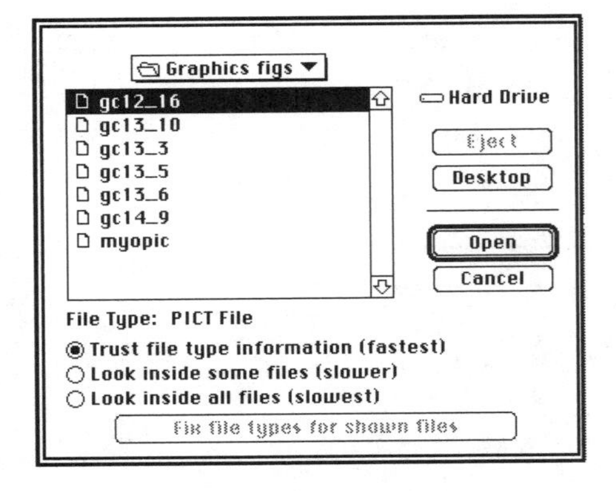

Figure 13.10:

Choosing a GIFConverter format.

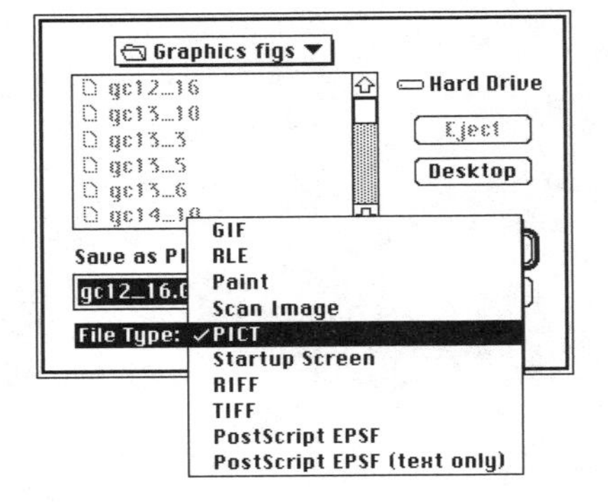

After you choose the format you want, click on OK. GIFConverter then saves the file in the format you specified.

REGISTERING YOUR SHAREWARE

Why should you worry about registering your shareware program? First, because that's the ethical thing to do. Second, because by doing so, you put yourself in the queue for any updates the author or company produces. For example, although GIFConverter can import RIFF files, trying to open a file created in Painter produced an error message. By making sure the copy of GIFConverter is registered, you are informed of updates when the new versions of the RIFF format are added to GIFConverter.

MANAGING GRAPHICS FILES

As you'll soon discover, graphics files can take up quite a bit of room. For the average PC or Mac user, a few graphics files on the hard disk is no big deal. But many files soon grow to be a bit of a problem. You're other programs run more slowly. The access time needed by your computer to read and write files becomes ridiculous.

Letting your hard disk get too full can be dangerous. Always use some kind of file compression utility to compress your graphics files when you're not using them.

The most popular file compression utility for PCs is PKZIP, created by PKWARE, Inc. PKZIP compresses data files—large or small—into zipped files you later restore by using the companion utility, PKUNZIP. PKZIP is one example of a tremendously successful shareware program that has become a standard in all realms of business use.

The flagship file compression program for the Mac is StuffIt!, a compression utility used by traditional business and graphics users. Many of the GIF files you'll find in on-line information services are compressed using StuffIt!. Not only does StuffIt! save space on your hard disk, it saves the transmission time it would normally take to download a large graphics file.

INSTANT REPLAY

This chapter rounded out Part Three—and the book—by exploring the world of graphics file conversion. In this chapter, you learned about the following topics:

INSTANT REPLAY

- ✔ Converting files with Paint Shop Pro
- ✔ Converting files with Graphic Workshop
- ✔ Converting individual files and file batches
- ✔ Converting files with GIFConverter
- ✔ Compressing graphics files

Now you've completed your Personal Trainer course and *The Graphics Coach*. As you let your creativity loose and begin to make your own masterpieces (and your own mistakes), remember that graphics technology is always caught up in a cyclone of new information. Register your shareware and other software products to make sure that you've got the most recent version. Keep on top of changes in technology that may affect the type of work you do. But most importantly, remember that every piece of art you create starts with a tiny spark of vision that has nothing to do with the computer you use, or the program you've purchased, or the quality your printer can produce.

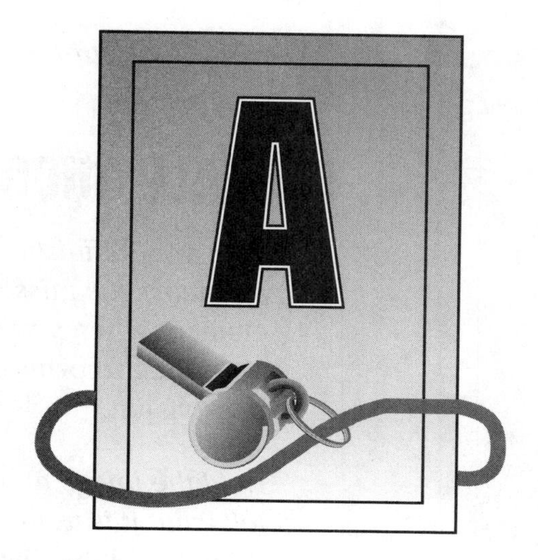

FINISHING GRAPHICS

And you thought you were done, right? Well, almost.

Depending on the type of work you do, simply creating the graphic and forgetting it might not be enough. You might need to place the image in a desktop published newsletter, for example. Suppose you need to get the image to a slide processing service so that you can add the art to an upcoming presentation. Perhaps you plan to add the images to a training manual or corporate report you've been working on.

In any of these cases, you're not finished with the graphic as soon as you create it. Other considerations include printing, translating to slides, and selecting paper, ink, and binding.

This appendix presents a hodge-podge of information that may (or may not) relate to the way in which you need to finish your graphics.

OVERALL SUGGESTIONS

After you're finished with the art, print it and go over it carefully for problems you missed. It's easy to overlook a stray line or misplaced element when you stare at the screen for hours. Sometimes switching to print provides a fresh look that helps you sharpen your vision.

Hold the image at arms length and look at its overall clarity. Can you tell what it is from a short distance? From a longer distance? If your graphic will be displayed on a projection screen, will the audience understand the image from several feet away?

Be careful with your color choice. Consider your output options—film? booklet?—and choose colors that are distinct and different from the other colors in the image. If you use four different subtle shades of blue, for example, the blues might all look the same after the publication is printed or converted to a slide. (If what you want is a subtle color progression, however, that's another story.)

Don't forget to check the spelling of text you use in your graphics. Nothing kills a good image faster than a misspelling. The artist or author suddenly can lose all credability.

PUBLICATIONS

If you're adding graphics to a publication, watch for resizing changes. When you reduce the size of an image, the image itself might be fine (at least if you're using a vector image), but if the image contains any text, the text might get jumbled or bumped to the next line. If possible, do the resizing of the image in your graphics program (or editor) before you import the file into the desktop publishing program. Then you can do a little adjusting, if necessary, but you won't have to make major size changes.

Make sure enough white space surrounds the image. Sometimes when you work on a piece of art by itself in a graphics file, you forget that at some point there will be text surrounding it. Art looks different when it's competing with text for your attention. You can cut down on the cluttered look and enhance the attention paid to your art by using a healthy border of white space to set off the image. Fight the temptation to make your art as large as possible to fill the space. Remember that eyes are drawn naturally to the white area on the page—strategically placing white space around the graphic will enhance the pull-power of your art.

Crop the item, if necessary. After all that work, all those lines, all those Zoom In/Zoom Out operations...now you're going to cut part of the image off? Sometimes cropping is necessary. In fact, from the desktop publisher's point of view, cropping is a valuable asset. You need to place three symbols on a page. Two of the symbols look similar. The other one has some extraneous detail work that won't look right when it's used beside the other symbols. Click on the cropping tool and remove the extra stuff. Voila! Three similar symbols. The artist may not like it (and the artist may be you). If it improves the consistency of the publication, however, just shrug and chock it up to creative license.

Don't use too many graphics on one page. Again, every image you create will be vying for attention on the page. If you place too many images on the page, you'll detract from the impact of all of them. Use the images sparingly, only when necessary, to highlight information, entertain readers, or reinforce the publication's message. Remember that one image goes a long way.

Make a copy of the graphics file before you import the file into a publishing or word processing program. It doesn't happen often, but it's awful when it does: you try to import a file, something bad happens, and the file is corrupted. If you don't have a backup, you don't have a file. Keep copies of all your work (preferably in a compressed file).

Make sure the publishing program supports the file format you're planning to import. Again, after all the work involved in creating and finishing a piece of art, it's maddening to get that Unrecognizable file type error. Look it up in your program's documentation to find out what graphics file formats are supported. Then, if necessary, use one of the graphics file conversion utilities to change the file into one supported by your application.

PREPARING A FILE FOR TRANSMISSION

Many high-end presentation graphics programs, such as Freelance Graphics for Windows, Microsoft PowerPoint, and Harvard Graphics, provide software links to slide service bureaus such as Autographix, Genigraphics, MagiCorp, and Slidemasters. Because you'll be relying on the originating programs for communications support, the programs offering this built-in service also include a communications utility that makes all the connections with the sponsoring service. Of course, you'll need your own modem.

Before sending a file the first time, call the service bureau to find out about transmission settings. Because you'll be sending files through the phone lines, it's important that you use the correct communications settings. Give them a call to make sure everything is set up properly before proceeding.

Find out about rates and deadlines. Different services charge different amounts for slide generation. Ask what their turnaround time is and, if you're working on a crunch project, ask about overnight processing or special delivery slides.

If you don't understand how the process works, ask, and keep asking, until you're clued in. Being new to the technology is nothing to be embarrassed about. And you'll make a better customer if you understand what's expected and provide files in a trouble-free format for the service.

Save the file in several formats so if one format doesn't "take," you can try another. Remember that the file you're sending is actually just a long stream of data: it will take some time before your data is printed as a slide. If you're sending a large volume of slides and this is your first time working with a slide service, ask them to do a few as a sample and return them to you before doing the entire batch. That way, if you see a problem in the slides (such as blurred color or alignment problems), you can make corrections before the whole project is run.

Find out more about communications possibilities. On-line services are a great place to find clip art, custom-drawn graphics, special graphics utilities, and editing tools. If you have access to a modem and communications software, you can explore an entire world through your phone line. For more information on working with communications, see *The Modem Coach*, published by New Riders Publishing.

CONSIDERATIONS FOR PROFESSIONAL PRINTING

If you're finishing a booklet, manual, report, or set of handouts that will be professionally printed, you have other issues to worry about. What kind of paper will you use? What about ink color? What type of binding—if any—do you need? Will you professionally print the piece, or will the copier do the trick?

Investigate paper weights. When you go to the printer, ask questions about the type of publication you're producing. Find out about their different paper weights and the corresponding costs. Typically, a 60-lb offset paper is good for newsletters and other materials that will be printed on both sides of the page; the paper is coarse enough to stand up to the use of more ink.

Look at the different paper types. You probably have a variety of finishes from flat to enamel, or high gloss. You also can choose from text stock or card stock. Card stock is a stiffer paper style than text stock and often is used for those annoying subscription cards that publishers stick in the middle of magazines.

Choose the right paper size. Think about whether your materials will be folded and bound, just folded (such as a brochure), or bound flat in 8 1/2-by-11 format. Remember that the size of the page has a lot to do with the effectiveness of the piece. Printers can work with many different paper sizes, although irregular sizes will cost more than traditional ones.

Think about your color options before you submit the work. Color is great, but if you don't need four-color process, don't pay for it. Make sure the color you use in your project is functional—that is, it has some reason for being there. A two-color book just for its own sake means nothing to readers; a two-color book that places important tips or instructions in second color can be both attractive and functional.

INSTALLING PROGRAMS FROM THE DISK

On *The Graphics Coach* bonus disk, you will find the three graphics file editing and conversion utilities that accompany *The Graphics Coach*. Each of these three programs represent a different group of users: Windows PC, DOS PC, and Macintosh.

The first utility, Paint Shop Pro for Windows, is stored in the Windows subdirectory of the *The Graphics Coach* bonus disk. The second program, Graphic Workshop, is stored in the DOS subdirectory. The final program, GIFConverter for the Mac, is placed in the Mac subdirectory.

You'll notice after you copy the files for Paint Shop Pro and Graphic Workshop to your hard disk that these files are compressed in a ZIP file. This means that PKZIP was used to compress the files so that they would all fit on one disk. PKUNZIP is also included on this disk so that you can unzip the file once you copy them to your hard drive.

MAKING A BACKUP COPY OF *The Graphics Coach* BONUS DISK

Before you begin using your *The Graphics Coach* bonus disk, it's always a good idea to make a backup copy, just in case. To make a backup copy on your PC, follow these steps:

1. Start with a blank, formatted diskette. Make sure that the disk is the same density—that is, stores the same amount of information—as *The Graphics Coach* bonus disk. A high-density 5 1/4-inch disk stores 1.2M of information; a low-density stores 360K. A high-density 3 1/2-inch disk stores 1.4M; a low-density stores 720K.
2. Place the Graphics disk in drive A (or whichever drive is the appropriate size).
3. Type **DISKCOPY A: A:** and press Enter. The computer will ask you to insert the source disk (the disk from which you are copying). Insert the disk in the drive and press Enter.
4. The computer begins reading the information on the file. After a moment, you are prompted to remove the source disk and replace it with the target disk (the disk to which you want to copy the information.) Remove the source disk and place the blank disk in the drive. Press Enter.

This process is repeated until the entire disk is copied. The process makes copies of all subdirectories and files on the disk. Remember to label the disk clearly and store the original away in a safe place.

To make a backup copy of your Mac file, place the disk in the Mac drive. When the disk icon appears on the desktop, double-click it to open the disk folder. Create a new folder to store GIFConverter

and drag the GIFConverter folder from the Mac disk to your hard disk.

INSTALLING THE PROGRAMS

The following sections tell you how to install and register the programs included on *The Graphics Coach* bonus disk.

INSTALLING PAINT SHOP PRO

To install Paint Shop Pro for Windows, put the Graphics disk in drive A and follow these steps:

1. If you have not started Windows, switch to the directory in which you want to place Paint Shop Pro for Windows by using the CD command, such as **CD WINDOWS**. Or, you can create your own directory (such as PAINT) and place Paint Shop Pro there. (Use the MD command to create a directory.)

   If you are in Windows already, you can start a DOS session by double-clicking on the DOS icon and then switch to the directory in which you want to place the file.

> **The Coach Says...**
> If you create your own directory using the MD command, remember to switch to that directory using the CD command.

2. After you switch to the appropriate directory, type **COPY A:WINDOWS\PSP.ZIP** and press Enter. This copies the PSP.ZIP file onto your hard drive.

The Coach Says...

A quicker way to copy the files from *The Graphics Coach* bonus disk to your hard drive when you are in Windows is to use the drag-and-drop method in File Manager. To do this, start File Manager and find the directory in which you want to place the Paint Shop Pro files (or use the Create Directory option in the File menu to create a new directory).

You then need to double-click on the drive A: icon to open the contents on the floppy disk, and then double-click on the WINDOWS directory to show the PSP.ZIP file. Press Shift-F4 to tile your windows and drag the PSP.ZIP file into the appropriate directory on your hard drive. (For more information on using Windows actions, see your Windows documentation.)

The file PSP.ZIP is compressed using the utility PKZIP, so you now need to uncompress it using the PKUNZIP.EXE file provided with *The Graphics Coach* bonus disk.

3. At the DOS prompt again, type **COPY A:PKUNZIP.EXE** and press Enter. This copies the PKUNZIP.EXE file onto your hard drive. You also can use the drag-and-drop method to copy the PKUNZIP.EXE file onto your hard drive. See the previous Note for more information on how to do this.

The Coach Says...

You can use the PKUNZIP.EXE utility anytime that you receive "zipped" files, which usually are named with a file-name extension of .ZIP. If you plan on using PKUNZIP.EXE a lot in your work, you might consider copying this file into your DOS directory. This way you can access PKUNZIP from any directory. See your *DOS User's Manual* for more information on using DOS commands.

You now need to uncompress (usually referred to as "unzip") the file that contains Paint Shop Pro using the PKUNZIP.EXE program.

4. Type PKUNZIP PSP.ZIP and press Enter. PKUNZIP uncompresses the PSP.ZIP file so that the individual files are on your hard drive. As the file unzips, your screen shows the files that are contained in PSP.ZIP.

CREATING THE PAINT SHOP PRO PROGRAM GROUP

After you unzip the file, you can start Windows (or return to Program Manager) and set up Paint Shop Pro as an item in a program group so that you can use it in a Windows session.

To do this, you first must decide if you want to place the Paint Shop Pro icon in its own program group, or place it in an existing one on your desktop. If you already have some graphics programs set up in their own groups, such as CorelDRAW!, Micrografx Designer, or even Windows Paintbrush, you might consider placing Paint Shop Pro in one of those groups. If you want to do this, skip over the next set of steps and go to the heading called "Creating the Paint Shop Pro Program Item".

You might, on the other hand, prefer to set up Paint Shop Pro into its own group, such as in a group called Paint Shop Pro or a group called Shareware. If you want to create your own program group, do the following steps:

1. In Program Manager, select the File menu and choose New to display the New Program Object dialog box.

Click in the radio button next to the Program **G**roup option, as shown in figure B.1. This tells Windows that you want to create a new program group.

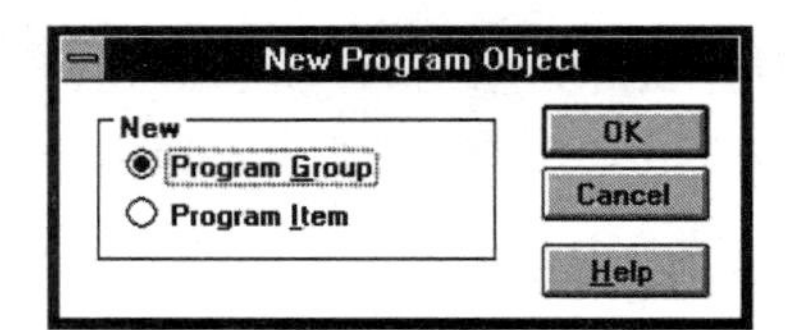

Figure B.1:

Selecting the Program Group option to create a new program group.

The Program Group Properties dialog box appears. This box enables you to tell Windows the name of the group in which you want to place the Paint Shop Pro item (called an *icon*).

2. In the Description field, type the name that you want to appear as the title of the group window. In this case, type **Paint Shop Pro** and press Enter. (Windows fills in the **G**roup File field automatically. You do not need to fill in that field.)

Your new Paint Shop Pro program group appears on screen, without any items (icons) in it. To place the Paint Shop Pro item in the new group, you need to create the program item.

CREATING THE PAINT SHOP PRO PROGRAM ITEM

You now need to create a program item in the program group in which you want the Paint Shop Pro icon to appear. If you created your own group as the preceding steps outlined, the Paint Shop Pro group should still be on your screen. If you want to place the icon in another program group, such as the Accessories group, make sure that program group is open. If it is in an iconized form, for example, double-click on it.

You now can place the new Paint Shop Pro program item in that active program group.

1. Select Program Manager's **F**ile menu and choose the **N**ew option. The Program Item Properties dialog box appears, which enables you to tell Windows the name that appears under the icon as well as where Windows can find the Paint Shop Pro program to associate with the icon.
2. In the **D**escription field, type in the name that you want to appear under the icon. In this case, you might want to use the name Paint Shop or some such. To do this, just type Paint Shop.
3. To tell Windows where to find the Paint Shop Pro program on your hard disk, type in the name of the directory in which it resides in the **C**ommand Line field. If, for example, you copied your Paint Shop Pro files into a directory called PAINT, you should type the following command:

   ```
   C:\PAINT\PSP.EXE
   ```

   This tells Windows where to find the Paint Shop Pro program called PSP.EXE) on your hard disk (see fig. B.2).

Figure B.2: The Program Item dialog box, with the Paint Shop Pro information.

Note that in the preceding example, the directory PAINT is a subdirectory off the root directory C:. Yours may differ, so modify your command line appropriately.

If you don't remember where you placed the PSP.EXE file, click on the **B**rowse button and browse through the directories and files on your hard disk until you find the one called PSP.EXE. Double-click on that file and Windows automatically places that file in the **C**ommand Line field.

4. Click on OK or press Enter and Windows places the Paint Shop icon in the Paint Shop Pro program group. (You do not have to fill in the **W**orking Directory field, because Windows does this automatically.)

You now can double-click on the Paint Shop icon to start Paint Shop Pro.

INSTALLING GRAPHICS WORKSHOP

To install Graphic Workshop, follow these steps:

1. Starting at the DOS prompt, create a subdirectory to store the Graphic Workshop files by typing **MD GWS** and press Enter.
2. Change to the GWS directory by typing **CD GWS** and press Enter.
3. Now copy the contents of *The Graphics Coach* bonus disk to the new directory by issuing the following command:

   COPY A:\DOS\GWS.ZIP

   and pressing Enter. DOS then copies the files from the GWS subdirectory on the Graphics disk to the new GWS directory you just created.

UNZIPPING FILES

Files with the extension ZIP are called zipped files. These files have been compressed to save space on the disk. To unzip the files, use PKUNZIP on drive A in the following format (PKUNZIP is included on *The Graphics Coach* bonus disk):

PKUNZIP *filename* C:\GWS

Enter the name of the file you want to unzip for *filename*. After you press Enter, PKUNZIP unzips the file and places the files in the C:\GWS directory.

After the files are unzipped and placed in the GWS directory, you can start GWS by typing **GWS** and press Enter.

INSTALLING GIFCONVERTER

To install GIFConverter, first double click on the Mac folder to open it. Then drag the GIFConverter 2.2.10 program icon to the Apple Menu Items folder (inside the System Folder). This places GIFConverter in the Apple menu so that you can easily access it from any point in your Mac applications.

REGISTERING YOUR SHAREWARE

It's not just the right thing to do—it's also the smart thing to do. Shareware is not free software; it's software licensing that calls for conscience. Shareware is based on the "try it before you buy it" idea. If you like it, pay for it. If you don't use it, don't worry about it.

Registration for Paint Shop Pro for Windows is $49.00 (with this payment you receive continual updates, a user manual, and technical support). To register Paint Shop Pro, contact:

JASC, Inc.
10901 Red Circle Drive, Suite 340
Minnetonka, MN 55343
(612) 930-9171
(612) 930-9172 (Fax orders)

To register Graphic Workshop, send $40 to Alchemy Mindworks, Inc., at the following address:

Alchemy Mindworks, Inc.
P.O.Box 500
Beeton, Ontario, L0G 1A0, Canada

For this price, the authors promise reasonable phone support, a free upgrade upon registration, update information, and—the best part—"good karma."

Finally, GIFConverter was created (and is maintained) by Kevin A. Mitchell. The author requests that users who, after 15 days, think the software is a "keeper" send $40 to

Kevin A. Mitchell
P.O.Box 803066
Chicago, IL 60680-3066

This investment entitles you to upgrade information, a well-done instruction manual, and a software key that disables the initial copyright message.

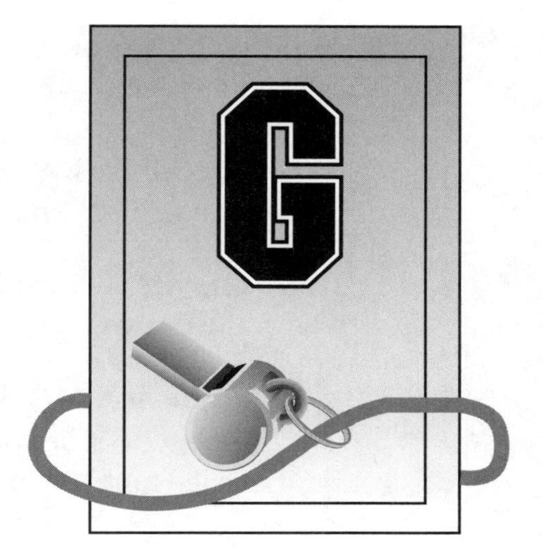

GLOSSARY

Attributes. Qualities of an image or text, such as font size, style, and color.

Backup. Making a copy of the current, or an original, file or disk.

Bezier curve. A type of curve created in object-oriented graphics that uses a calculation to draw the curve and prevent distortion.

Bitmap. A type of graphic that is actually a pattern of dots, or pixels, on the screen.

BMP. A bitmapped graphics file format used by Microsoft Windows.

CDR. The vector file format used with CorelDRAW!.

CGM. The vector file format that is widely accepted among both DOS and Windows applications. The acronym stands for Computer Graphics Metafile.

Checkboxes. A type of option in dialog boxes that enables you to turn an item on and off by clicking in the box.

Clip art. A type of art you can purchase that has been professionally drawn.

Clipboard. May be used to refer to the Windows clipboard, which is used to store data that is copied, cut, or pasted. Other DOS-based and Macintosh programs also use clipboards to store data.

CPU. The microprocessor that runs all processes in the computer.

Dialog boxes. Popup boxes that enable you to enter settings for a command you've chosen.

DIB. A bitmap graphics file format that is the standard format for OS/2 applications.

Drawing tools. A set of art tools in a drawing program that help you create object-oriented graphics.

DRW. The vector file format in which Micrografx Designer and Draw images are saved.

EGA. A graphics standard that used to be the high end of graphics display and now represents the low standard.

EPS. A graphics file format (Encapsulated PostScript) that can store both bitmap and vector images.

Extended VGA. A newer video display technology that provides an on-screen resolution of 1024×768.

Flipping. Turning the selected graphic so that it is in a different position on the page (such as left to right or top to bottom).

GIF. A bitmap graphics file format (Graphics Interchange Format) that is used with both Macintosh and PC computers. GIF graphics files first became popular on CompuServe forums.

Graduated patterns. A shaded or mixed pattern that uses two colors and gradually fades one into another.

Graphics adapter. The plug-in board the controls the transmission of video data from the CPU to the monitor.

Graphics tablet. An electronically sensitive surface on which the users writes or draws with a stylus, or pen. The information is transmitted from the tablet to the CPU.

Grouping objects. The process of merging individual lines or objects into one object.

Handles. The small squares that appear along the edge of a selected object.

HPGL. A language created by Hewlett-Packard to drive the pen plotters produced by the same company.

Image editor. An add-on utility that provides additional editing capabilities not supplied by most paint programs.

Landscape orientation. A setting that produces an 11-by-8 1/2-inch printout or display of graphics or text.

Multimedia. A technology that, if you have the right hardware, lets you integrate video and sound clips in presentations.

Object. Any graphic item that can be selected and manipulated with the selection tool. Used in vector graphics.

Object-oriented graphics. The type of art created in a draw program. Also called *vector* graphics.

OCR software. An acronym for *Optical Character Recognition*, this type of software enables you to turn scanned text into "real" text that you can use as normal text, or with fonts, styles, and sizes.

Orientation. A term used to describe the way the page is printed. Landscape prints horizontally (11 by 8 1/2) and portrait prints vertically (8 1/2 by 11).

PCL. An acronym for *Printer Control Language*, now in its fifth generation. Early PCL printers could not support scaleable fonts, but the most recent versions of PCL support scaleable fonts and are compatible with PostScript and AppleTalk printers.

PCX. A bitmap graphics file format first made popular by PC Paintbrush. Now an industry standard, supported by all major graphics applications.

Picas. A unit of measurement. (Seven picas is roughly equivalent to one inch.)

PICT. The standard format for Macintosh graphics files.

Pixel. The smallest point, or dot, in a bitmapped graphic.

Plotter. A pen-based graphics device that is used in CAD applications to produce large printouts using different colored pens.

PostScript. A page-description language created by Adobe that communicates information to the printer (and writes graphics files) in a special code understood by printers using the same language.

Points mode. Points mode allows you to add and move small points on a created graphic.

Portait orientation. A standard, 8 1/2-by-11 business-document format for printing or display.

Raster images. Another name for bitmapped, or paint, graphics.

Replicating. The process of making a copy and placing the copy immediately on the page.

Rotating. Turning a selected object in any angle.

Rulers. On-screen drawing rulers that help you with precise measurements and placement. Most graphics programs allow you to choose the unit of measurement you're most comfortable with.

Scanners. Devices that turn hardcopy printouts of graphics and text into digitized, electronic files. Types of scanners include handheld, half-page, and flatbed scanners.

Special effects. In image-editing utilities such as Photo Styler, special effects include smudging, sharpening, and color fading or enhancing.

Super VGA. A newer standard of video technology that displays on-screen resolution of 800 × 600.

TIF. A bitmap graphics file format (Tagged Image Format). TIF files are an accepted standard for many DOS, Windows, and Macintosh applications.

Undo. A command available in most graphics programs that allows you to reverse the last action performed.

Ultra VGA. The highest current video standard, providing an on-screen resolution of 1280 × 1024.

Vector images. A name for the type of graphic created in a draw program.

VGA. A commonly accepted standard of video display. VGA provides 640 × 480 on-screen resolution.

WMF. A graphics file format capable of storing both bitmap and vector graphics. A format unique to Microsoft Windows.

Work area. The area of the screen in which you create graphics.

Zoom In. The command used to magnify the screen in both paint and draw graphics programs. (You can only display pixel mode in paint programs, however.)

Zoom Out. The command that reduces the page magnification, perhaps returning the page to normal view.

INDEX

SYMBOLS

A

B

E

F

G

H

R

S

T

U

V

W-Z